I0314448

Working for the clampdown

Manchester University Press

Working for the clampdown

The Clash, the dawn of neoliberalism and the political promise of punk

Edited by Colin Coulter

Manchester University Press

Copyright © Manchester University Press 2019

While copyright in the volume as a whole is vested in Manchester University Press, copyright in individual chapters belongs to their respective authors, and no chapter may be reproduced wholly or in part without the express permission in writing of both author and publisher.

Published by Manchester University Press
Altrincham Street, Manchester M1 7JA
www.manchesteruniversitypress.co.uk

British Library Cataloguing-in-Publication Data is available

ISBN 978 1 5261 1420 4 hardback
ISBN 978 1 5261 1421 1 paperback

First published by Manchester University Press in 2019

The publisher has no responsibility for the persistence or accuracy of URLs for any external or third-party internet websites referred to in this book, and does not guarantee that any content on such websites is, or will remain, accurate or appropriate.

Typeset by Servis Filmsetting Ltd, Stockport, Cheshire

This book is dedicated to the memory of

Professor İsmet Emre Işık (1969–2016)

Dünle beraber gitti cancağızım
Ne kadar söz varsa düne ait.
Şimdi yeni şeyler söylemek lazım.
(Mevlana Celaleddin-i Rumi)

Contents

List of contributors ix
Acknowledgements xii

Working for the clampdown: an introduction 1
Colin Coulter

PART I: 'No Elvis, Beatles or the Rolling Stones': The Clash, the politics of pop and the neoliberal conjuncture

1 The Clash, revolution and reverse 35
  Jason Toynbee

2 The Clash and musical artistry: against the corporate voice 52
  Caroline Coon

3 'Up in heaven (not only here)': The Clash, left melancholia and the politics of redemption 69
  Colin Coulter

PART II: 'Back in the garage with my bullshit detector': The Clash and the cultural politics of punk

4 'Are you going backwards, Or are you going forwards?' – England past and England future in 1970s punk 89
  Ruth Adams

5 Retrieving the messianic promise of punk: The Clash in 1977 107
  Kieran Cashell

6 What if Keith Levene had never left The Clash? Punk and the politics of novelty 129
Pete Dale

7 'The beautiful people are ugly too': The Clash as my 'true fiction' 144
Martin James

PART III: 'It could be anywhere, Most likely could be any frontier, Any hemisphere': The Clash around the world

8 'Up and down the Westway' or 'live by the river'? Britishness, Englishness, London and The Clash 161
Conrad Brunström

9 'Cashing in the bill of rights'? The Clash in New York, in myth and reality 178
Harry Browne

10 The one struggle: The Clash, Gary Foley, punk politics and Indigenous Australian activism 194
Alessandro Moliterno

11 Brigade Rosse: The Clash, Bologna and Italian punx 209
Giacomo Bottà and Ferruccio Quercetti

Index 223

Contributors

Ruth Adams is a Senior Lecturer in Cultural and Creative Industries at King's College London. She teaches, among other things, about youth subcultures and international heritage and cultural tourism. Her research interests include Englishness, the postcolonial city, class, culture, gender, museums, digital media, grime music and 'stately homes'.

Giacomo Bottà has a doctorate in comparative cultural studies from IULM Milano and he is currently adjunct professor (docent) in urban studies at the Department of Social Research, University of Helsinki. His research has dealt with urban cultural studies on a comparative European level to determine how art and cultural expressions can be used to better understand space and spatialities on the one hand, and communities and societies on the other.

Harry Browne is Senior Lecturer in the School of Media, Technological University Dublin, where he coordinates the Centre for Critical Media Literacy. His journalism has appeared in numerous publications, including the anthology *Great Irish Reportage* (Penguin, 2013). He is the author of three books: *Hammered by the Irish* (Counterpunch/AK Press, 2008), *The Frontman: Bono (In the Name of Power)* (Verso, 2013, with Spanish and Italian editions by Sexto Piso and Edizioni Alegre respectively) and *Public Sphere* (Cork University Press, 2018).

Conrad Brunström is a Senior Lecturer in English Literature at Maynooth University, Ireland. An eighteenth-centuryist with special interest in the fields of religious poetry, theatre history and oratory, his most recent work engages issues of national identity and conflict. He is the author of two monographs: *William Cowper: Religion, Satire, Society* (Bucknell University

Press, 2004) and *Thomas Sheridan's Career and Influence: An Actor in Earnest* (Bucknell University Press, 2011).

Kieran Cashell is a Lecturer in Critical and Contextual Studies at the Limerick School of Art and Design. He is the author of *Aftershock: The Ethics of Contemporary Transgressive Art* (I.B. Tauris, 2009) and contributor to Ian Peddie (ed.), *Popular Music and Human Rights* (Ashgate, 2011) and Sean Campbell and Colin Coulter (eds), *Why Pamper Life's Complexities? Essays on The Smiths* (Manchester University Press, 2010). He is currently completing a book on the British artist Richard Billingham.

Caroline Coon is an artist with a unique place in British culture: as a countercultural activist in the 1960s she founded Release to give advice to young people arrested for drugs, and in the 1970s she documented in writing and photography the emerging punk movement. She managed The Clash from 1978 to 1980. Feminism has always informed her work. http://www.carolinecoon.com/

Colin Coulter is Senior Lecturer in the Department of Sociology, Maynooth University, Ireland. He is the author of *Contemporary Northern Irish Society: An Introduction* (Pluto, 1999), as well as the co-editor of four books including *Why Pamper Life's Complexities? Essays on The Smiths* (Manchester University Press, 2010) and *Ireland under Austerity: Neoliberal Crisis, Neoliberal Solutions* (Manchester University Press, 2015).

Pete Dale studied communication studies at Sunderland Polytechnic from 1989 to 1992. On graduating, he played in several indie/punk underground bands and set up the cult DIY label/distributor Slampt, which ran from 1992 to 2000. Taking up school teaching in 2001, he completed an MA in music and a PhD at Newcastle. After an early career fellowship at Oxford Brookes in 2012–13, he has worked as Senior Lecturer in Popular Music at Manchester Metropolitan University. His monographs include *Anyone Can Do It: Tradition, Empowerment and the Punk Underground* (2012), *Popular Music and the Politics of Novelty* (2016) and *Engaging Students with Music Education: DJ Decks, Urban Music and Child-Centred Learning* (2017).

Martin James is Professor of Music Industries at Solent University (Southampton), where he lectures on British popular culture, in particular late twentieth-century alternative punk, post-punk and electronic music, music memoir, social media and music journalism. He is co-author of *Understanding the Music Industries* (Sage, 2012) and author of several books about music, including *State of Bass: Jungle – the Story so Far* (Boxtree, 1997) and *French Connections: From Discotheque to Discovery*

(Sanctuary, 2004). He has also written biographies of Dave Grohl, The Prodigy and Moby.

Alessandro Moliterno is a PhD student at the Australian National University, Canberra. He is currently undertaking his candidature as part of the Research School of Humanities and the Arts in the Interdisciplinary Humanities Group. His dissertation focuses on a comparison between the political aspects of punk in the UK and Australia from a historical perspective.

Ferruccio Quercetti is a PhD research student at the University of Glasgow. The main focus of his research is the impact of first-wave punk rock on late-1970s Italy. His work is aimed at contributing to a better understanding of Italian youth culture, in the context of a very tense moment of Italian contemporary history which is commonly referred to as the *Anni di Piombo* ('the years of lead'). In this context, the reception of early punk rock in Italy can be seen as an example of the ways in which the country perceives, absorbs and reworks international popular cultural phenomena.

Jason Toynbee was Senior Lecturer in the Department of Sociology at the Open University. His most recent books are *Bob Marley: Herald of a Postcolonial World?* (Polity, 2007) and, as co-editor, *The Media and Social Theory* (Routledge, 2008, with David Hesmondhalgh), *Migrating Music* (Routledge, 2011, with Byron Dueck) and *Black British Jazz* (Ashgate, 2014, with Catherine Tackley and Mark Doffman). He is currently working on a book about the countryside in England and Wales from the viewpoint of a cycling Marxist.

Acknowledgements

The essays gathered together here owe their origins primarily to a conference held in Belfast on 20–21 June 2014. I would like to express my gratitude to all the people who contributed to making that weekend in my home town such a memorable one. In particular, I would like to thank Patricia Lundy, Niall Gilmartin, Ruairi Shirlow, Eimear Rosato, Seamus Reynolds, Bernard Mahon, Stuart Bailie, Jonny Tiernan, Jamie Webb, John Thompson, Paul Notman, Maureen Lawrence, Maeve Quigley, Paul Burgess, Jack Forgie, Henry McDonald, Jason Toynbee, David Hesmondhalgh, Caroline Coon, Adrian Boot, Gavin Martin and Chris Salewicz. Thanks also to Tom Dark and Rob Byron at Manchester University Press for their help in bringing the book into being. Finally, I would like to record my gratitude to the National University of Ireland and to Maynooth University for providing financial support in the form of publication grants.

Working for the clampdown: an introduction

Colin Coulter

The Ulster Hall in the heart of Belfast takes pride of place in the city's cherished musical heritage. Over the last half century – as Northern Ireland's seemingly intractable war eventually shaded into its seemingly intractable peace – the venue has played host to scores of gigs that have over time passed into legend. This rich musical pedigree is curated on the foyer walls of the ornate Bedford Street building. On entering, visitors are reminded instantly that the venue has witnessed concerts by some of the most revered acts in the history of popular music, among them Led Zeppelin, Pink Floyd and the Rolling Stones. Sharing wall space with these rock luminaries is, ironically, another band who once promised to be their pallbearers.[1] London punks The Clash played the Ulster Hall on two separate occasions. The permanent exhibition that graces the foyer of the venue does not, however, centre on this brace of gigs that actually took place but rather, curiously, on one that never quite came to pass.

On 20 October 1977 The Clash were scheduled to open their 'Sort it Out' tour in the Ulster Hall.[2] At the time, the punk scene remained at the centre of a sustained moral panic that gave rise to a stream of lurid tabloid tales documenting its alleged appetite for destruction. In May that year, fans of The Clash had caused widespread damage when the four-piece had played their biggest gig to date in the Rainbow Theatre in London.[3] The reputation for violence that preceded punk bands on tour prompted the insurers of the Ulster Hall concert to withdraw cover only a matter of hours before The Clash were due to take the stage.[4] When news spread that the gig had been cancelled, fans of the band vented their anger by blocking the road outside the venue, leading to an altercation with police that many have chosen to remember as a 'riot'.[5] Other observers, more familiar perhaps with the serious and sustained instances of violence that routinely convulsed Belfast at the time, have, however, been wont to dismiss the so-called 'Battle of Bedford Street' as little more than a minor skirmish.[6]

The disputes over what really happened when the Ulster Hall gig was cancelled at short notice have not, of course, prevented a certain version of events that evening from passing into Belfast's hallowed musical lore. In cultural accounts of that most troubled period of recent Northern Irish history, the *gig that never happened* has come to assume almost mythical status. The most prevalent rendition casts The Clash as heroic figures who, in coming to Belfast, promised to break the cultural embargo imposed on the city since the onset of the conflict.[7] While the much-anticipated gig might not have gone ahead, those young punks who gathered outside the Ulster Hall only to be disappointed are said to have come away in the realisation that they were now part of a subculture that was rather more extensive than previously anticipated, and that offered alternative and more progressive forms of cultural affiliation. In the account that tends to be aired most frequently, The Clash coming to Belfast only to be refused a stage is identified as the point of origin of a punk scene that would produce several legendary acts and provide a space in which young people from different backgrounds could at last transcend Northern Ireland's notoriously stifling sectarian divisions. This highly romanticised version of events has been recounted largely uncritically in journalistic and academic accounts of the period[8] and was trapped in amber in 2013 with the release of *Good Vibrations*, a movie devoted to Belfast's most famous record store which issued some of the seminal singles from the city's first wave of punk bands.[9]

While the first visit that The Clash paid to Northern Ireland appears in the main to be remembered fondly, there is, inevitably, a rather more critical reading of the events that unfolded that day. For a band whose songs centred so often on themes of *hate and war* Belfast provided an obvious and enticing visual backdrop. It was entirely predictable then that The Clash would use their brief stay in the city as a photo opportunity. In advance of the gig, Adrian Boot shot the band in various contexts that captured the militarised and divided nature of the Northern Irish capital.[10] These images, which appeared in several of the *inkies* the following week, show the four members of the band posing in front of military fortifications and being frisked when going through the security cordon that once passed for normal life in Belfast's central shopping district.[11] In one especially memorable shot, we see front man Joe Strummer passing some presumably mischievous remark in the direction of an unwitting British squaddie patrolling the streets. These stark images of The Clash taken in Belfast in the midst of the Troubles have been the source of no little ire ever since. For many critics, Adrian Boot's arresting photos represent a form of cultural pornography indicative of the band's weakness for cultivating radical chic through flirtation with violent political contexts and causes of which, in reality, they knew little and perhaps cared less.[12] The group's Inquisitor-in-Chief,

Marcus Gray, for instance, goes so far as to suggest that the Belfast gallery represented the 'crassest and most credibility-damaging error of judgement' made by The Clash in the early part of their career.[13] It seems that there are quite a few residents of the city who would echo that critique. In 2014 I organised a conference on The Clash in Belfast from which this book, in part, derives and which took as its point of departure the mythical *gig that never happened*. The occasional voices of criticism that were raised against the event almost invariably centred on the photos taken of the band around the city on that overcast day in the winter of 1977. Even four decades on, there remains anger among those who feel that The Clash treated Belfast as little more than a convenient canvas to further burnish their own outlaw mythology before moving on to the next port of call and the next photo opportunity.

The controversies that continue to surround the first time The Clash visited Belfast tell us a great deal about the band and not least about their enduring ability to divide opinion. The accounts of the group's fans often bear lucid testimony to the power of popular music to change people's lives. Those who saw the group live often recount the experience as a moment of epiphany that led them to form a band or pursue some other creative course that had previously seemed out of reach.[14] The evangelical tone of those who cherish The Clash finds its mirror image in the air of apostasy that frequently pervades criticism of the band. Those who are the most ardent critics of the band are often lapsed fans who took their radical pronouncements as gospel and became disillusioned when, inevitably perhaps, words failed to materialise fully as deeds.[15]

The particular vehemence of the arguments that rage on either side of the debate only serves to underscore that The Clash were – perhaps *are* – a band with a very singular importance. The familiar refrain that they were the *only band that matters* was, of course, entirely absurd from the very outset. That the phrase owes its origins to a record company publicity drive only serves to underline its absurdity.[16] While The Clash may not have been the only band that matters, they clearly still matter a great deal to a great many people. The enduring significance of the band finds expression across a range of cultural forms. As a band whose self-image entailed a profound and knowing sense of 'cinematic romance'[17] it is particularly fitting that The Clash have been celebrated so frequently on the silver screen. In the decades since their demise, they have appeared on the soundtracks of movies as diverse as *Billy Elliot*, *The Royal Tenenbaums*, *Knocked Up* and the *Trainspotting* sequel. Moreover, the 2018 winner of the Oscar for Best Movie, *Three Billboards Outside Ebbing Missouri*, was written by playwright turned scriptwriter Martin McDonagh, who has frequently cited The Clash as an inspiration for his work.[18] In the course of the movie, there is only one scene where we encounter the young woman whose sexually violent death prompts the eponymous advertising hoardings demanding that the police pursue her killer with greater urgency. In this passage, we are taken momentarily into her bedroom whose walls are a clutter of pop cultural references. In the centre of the frame is a classic image of Joe Strummer, eyes closed and temples throbbing, hunched over his trusty Telecaster and presumably on the verge of declaiming some heartfelt universal truth to an audience that is out of shot but doubtless hanging on every word. If you are aware of the cultural reference point here, what it signifies becomes instantly legible. As a fan of The Clash, McDonagh presumably includes the reference to the band's iconic front man as an invitation to read the young female victim in a particular way – as a person of genuine heart and depth – that leads us to identify even more strongly, if that were possible, with her plight.

While the enduring cultural significance of The Clash might be apparent to anyone who goes to the cinema with any regularity, it has yet to be acknowledged widely in the world of academia. The career of the band, as we shall see, illuminates some of the critical debates across the various fields that comprise what is often termed 'cultural studies'. There would appear, however, to be remarkably little appreciation of this among scholars writing about popular culture. While there has been a host of journalistic accounts of the band, there have to date only been two academic books devoted to The Clash, one of which focuses primarily on the group's charismatic front man.[19] In view of the commercial appeal and critical acclaim of the band, the relative dearth of scholarly work devoted to The Clash arguably represents a glaring and perplexing oversight. The intention and ambition of this volume is to help redress this curious near silence in the academic study of popular culture. Drawing on the work of scholars from a range of disciplines and based in various parts of the world, the essays collected here seek to provide a rigorous but accessible account of one of the most influential and controversial bands ever to have graced a stage.

There are, of course, various perils associated with a project of this nature. While all bands harnessing the energies of talented and driven young people tend to be complex and contradictory, this was notoriously so in the case of The Clash. As anyone familiar with them will attest, this was a band that managed to be many very different things at different times, indeed often at the same time. The Clash were, after all, a group who raged against the power of capital while turning a hefty profit for several major global corporations;[20] who expressed their horror at the iniquities of war while dressing up in military attire;[21] who nurtured many female artists in their peer group while exuding a 'radical machismo';[22] who appeared to be in pursuit of some higher truth yet all the while engaged in convenient acts of revisionism;[23] who were famously generous to their fans but at times rather less humane to those in their inner circle and indeed to one another.[24] Seeking to capture the complex and often bifurcated nature of The Clash represents one of the fundamental challenges facing a collection such as this. Over the course of the book, we set out to provide a critical engagement with the cultural politics of the band. This critique is inevitably more to the fore in some chapters than others. In his essay, for instance, Pete Dale suggests that The Clash were in fact a more musically conservative band than is often assumed. And in his contribution, Kieran Cashell breathes the heresy that *London Calling* is perhaps not quite the masterpiece that many of us have chosen to believe.

While the depiction of The Clash offered in the book is at times critical, it is more often celebratory. As Simon Frith argues in *Performing Rites*, even in the 'oddly bloodless' world of academic writing there has to be room for the subjective expression of aesthetic pleasure.[25] Many of the writers here approach this subject not only as scholars but as fans, and these dual identities are at times closely bound up with one another. For many of us, this writer included, it was encountering The Clash at a pivotal age that opened doors and nurtured interests that would in time lead to academic careers. If it were not for the band, we might never have published a single word about anything at all, let alone about them. In that sense not least, this is a book that could never have happened without The Clash. The formative influence of the band on many of the contributors inevitably reveals itself in the tone and balance of the collection. While the essays gathered here certainly offer critical perspectives on the band, they also seek to underscore that they had an aesthetic and political power that speaks from beyond the grave. Among the threads running through the collection is the conviction that The Clash not only mattered a great deal in a time of crisis in the distant past but also that they still do in the time of crisis in which we currently find ourselves. The book might be seen, then, as an invitation to listen to The Clash anew and as though they were a contemporary band.

There are, of course, certain dangers that come with calling to mind any group that parted company so long ago and these have only been amplified in the age of digital reproduction. The specific pitfalls associated with these acts of remembrance are important for our purposes and we shall, therefore, return to them at some length in due course. In advance of doing so, it would be prudent perhaps to provide a necessarily brief biography of The Clash for the benefit of those readers who are not familiar with the finer detail of the band's celebrated and controversial career.

'Something about England'

In his abidingly influential text *Noise*, Jacques Attali advances a robust case for the importance of music in our understanding of the social world. Attali contests that 'change is inscribed in noise faster than it transforms society' and that music is, therefore, a 'herald' that foretells our future.[26] If we are interested in the likely course of social change, he suggests, we merely need to acknowledge the predictive power of music and 'lend it an ear'.[27]

The logic at the heart of the seemingly quixotic thesis that Attali advances becomes readily apparent once we consider the illustrious recording career of The Clash. Those songs that the group committed to vinyl in the late 1970s and early 1980s served after all to chronicle and indeed herald facets of a social transformation that would prove so profound that we are still living with its repercussions today.

In the three decades that followed the Second World War, Western societies came to experience unprecedented levels of political stability and economic prosperity. The growing living standards that defined *les trente glorieuses* were often attributed to the adoption of Keynesian strategies that saw the state intervene both to stimulate the economy and to guarantee the welfare of citizens. That this golden age of social democracy came to an unanticipated end would owe much to the response of certain Arab states to the support that some Western countries gave Israel during the Yom Kippur War in October 1973.[28] In the year that followed the conflict, the principal oil producers in the Middle East raised the price of the commodity fourfold and accelerated an incipient global economic crisis. The impact was felt with especial gravity in a British context and the United Kingdom would soon earn the unfortunate tag of 'the sick man of Europe'.[29] As oil prices rose steeply, many factories were required to operate a 'three-day week' and the numbers out of work continued to grow. The escalating crisis in the British economy would find perhaps its starkest illustration in 1976 when the growing void in the public finances required the Labour government to go cap in hand to the International Monetary Fund (IMF) for an emergency loan of $3.9 billion.[30] A country that was within living memory a major player on the world stage now found itself reduced to the humiliating status of mere ward of the institutions of global finance.

The economic crisis that overtook the United Kingdom in the mid-1970s was inevitably the occasion of widespread social and political upheaval. The decade was marked by levels of union militancy that governments of various shades would find impossible to tame. In 1974 the Conservative government of Edward Heath fell primarily due to its inability to face down the most combative element within the labour movement, the National Union of Mineworkers.[31] The Labour administration that followed might have been expected to have had rather more cordial relations with the trade unions, but the reality would prove otherwise. One of the terms of the IMF loan was the introduction of measures to restrict the growth of pay. The implementation of an 'incomes policy' at a time of rampant inflation meant that workers were in real terms experiencing serious cuts in their wages.[32] The alienation that grew inevitably within the union movement came to a head in the 'winter of discontent' in 1978–79 when a series of strikes saw the disruption and suspension of essential services in British cities.[33] Images of refuse piled high in public places and tales of council workers refusing to bury the dead would become emblematic of a society that appeared to be in the process of unravelling. Among the potential beneficiaries of the political chaos of the time were the forces of the far right. In the mid-1970s, the National Front represented not only a menacing presence on the streets of many British cities but also a potentially important electoral force.[34] While the spectre of fascists making a genuine breakthrough at the ballot box never came to pass, the influence of the National Front on the politics of the period was important nonetheless, not least in shifting public debate on immigration even further to the right.

Among the various cultural texts that emerged to document the crisis of British social democracy in the mid-1970s, there are few that summon the period quite so vividly as the early songs of The Clash. Instructed by their charismatic but fractious manager to ditch the love songs and write about the world around them, Joe Strummer and Mick Jones set out to capture the violence and sclerosis of living in London at the time. The outcome was the collection of tracks that would feature on the band's eponymous debut album, released in April 1977 on the major record label CBS.[35] The songs that appeared on *The Clash* offer a deeply dystopian account of British society that was at the time widely hailed for its authenticity. In his review for the *New Musical Express*, for instance, Tony Parsons proclaimed that the album captured 'what it's like to be young in the Stinking Seventies better than any other'.[36] The classic social realism of *The Clash* depicts the band's home town of London as grey and desolate,[37] a cityscape populated by empty tower blocks through which the wind blows 'looking for a home'. The lengthening dole queues mean that there is little chance of life getting better for young people in particular. From the jaundiced vantage point of 'Career Opportunities', the only jobs available are entirely menial – like making tea at the BBC or opening potential letter bombs for the Royal Mail – and designed purely to forestall juvenile delinquency, to 'keep you out the dock'. While the working day offers little in terms of stimulation, leisure time provides equally meagre fare. In the songs compiled on *The Clash*, London is far removed from the glossy, perpetual motion, world city that dominates its representation today. The public houses in the capital, the single 'Remote Control' reminds us, were required to close at eleven o'clock at night. Those in search of further entertainment are left with the not entirely appetising alternatives of returning home to 'face the new religion' of television – which closes down not long after the end of licensing hours – or driving aimlessly all night 'up and down' the Westway. This elevated urban motorway, central to the 'urban hyperrealism'[38] of The Clash's early iconography, should offer the prospect of escape from the city, but instead represents here one of its many snares.

The songs that appear on *The Clash* not only document the multiple ills of a society in the throes of seemingly terminal crisis, but also identify those deemed responsible for this state of affairs. Over the course of the album, the United Kingdom is depicted as falling far short of its democratic pretensions. Those in public office are held to exercise an autocratic form of 'remote control' whether from the 'civic hall' or the national parliament. The real power within British society does not, however, lie with the 'fat and old' filing into the Palace of Westminster but rather with those 'rich enough to buy it'.[39] Given the vested interests of the politicians who appear to run the country and the kleptocrats who actually do so, there would seem little prospect of real change within the existing order of things. The cause of political progress will, therefore, demand a more revolutionary course of action.

The prospect of a form of political change that is radical – and in all probability violent – invites a response from The Clash that might be said to be characteristically ambivalent. This ambivalence is readily apparent in the songs twinned on the band's debut single. The B-side of the record, '1977', offers yet another bleak prognosis of a British society depicted as on the verge of widespread and perhaps indiscriminate violence. The future foretold here is one in which there will be 'knives' in the racially diverse London postcode 'West 11' and 'sten guns' in the exclusive district of Knightsbridge. On first release, '1977' was widely heard as harbouring ambitions towards armed insurrection. In subsequent interviews, however, Joe Strummer was at pains to clarify that his lyrics were intended not as a call to arms but rather as a warning of the capacity of regressive forces to advance their goals through violent means.[40]

The prospect of political violence seems to invite a rather less squeamish response on the lead track of the band's debut single. Perhaps the best known of the early songs written by The Clash, 'White Riot', like its equally incendiary B-side, owes its origins to a key political event that would quickly become central to the radical iconography of the group. Among the many tensions simmering within British society in the mid-1970s was that between immigrant communities and a police force prone to what would later be termed 'institutionalised racism'. The scale of this mutual antipathy became dramatically apparent at the Notting Hill carnival held at the end of the long hot summer of 1976. When police attempted to arrest a young black man, they came under a hail of missiles that would prove the harbinger of the largest riot in Britain for two decades, with 60 arrests and 456 people injured.[41] Two members of The Clash, Paul Simonon and Joe Strummer, as well as their manager Bernie Rhodes, had happened along to the carnival and found themselves caught up in the violence. Both Simonon and Strummer would later recount what happened in Notting Hill as exhilarating and inspirational, and the events that day would certainly have an immediate and indeed lasting effect on the band.[42] Rocco Macauley's image of a police line charging towards rioters gathered in the shadow of the Westway was adopted as the back cover of the debut album and would feature as the striking backdrop to many of the band's early gigs. The violence at the carnival would also inspire Joe Strummer to write the lyrics of 'White Riot'. Although misinterpreted in some quarters as a racist anthem, the song was precisely the opposite.[43] Written in homage to those black youths who had vented their anger at the Metropolitan Police, the song invites their white counterparts to summon the courage to follow suit. 'White Riot' might perhaps be read as the first inchoate manifesto issued by The Clash, one that committed them to the causes of multiculturalism and radical, perhaps even violent, political change. These commitments would, of course, offer many hostages to fortune and would time and again provide ready ammunition to the band's many detractors.[44]

While the band's commercially successful and critically acclaimed debut album was recorded at breakneck speed over three consecutive weekends,[45] its successor would have a longer and more arduous gestation. Like many bands before and since, The Clash found themselves short on inspiration when it came to finding songs for their second LP. The pressures arising out of sustained writer's block were compounded by those coming from the record company for a more polished album with the potential to breach the lucrative US market. Columbia Records – the American sister corporation of CBS – had refused to release *The Clash* on the grounds that the album had not been produced to a sufficient quality, and the corporation insisted that the follow-up would require someone at the helm capable of making the new album more 'radio friendly'. After considerable wrangling, Sandy Pearlman was appointed as the producer with the task of breaking The Clash to a mainstream American audience.[46]

Eventually released in November 1978, *Give 'Em Enough Rope* experienced a rather less rapturous reception than its much less expensively produced predecessor. The distinctly polished sound of the record would, ironically, prove abrasive for many fans whose conception of the band was bound up with the more 'primitive' production of the debut album. Critics of The Clash were quick to seize on the 'American sheen'[47] of *Give 'Em Enough Rope* as fresh evidence that the group were already moving away from the *lo-fi* punk manifesto they had sketched on the early song 'Garageland'. The new album marked a shift not merely in the sound of the band but in their political field of reference as well. As Cohen notes, on *Give 'Em Enough Rope* the lyrical concerns of The Clash move beyond their native land and begin to become rather more international in reach.[48] The increasingly global concerns of the band were suggested in a poster depicting hot spots of political violence across the world that was originally intended to accompany the album but was withdrawn at the last minute due to a printing error.[49] This widening focus was also made apparent in two of three tracks that provide *Give 'Em Enough Rope* with an exhilarating, breathless opening that the rest of the album simply cannot sustain. The lead track on the record, 'Safe European Home', records the culture shock and sheer terror experienced when Joe Strummer and Mick Jones relocated briefly to Jamaica in search of songwriting inspiration. The painful realisation that the iniquities of west London paled in comparison to the poverty and violence that existed in many places outside the 'Western world' finds further voice on the third and final track of *Give 'Em Enough Rope*'s incendiary opening sequence. Released as the lead single from the album, 'Tommy Gun' takes aim at the ease with which some in comparatively wealthy countries lend their support to the cause of revolutionary violence elsewhere. As often, critics of the band had reasonable grounds for pointing out that the 'romantic cops 'n' robbers world'[50] of lyricist Joe Strummer frequently saw him indulge in similar dalliances.

On *Give 'Em Enough Rope* we encounter the 'world service broadcasts'[51] that would become ever more common as The Clash's career progressed. The album does also, however, feature several numbers whose focus is closer to home. In these songs, London is once more depicted as oppressive and claustrophobic, with the band subject to the surveillance of both the Metropolitan Police drugs squad and Criminal Investigations Department (CID)[52] as well as the ever more insistent sniping of journalists and fanzine writers keen to pounce on the slightest evidence that they had 'sold out' the punk cause.[53] The air of menace and perhaps impending doom summoned in these songs finds sharp relief on one of *Give 'Em Enough Rope*'s standout tracks. In common with the track '1977' discussed earlier, 'English Civil War' offers a premonition of the serpent's egg hatching within the crisis of British social democracy at the time. The track was released as a single in March 1979 in the midst of the chaos summoned by rolling public sector strikes and a mere two months before what would prove to be a pivotal General Election.[54] With its dire warnings of a violent future in which a fascist 'new party army' has seized power, 'English Civil War' provides a dramatic reminder of that critical moment in which the battle of forces within an increasingly disordered British society was rapidly coming to a head.

Broadway

The crisis of social democracy in the UK in the mid-1970s would indeed give rise to a period of radical social transformation, but this would assume a form altogether different to that desired by the radicals who had come to gather beneath the standard of punk rock. On 4 May 1979, Margaret Thatcher assumed the office of Prime Minister of the United Kingdom. Over the next decade, her 'authoritarian populist'[55] regime introduced policies that would leave British society barely recognisable. At the heart of the Thatcherite project was the neoliberal conviction that it is the market and not the state that facilitates the efficient allocation of resources that is understood to be the wellspring of economic prosperity.[56] This faith in the free play of market forces would lead to the removal of government subsidies to nationalised industries, which in time would be sold off one by one to the private sector. The inevitable outcome was a further acceleration of unemployment and in the first two years of the Thatcher government the jobless total trebled to the historically unprecedented level of three million. In the early summer of 1981, the polarisation gnawing at British society came dramatically to the surface when violence erupted in a south London neighbourhood with which The Clash had come to be intimately associated.[57] The disturbances in Brixton swiftly sparked a sequence of riots in various cities across the country, producing scenes that were more immediately reminiscent of the habitual chaos then reigning in Belfast and Derry.[58]

It was widely anticipated among fans of the band that The Clash would be in the vanguard of the cultural resistance to Thatcherism.[59] This assumption was premised in part on the decision of the group to release another set of critical cultural broadsides – the four tracks that comprised *The Cost of Living* EP – on the same day that Thatcher swept to power.[60] It soon became apparent, however, that the principal preoccupations of The Clash no longer centred on the urban neuroses of an increasingly polarised British society. There was, of course, a hint that the band's field of vision was changing in one of the tracks featured on the record released to mark the dawn of Thatcherism. While the lyrics of 'Gates of the West' document a sense of being torn between the call of home town London and the lure of the exotically alien New York, this dilemma would in time be resolved decisively in favour of the latter. The increasingly global frame of reference of The Clash – albeit one focused primarily on the United States – would in the first instance find reflection in a growing willingness to embrace different musical styles. This cultural openness was apparent even in their early days, most notably when they decided to dispense with the stylistic constraints of punk and include a song by the Jamaican artists Junior Murvin and Lee 'Scratch' Perry on their debut album. The band's celebrated cover of 'Police and Thieves' was not only an expression of their genuine respect for reggae – bassist Paul Simonon especially was an aficionado – but also a declaration of multicultural solidarity with those West Indian communities that were routinely subject to the suspicion and surveillance of the state.[61] The musical curiosity that was evident from the outset would really begin to flourish, however, during the sessions at the Vanilla rehearsal space that began within days of Thatcher arriving in Downing Street. Around their notoriously robust daily games of football,[62] the four members of the group began to sketch a collection of songs that would explore a diversity of influences including rockabilly, reggae, ska, funk and rhythm and blues. The outcome of these sessions was *London Calling*, a nineteen-track double album retailing for the price of a single album that was released in December 1979 and would become celebrated as the band's masterpiece.[63] Released a mere twelve months later, the follow-up album, *Sandinista!*, featured no fewer than thirty-six tracks spread across three LPs, once more for the price of one, and if anything proved even more eclectic in its range of musical sources, with gospel and calypso being added to an ever expanding repertoire. While the sprawling *Sandinista!* would be widely panned by critics, it showcased the growing appetite and respect of The Clash for new and different cultural forms. Among the standout tracks in a notoriously uneven collection was the hypnotically relentless opening number 'The Magnificent Seven', which would come to be acknowledged as the first time white artists had drawn on the then emerging black urban American style of hip hop.[64]

The widening of the band's horizons signalled by their ever more eclectic musical tastes was mirrored in their growing preoccupation with world politics.[65] There were, of course, gestures towards global political crises from the very beginning of The Clash's recording career: the Watergate scandal features prominently in the indictments levelled at the American government in 'I'm So Bored with the USA' on the debut album; the lead single from its successor, 'Tommy Gun', offers, as we saw earlier, a perhaps autobiographical exploration of the glamorous allure of international terrorism; and *London Calling* features the track 'Spanish Bombs', which oscillates back and forth between the ascent of fascism on the Iberian peninsula in the 1930s and the rise of package holidays there four decades later. The internationalism that informed the work of The Clash from the outset would, however, come into bolder relief on the final two albums recorded by the 'classic' four-member version of the group. A song that might be taken as emblematic here is 'Washington Bullets', which centres on a searing critique of US foreign policy, especially in the context of Latin America.[66] When recording the track, Joe Strummer spontaneously cried out 'Sandinista!' in homage to the left-wing guerrillas who had seized power in Nicaragua the previous year, inadvertently inspiring the title of the band's ill-starred triple album.[67]

The theme of global injustice prominent on *Sandinista!* became sharper still on the final album by The Clash to feature the songwriting partnership of Joe Strummer and Mick Jones. By the time they came to record the tracks that comprise *Combat Rock* the growing fascination of the band with the United States was in full flower. In the summer of 1981, The Clash played a legendary series of seventeen consecutive concerts in Bond's Casino on Times Square.[68] At a time when they were the object of incessant criticism from the London music press, the band suddenly found themselves the toast of New York's (sub)cultural elite. This love affair between the group and the city would be reflected and refracted in the songs recorded later in the year. The dozen tracks that appear on *Combat Rock* represent arguably the most thematically coherent set of songs the band had recorded since their debut LP.[69] The album returns time and again to the aftermath of the United States' disastrous war in Vietnam and to the fabled streets of New York.[70] Opening the record is what sounds instantly like a classic protest song, the lead single 'Know Your Rights'. Against the backdrop of an unremitting, metallic rockabilly beat, front man Joe Strummer barks what our human rights are meant to be and how these are qualified in the face of wealth and power.[71] Hence, while we have the right 'not to be killed', this entitlement disappears should we fall victim to 'a policeman' or 'an aristocrat'. The tone of outrage that opens the album is sustained in the following track, the spellbinding and inexplicably often overlooked 'Car Jamming'. For the first time but not the last, we are introduced to one of the many victims of the conflict in Vietnam, a 'shy boy from Missouri' who had his 'boots blown off' in a 'sixties war' and is forced to move on 'aluminium crutches' from 'door to door' in search of a 'welfare kindness' that will never materialise.

The mood of belligerence that marks the beginning of *Combat Rock* soon dissipates and the passion of that opening pair of tracks gives way to an increasingly pervasive air of pathos. One of the tracks that lends voice to the sense of abjection running through the album is 'Ghetto Defendant', featuring guest lyrics and vocals from Allen Ginsberg.[72] Here we find Joe Strummer interweaving lines with the esteemed Beat poet as the pair document the debilitating impact of hard drugs on the poor. It is not, they insist, the 'tear gas or baton charge' of the state that prevents radical social change but rather the scourge of 'heroin pity'. The sense of melancholy summoned by a track like 'Ghetto Defendant' reaches its apogee in one of the songs chosen for a double A-sided single that was the last to be released from the album.

'Straight to Hell' represents perhaps the last of the many great songs crafted by the partnership of Joe Strummer and Mick Jones. The track is considered in some detail in a later chapter, so for the time being we will restrict ourselves to a relatively brief account. In one of his most ambitious and moving lyrics, Strummer takes us on a tour of a planet scarred by the twin iniquities of poverty and war. We witness first the British steel mills rusting as the Thatcherite project of deindustrialisation gathers pace, encounter the mixed-race children abandoned in Vietnam after the war by their US servicemen fathers, and bear witness to the catatonia of an American society mired then as now in a crisis of opioid addiction. The song offers a compelling panorama of a world in which conflict and injustice are genuinely universal. The instances of human rights abuses documented here are held to be ones that can, indeed do, happen 'anywhere', on 'any frontier', in 'any hemisphere'. While such injustice ordinarily moves the band's front man to full-throated indignation, the tone here is rather closer to sullen resignation. There seems little purpose in pursuing justice in a world where there is none – 'King Solomon he never lived round here' – and the only prospect that remains for the wretched of the earth is to 'go straight to hell'.

The release of *Combat Rock* in May 1982 saw The Clash attain a level of commercial success in the US that had seemed on the cards since the media frenzy surrounding the Bond's Casino gigs the previous summer. The burgeoning appeal of the band to an American audience was confirmed in the chart success of the single 'Rock the Casbah' and was visually framed by the vast crowds that rapturously received their performances at Shea Stadium in support of their cultural forbears, The Who.[73] At the precise moment that The Clash were finally experiencing the commercial success for which they had worked so hard, they were, however, falling apart for precisely the reasons that bands almost always do. In the month that *Combat Rock* was released, the group sacked Nicky 'Topper' Headon on the grounds that his long-running drug addiction was becoming an ever greater impediment to his performance.[74] While competent replacements would be found for the drummer, the band had now lost the member who was, arguably, their most naturally gifted musician and who was the principal author of their biggest ever American hit single. The departure of Topper Headon did not, however, address what was in fact the principal fault line within the band from the very outset of their career. By the time The Clash came to record *Combat Rock* there were ever greater, and seemingly irresolvable, musical differences – both literal and metaphorical – between Mick Jones and the other members of the group. The increasingly temperamental behaviour of the guitarist would in time bring the long-running tensions within The Clash to a head. As the summer of 1983 drew to a close, it was announced that Mick Jones had been asked to leave the band, sundering one of the most fruitful writing partnerships in the history of popular song.[75]

In the wake of the departure of the guitarist who had written the music for almost all of the band's back catalogue, the remaining members Joe Strummer and Paul Simonon took the ultimately foolhardy decision to carry on as The Clash. Three younger musicians were recruited with a view to taking the band back to their original roots in punk rock.[76] This five-piece version of The Clash toured intermittently for a couple of years and recorded what would transpire to be the band's final album. However, while *Cut the Crap* bore the name of The Clash, it was in fact largely the work of Machiavellian manager Bernie Rhodes, finally realising his long-standing delusion that he was actually a member of the band.[77] When the album was released in October 1985, it was greeted with almost universal derision. Although Jon Savage emerged as an early and perhaps unlikely champion of *Cut the Crap*, he would remain very much in the minority.[78] Even the inclusion of the infectiously bleak social realist single 'This is England' cannot salvage an album that is a collage of hackneyed imagery, football terrace chants and music that barely merits the name. It would be hard to imagine an epitaph less worthy of a band of the stature of The Clash. Indeed, perhaps out of respect for how truly great they once were, many biographers have chosen simply to airbrush the final, calamitous incarnation of the group out of the story altogether.[79]

There is, of course, a certain temptation to replicate this familiar act of historical revisionism when talking about The Clash. The abridged version of events that marks the demise of the band as the moment when Mick Jones was sacked does after all lend the story a particular, appealing symmetry. Looking back, the career of The Clash clearly maps out a period of social transformation of such gravity that we are still experiencing its aftershocks today. The early songs of the band, as we noted earlier, provide the most compelling cultural document imaginable of that moment in the mid-1970s when the long global economic boom turned to bust and heralded the demise of the post-war Keynesian political settlement. While the 'utopian heresies'[80] of punk issued promises towards a more progressive future, the crisis of social democracy would in time be resolved in favour of more reactionary forces. The ultimate victory of the neoliberal project would find obvious echoes in the songs that mark the end of The Clash's career, or at least that of the band's classic line-up. Those tracks that appeared on *Combat Rock* were written against the backdrop of Ronald Reagan entering the White House, and the release of the album coincided with the outbreak of the Falklands War, a needless imperial skirmish in the south Atlantic that would claim almost a thousand lives and see the previously widely unpopular Margaret Thatcher return to power for her second, genuinely revolutionary period in office. The album documents, then, that moment when the tide of history shifted in favour of the forces of neoliberalism. While some of the songs on *Combat Rock* showcase a trademark righteous belligerence, the overall tone of the album is rather closer to political acquiescence. Listening to the likes of 'Ghetto Defendant' or 'Straight to Hell', there is a mood of abjection that suggests that there is no alternative to an ascendant political order that would only compound the injustices depicted on those tracks. While the victory of neoliberalism would in time assume many cultural forms, one of the first becomes audible if we listen closely to the tracks that make up what most fans choose to recall as The Clash's final album. It was perhaps fitting then that when Margaret Thatcher won the General Election in June 1983, it was only a matter of weeks before Mick Jones departed and The Clash ceased to exist as a genuinely creative cultural force.

'In these days of evil Presidentes'

The songs that The Clash committed originally to vinyl narrate with a particular vividness that critical moment of rapid political transformation that saw the crisis of social democracy prepare the ground for what would in time be termed 'the neoliberal revolution'. While this narrative threads its way through the band's entire body of work, it is rendered with especial clarity at certain specific moments in their extensive back catalogue. A case in point is one of the few numbers on *London Calling* that doesn't stray far from the musical conventions of rock. Track nine on the band's magnum opus is listed on the back cover as 'Clampdown' but appears on the inner sleeve lyric sheet as 'Working for the Clampdown'. The latter rendition, citing the phrase that recurs throughout the song, has a rather more pleasing ring to it and has accordingly been adopted by many fans as its 'real' name. In the discussion that follows we will follow this informal convention by using this fuller, more resonant version of the track's title. In a characteristically dense and arresting lyric, 'Working for the Clampdown' sees Joe Strummer summon once more a bleakly oppressive world animated by the rapacious desires of Capital and Empire ('The kingdom is ransacked, all the jewels taken back' he drawls during the track's barely decipherable preliminary verse). The new order that reigns here is one that immediately draws our minds back to a previous era of fascist rule. Someone wearing a turban has his headwear summarily removed by those keen to ascertain whether he is a Jew. And ideologues are at work with their 'twisted speech' to ensure that the next generation of 'blue-eyed men' become 'true believers'. While the insidious practices documented so vividly here evoke a distant political past, 'Working for the Clampdown' insists that these are also part and parcel of a political present that would persist long enough to define our own. The jagged lines delivered interchangeably by Joe Strummer and Mick Jones express the fear that the newly installed Thatcher government marks a shift towards the right that will see the British state become increasingly oppressive and racist. These concerns would in short order prove to be well founded, and the lyrics of 'Working for the Clampdown' might be said to represent one of the more prescient commentaries that emerged to mark the dawn of neoliberalism. There can be few lines in popular song quite as prophetic, for instance, as the one that foresees the baleful materialism that would soon become a cultural hallmark of the Thatcher era: 'They put up a poster saying we earn more than you.'

The construction of this oppressive new order – the 'clampdown' that gives the song its title – prompts Joe Strummer to advocate forms of political resistance that chime with the outlaw mythology he wove around himself and his band. Invoking a familiar refrain from the various traditions of popular song, 'Working for the Clampdown' incites the young to free themselves from the constraints of parental authority. In one of many lyrical detours, Strummer insists that while capitalism promises that hard work will lead to a life of luxury, these assurances will in time prove to be empty. The factories are full of men who are 'old and cunning' and who would seek to groom younger workers into repeating their own folly of a lifetime devoted to the same menial job. If the next generation are to avoid the same fate then they must realise that 'there's nothing coming' to them and flee the suffocating world of their parents: 'You don't owe nothing, so boy get running.' This familiar fantasy of youthful rebellion sketched in the lyrics of 'Working for the Clampdown' takes its place as part of the wider social transformation advocated in the song. In perhaps the most memorable passage, Strummer declares that 'anger can be power' and that if we 'let fury have the hour' then we can 'cause governments to fall'. It is hardly surprising then that 'Working for the Clampdown' is among the songs cited most readily by those keen to burnish the status of The Clash as a band that embodies the potential of popular music as a voice for radical political change.[81]

While 'Working for the Clampdown' certainly appears at first glance to be a crucial early instance of cultural resistance to the nascent neoliberal turn, its lyrics may on closer inspection prove ironic in ways that invite a more critical reading. In the venerable tradition of leftist political theory, there is a prominent thread – associated most famously with Theodor Adorno[82] – that insists that those cultural forms that seek to critique capitalism while operating within its orbit will ultimately only replenish that which they claim to wish to destroy. This conviction has formed the kernel of much of the substantial and often bitter criticism that has been levelled at The Clash over the course of the last four decades. In the eyes of their many detractors, the band are held to have channelled legitimate disgust at the iniquities of capitalism not into real political action, but rather into cultural commodities that are easily and profitably accommodated within the prevailing order of things. From this more jaundiced perspective, the radical sentiments expressed in a track such as 'Working for the Clampdown' become, at best, deeply ironic. While the song may well have been intended as a critique of the escalating power of capital in a world turning sharply to the right, it was released on an album that generated a substantial profit for a major capitalist enterprise that was in turn part of a wider conglomerate engaged in nefarious business practices across the globe. Regarded against this backdrop, a radical protest song such as 'Working for the Clampdown' invites another, more critical response. For those who would seek to puncture the enduring mythology of The Clash, it is at the very least problematic that the band encouraged people to resist the neoliberal turn signified in the song title even though they were themselves 'working for the clampdown'.[83]

Although arguably a poor relation to the many other gilded tracks that grace the *London Calling* double album, 'Working for the Clampdown' is nonetheless a compelling song that rewards a closer listen. Over the course of 3 minutes and 49 seconds, the track tells us a great deal about the nature, the power and the contradictions of The Clash. Here was a band who were vehemently opposed to the shift towards political reaction marked by the dawn of neoliberalism; who felt that resistance to the new order was possible at a personal and political level; but who ultimately were compromised by their proximity to a system that they claimed to despise, cogs in the machine of global capitalism when they had promised to be spanners in its works. These crucial characteristics of The Clash and their body of work that are illuminated in 'Working for the Clampdown' represent themes that in myriad ways inform all of the chapters that follow. It seemed only fitting then that we should name this collection of essays after the song, or, more precisely perhaps, after the phrase that features most frequently in its incensed, inspirational and, ultimately maybe, ironic lyrics.

A close reading of a track such as 'Working for the Clampdown' clearly illustrates the manner in which The Clash documented and indeed bookended that critical moment of global political transformation that would in time come to be known as the 'neoliberal revolution'. In acknowledging this, there might be a temptation to regard the band as merely a cultural relic of some distant bygone age. To do so would, however, be to squander an important opportunity. Perhaps a band that captured so vividly that period when neoliberalism turned the balance of political forces in its favour might have something to say to us about our own current age of crisis, heralded by the unravelling of that same ideological project. There might be a case for returning to The Clash and listening to those songs as if for the first time and as if they were written in the present moment. As with all cultural artefacts, however, there are very real dangers in taking popular music out of its time and place, and it is to these that we turn our attention next.

'Phoney Beatlemania has bitten the dust'

On 21 October 2017, Trinity College in Dublin hosted a symposium marking the fortieth anniversary of the first time The Clash performed in the city. Fresh from the disappointment of the cancelled concert in Belfast the day before, the band played a pair of blistering gigs in the incongruously ornate setting of the university's Examinations Hall that would instantly attain legendary status.[84] Perhaps the star turn during a hugely entertaining day devoted to this most cherished moment in Dublin's pop cultural folklore was Don Letts, the second-generation Jamaican Londoner who soundtracked and chronicled the punk scene that flourished in his native city in the mid-1970s. Liberated by a roving microphone, Letts paced among a captive audience comprised overwhelmingly of men of a certain age. At one point, the legendary DJ and film-maker chose to invite the gathering to reflect on the incongruity of the moment we were sharing. While one of its principal animating impulses was an unforgiving iconoclasm, punk had from the outset insisted upon hushed reverence for the endless sequence of commemorations staged to honour its own relics and martyrs. Pausing for effect and somehow looking everyone squarely in the eye simultaneously, Letts insisted that the audience reflect on that particular irony by saying something previously presumed to be unsayable: 'Why are we still talking about all this?'

While delivered with an amiable air of faux exasperation, the comments that Don Letts made in Dublin to a gathering of ageing Clash fans gesture towards matters that are very serious indeed. There are certain real perils involved in the endless recollection of bands from distant eras that come into stark relief when we turn to examine the nature of cultural production under late capitalism. In his influential account of the rise of postmodernism, the literary critic Fredric Jameson suggests that the era has entailed the collapse of a sequence of cultural barriers, and not least those that once marked the boundaries between distinct historical periods.[85] Over several decades, the culture industries have sought increasingly to purloin styles and personalities from the past and to splice and recycle these as commodities in what can barely summon the energy to call itself the present. The impact of this form of blank parody or 'pastiche', Jameson suggests, has been the debilitating historical amnesia that finds expression in an ever more ubiquitous and oppressive tendency towards cultural nostalgia.[86]

The backward glance of the culture industries that is the hallmark of late capitalism is, of course, no more apparent than in the world of popular music. In his book *Ghosts of My Life*, the astute cultural commentator Mark Fisher asserts that in this century, popular culture has fallen prey to an unprecedented and 'extraordinary accommodation with the past'.[87] The return of songs and figures from often long-distant eras in the age of digital reproduction means that it frequently seems that there is no genuinely *contemporary* popular music, that 'there is no now'.[88] The pervasive nostalgia that grips the twenty-first century, Fisher suggests, has prompted not merely the slowing down of cultural time but also the closing down of political space. Haunted by its own revered back catalogue, popular music no longer represents a space in which to reimagine the world because it has lost that gift for 'future shock' that was once its calling card.[89]

The diagnosis set out in *Ghosts of My Life* does perhaps tend to overstate the paralysis of contemporary popular culture. Looking on from the vantage point of early middle age, Fisher was, arguably, blind to the flashes of creativity that still occur in the world of pop music and there are times when his analysis comes rather close to a certain cross-generational condescension – *if only the millennials could summon our spirit and have their own version of punk rock*. These shortcomings take little away, however, from the essential veracity of the argument that Fisher set out shortly before his early and tragic death. Over time, it has become more and more painfully apparent that popular music has largely lost its facility to shock and originate, and that these critical faculties have migrated to other, more visual cultural forms. The diminished power of pop to produce fresh memories finds especially stark reflection in the abiding and indeed escalating preoccupation with that 'firefly'[90] moment of creativity that marked the birth of British punk.

In their recent account of the period, Richard Cabut and Andrew Gallix denounce what they see as a current widespread prohibition against nostalgia and make the case that 'punk's cultural importance should ... be officially recognised in museums and galleries'.[91] It would be hard to think of a characterisation that sits more at odds with contemporary cultural realities.

The potential significance of the scandals and heresies that punk scattered along its path was in fact recognised more or less instantly by the culture industries. As the movement slipped its own exclusive subcultural moorings in the days after Sex Pistol Steve Jones turned the air blue on national television, corporate interests sought to harness its energies through the long-established strategies of commodification and commemoration.[92] The original diversity of expression that had defined the early punk scene would soon cohere into an infantile uniform to be purchased off the rack or by mail order, immediately giving the movement its 'curiously petrified quality'.[93] And over time the cultural treasure of the original movement would come to be acknowledged endlessly in museums and galleries all over the world. The impact of the familiar strategies of the culture industries has, predictably, been to defuse the original radical political charge of punk rock. As its artefacts and personalities have come to circulate within the mainstream in ever heavier rotation, it has become more and more difficult to remember that this was in fact a cultural movement that for a time genuinely threw the British political establishment into a profound moral panic. The timeless facility of the culture industries to accommodate radically oppositional energies and turn them into profit becomes instantly apparent when we consider the fate of the young man who was the public face of punk's threatened/promised cultural insurrection. Once the *enfant terrible* who threatened to spoil Elizabeth II's Silver Jubilee celebrations, John Lydon now seems entirely housetrained, reduced to the role of yet another loveable rogue in a comfortingly familiar gallery of amiable English eccentrics, selling some brand of butter or other to a society on which he once threatened to rain anarchy.[94]

The particular ways in which the punk movement has been called to mind have tended, therefore, to dilute its original inflammatory political power. This mode of historical revisionism becomes especially insidious when we locate it in the context of the turn towards nostalgia that, as Owen Hatherley points out, British society has taken since the onset of austerity.[95] In June 2016, the UK voted by a slim majority to rescind its membership of the European Union. At the forefront of the Leave campaign was the prominent Conservative Boris Johnson, whose support for exiting the EU was widely seen as informed more by personal ambition than political principle. Until a few weeks before the critical referendum Johnson had been Mayor of London, and one of his final responsibilities in that capacity was to announce a sequence of cultural events to mark the birth of British punk in the capital some four decades before.[96] That particular combination of roles might – at first glance at least – appear to be an unlikely one. It seems a little odd after all that a conservative figure who was one of the most influential advocates of a political direction that threatens to narrow many British people's cultural horizons should almost in the same breath have been a vocal proponent of events organised at public expense to celebrate a radical cultural movement that promised to widen many British people's cultural frame of reference. That the Tory leadership contender was able to square those competing cultural impulses tells us a great deal not only about his own capacity for doublethink, but also about how its seemingly endless commemoration has rendered punk in the popular imaginary of contemporary British society.

While the practices and styles of the punk movement were initially conceived as a deliberate affront to those of parents deemed still to be basking complacently in former wartime glories,[97] the cultural artefacts of both generations now nestle genially beside one another in the same line of English heritage. Looking back from a distance of several decades, there are times when punk appears merely another free-floating signifier of a certain ineffable sense of Englishness, indistinguishable almost from the sepia tones of Ealing comedies or newsreel footage of rationing coupons and national service. A subcultural impulse that was intended to arrest historical time – to declare the advent of 'year zero' no less – has perhaps instead been arrested by its blurring. It often appears, in other words, that punk has become simply another referent to a particular historical moment in a digital age that acts to obliterate all such temporal distinctions. In the breathless stream of television programmes that slice historical time neatly into decades, those images of spikey hair and gently arcing phlegm become ever more jaded metaphors for that sequence of time when the promises of social democracy began to evaporate, and are now oddly interchangeable with Laura Ashley fabrics, Merchant–Ivory movies and Henry Cooper larking about with Kevin Keegan to promote a certain pungent brand of aftershave.[98] All those everyday artefacts of a mythical, lost England – the safety pin, the saucy seaside knotted hanky, the fawning tributes to the House of Windsor – now sit side by side with their satirical doubles that were subject to the *détournement* of Jamie Reid and others in the same cultural mausoleum that has been under construction for quite some time in preparation for the new golden age of *Brexitannia*.

The cultural processes that have shaped punk in general over the last forty years have inevitably applied with particular force to The Clash. It would be difficult to imagine another band that encapsulates quite so vividly the dilemmas – 'the play of resistance and incorporation'[99] – that face all radical artists operating in the orbit of the mainstream culture industries. While The Clash would time and again rail against the power of multinational capital, they would do so while generating no little fortune for a major corporate concern. The considerable ambition that fuelled the band from the outset ensured that it was entirely inevitable that they would sign to one of the major record companies.[100] In the endlessly recited official version of the story of punk, it is this development, invariably, that is highlighted as the moment that the movement fell from grace. In an outburst so familiar that it scarcely requires repetition here, the fanzine writer Mark

P(erry) alleged that 'punk died the day The Clash signed to CBS'.[101] The decision to go with a mainstream company would become the principal weapon in the arsenal of those who held the band to have fallen far short of the ambitious political claims that they had made to eager journalists as young men in the first flush of fame. While these allegations that The Clash had 'sold out' would accumulate over time, they were sharply at odds with the modest lifestyles that the band maintained for most of their career. The band's legendary generosity to their fans led them to insist that the price of concert tickets and albums should be pegged at rather lower than the going market rate. As a result, touring often lost them money, while even releases that charted strongly often brought in minimal income in the immediate term. In spite of the constant taunts of 'sell out', the members of The Clash spent most of their recording career flat broke. While joining the band had allowed Joe Strummer to experience recurrent mainstream chart success, the financial rewards were so meagre that he continued living in a sequence of London squats. When The Clash front man decided in 1980 to take the plunge and finally buy somewhere to live, his financial circumstances were such that his application for a mortgage was turned down.[102]

Chastened perhaps by the austerity that resulted from their commitment to giving value for money, The Clash would become rather more pragmatic in the latter years of their career. They accepted, as we saw earlier, a lucrative invitation to support The Who on some of the US dates on what was billed, not for the last time, as the latter's farewell tour.[103] In addition, the group received no less than $500,000 for playing a single gig at the Us Festival organised by Apple co-founder Steve Wozniak.[104] That chaotically bipolar performance in San Bernardino, California would be the last time that Mick Jones played live as a member of The Clash. The compromises that the band made at the tail end of their career would, of course, set the tone for what came after. Since the members of The Clash parted company, their music has been licensed to sell the wares of a range of multinational corporations, ranging from Levi's jeans to Jaguar cars to Technics exclusive range of hi-fi equipment.[105] The escalating commercialism of the band has also given rise to a slew of expensive and ever more elaborate retrospectives designed to cash in on their enduring appeal in an era of ever deepening cultural nostalgia. This process of relentless reissuing and repackaging reached its nadir perhaps in 2013 when Sony – which had bought out the band's original label CBS fifteen years earlier – released *Sound System*. Housed in a sleeve shaped like a Boom Box, this exhaustive retrospective featured no fewer than thirteen compact discs as well as a range of memorabilia including a poster tube in the shape of an outsized cigarette, a gesture towards one of the band's shared vices that played no little part in their distinctly cinematic presentation of self. At the time of its release, any American fan of The Clash eager to get their hands on this treasure trove of material would have been required to part with almost $200.

The remarkably lucrative commercial afterlife of the band is both symptom and cause of the growing critical reputation they have come to enjoy since they parted company. Over time, The Clash have come largely to be remembered as merely one more in a rich lineage of classic English rock bands. While often conceived with the best of intentions, retrospectives devoted to their career tend increasingly to sanitise the group politically. The radical political agenda of The Clash becomes mere autobiographical colour, in an American context perhaps simply more endearing evidence of a certain *limey* eccentricity. Beliefs that were once very firmly held indeed – the early commitment to being *anti-fascist, anti-racist, anti-violence and pro-creativity* springs to mind here[106] – enter the haze of accelerating digital information and are leached of most of their political meaning and valence. That the ways in which they have come to be remembered tend to obscure the radical politics of The Clash becomes particularly evident when we consider the fate that has befallen the title track of the album widely regarded as their finest hour. Written in the wake of Margaret Thatcher's ascent to power, 'London Calling' envisages an immediate future – or perhaps an immediate past (*yes, I was there too*) – where society has unravelled, famine and nuclear war have descended and the English capital is under water. This bleak prognosis crafted at a time of genuinely grave geopolitical uncertainty has been used countless times since as the score for a range of visual media, and almost always in ways and in contexts that are quite breathtakingly inappropriate. It has over time become almost obligatory for advertisers promoting more or less any event in the UK capital to employ 'London Calling' as the soundtrack. The song would, for instance, become an official anthem of the 2012 London Olympics.[107] Hence, we were treated time and again that gilded summer to the disorientating spectacle of a global audience being invited to enjoy two weeks of sporting entertainment against the backdrop of a track depicting the location of the festivities as submerged in contaminated water and shrouded in nuclear winter. Over the years, 'London Calling' has been cited inappropriately so often that the song really seems to have lost all meaning, and this practice is likely to accelerate in the near future. It is, for instance, entirely conceivable that the classic single will be employed to sell London to international investors should the UK fulfil its commitment to leaving the European Union. We might yet then be required to stomach the final indignity of hearing a song crafted by a band that railed against global capital used as the siren call for the various additional forms of dirty money that will potentially be lured to the City in the aftermath of Brexit.

'I'm hearing music from another time'

The ways in which the culture industries have come to venerate and commemorate The Clash have left us, then, with a distorted recollection of the band, one that serves, predictably, to deflect and defuse their radical politics. That this is so should perhaps give pause for thought for those involved in a project such as this one. There is, after all, at least the chance that a book like this might itself simply replicate the problems we have just diagnosed, that the text might, in other words, become just another moment when The Clash are inaugurated yet again into the pantheon of what the arch English satirist Luke Haines has dismissed as 'heritage rock'.[108] How are we to remember the band without laying on them – in Simon Critchley's words – 'the dead hand of commemoration'?[109] There are two principal strategies that suggest themselves here, and we shall consider each in turn.

The first is perhaps the more obvious and requires us to resist the de-historicising practices often beloved of the culture industries. The story of The Clash has, as Marcus Gray reminds us, long since passed into popular cultural mythology.[110] When retracing the steps of a band that more perhaps than any other seemed intent on writing the score of their own legend for the big screen,[111] it is easy to forget that these were real people with real ambitions and pressures living under very real political circumstances. One of the principal intentions and responsibilities of a collection such as this must be to acknowledge and delineate these specificities, to relocate The Clash in their own time and place. While some of this work has been completed in earlier parts of this introduction, it features also in several of the essays to come. Of particular note in this regard is the essay by Jason Toynbee, which places The Clash against a wider geopolitical canvas and suggests that their songs might be heard as a herald of what he terms the 'neoliberal conjuncture'. The task of relocating the group in history is a critical one that allows us to arrive at a more faithful understanding of what they meant and indeed perhaps what they still mean. When we acknowledge The Clash in their own time and their own space, after all, we discharge them from the 'everlasting present'[112] of the culture industries and release a political energy that has long since seemed defused in the age of digital reproduction.

The second strategy available to us takes a rather different tack that at first glance might seem to mimic some of the cultural practices that we have set out to resist. As with all genuinely great popular music, the songs of The Clash are both utterly of their time and entirely timeless. One of the ways that we might arrive at a more critical understanding of the band would, then, be to take them out of their own very particular historical context. There is, of course, the danger that in de-historicising The Clash we might end up doing the same violence to them that the culture industries have over several decades now. In order to avoid this pitfall we might perhaps follow the path mapped out for us by one of the most elusive and supple cultural theorists of the previous century. The insights offered by Walter Benjamin are examined in some detail in two subsequent chapters – in Kieran Cashell's apostate claim that the cultural power of The Clash was already spent in the 'year zero' of 1977, and Colin Coulter's account of the band's powerful channelling of a certain strain of 'left melancholia' – and hence we will restrict ourselves here to a brief preview.

In his writings, Benjamin offers a worldview that famously conjoins the material and the messianic.[113] The defeats that progressive forces have endured in the past, he insists, leave traces that will in time prove to have a redemptive force. It is the role of the revolutionary mind to curate these cultural artefacts, to act as a 'ragpicker' gathering from the field of battle relics of the fallen and tales of the vanquished.[114] These have a political charge that will only become apparent at some point in the future when the field of political possibility widens once more. In such 'moments of danger' we must call to mind the tributes of the 'ragpicker', the cultural traces bequeathed to us by our fallen predecessors. It is this act of recollection, Benjamin insists, that allows us to make that 'leap in the open air of history', that moment of revolutionary transformation in which the future is rewritten and the past redeemed.[115]

In his enigmatic, messianic writings, Walter Benjamin offers a model of recollection that suggests that if we are to recall properly a band such as The Clash, we need to take them out of their own time and place, to 'blast' them out of history, as he would have put it.[116] Benjamin's argument that we must recall the cultural artefacts of past reversals if we are ever to summon the courage for future victories has a real resonance for our purposes here. It is, of course, tempting to hear the songs of The Clash as the soundtrack of a particularly profound moment of political defeat. This was after all a band that issued a challenge to the music industry, only to become a cog in that notoriously exploitative machine; that dispatched various radical political manifestos that they would, inevitably, never come close to fulfilling; that raged against the rise of those very neoliberal forces that would in short order eclipse them. It would be entirely understandable if such a litany of failure were to induce a certain pessimism of both intellect and spirit. Benjamin reminds us, however, that it is precisely the cultural traces that we inherit from these moments of abject reversal that we need to recall if we are ever genuinely to imagine that another world is possible. And maybe that is the spirit in which we need to approach the complex and contradictory story of a band like The Clash. If we are truly to remember the group properly we need to see them in their time and in their place. We need also, however, to 'blast' them out of their historical context and to relocate them in our own, to listen to them as though they were still with us and as though we were hearing them for the very first time.

The particular model of cultural memory that we find in the writings of Walter Benjamin finds certain echoes in the diverse contributions to this collection. In the essays that follow, a range of authors underline that The Clash left us various cultural gifts and that these retain a certain political charge even, or perhaps especially, after all this time. The principal legacy of the band is, of course, a prolific and eclectic body of work that has an enduring aesthetic power and political resonance. In her contribution, former manager Caroline Coon provides some first-hand insights into the origins of these songs, charting the struggle of The Clash to shake off the *do-it-yourself* orthodoxies of the punk era in order to reach creative heights that none of their peers would ever match. The burgeoning ambition of the band would find form in their willingness to embrace a range of musical influences and styles. In her chapter, Ruth Adams underlines that the passion of The Clash for reggae in particular was an important multicultural gesture at a time of febrile racial tensions in the UK and, in hindsight, a formative step in the progressive *outernationalisation* of British society. The appetite of the band for diverse musical forms suggested an openness of mind that would over time give rise to a growing interest in world affairs. One of the greatest legacies of The Clash was in drawing injustices both at home and abroad to the attention of a mass audience that would otherwise perhaps have remained oblivious.[117] The final section of the book draws together four essays that illustrate the power of the band to bring a radical political message to, and about, very different political contexts. While Conrad Brunström's contribution considers the importance of The Clash to the cultural politics of their native London, Harry Browne reflects on the complex ways in which the band connected to the city, New York, that would for a time become their adopted home. In his contribution, Alessandro Moliterno documents the manner in which The Clash used their 1982 tour of Australia to highlight the abuse of Aboriginal rights in that country. While this intervention seemed to resonate with audiences, the political message of The Clash was not always received quite so enthusiastically. In their chapter, Giacomo Bottà and Ferruccio Quercetti document vividly the hostility that the band encountered in 1980 in Bologna at the hands of local *punx* who were less than impressed with their political credentials. While The Clash opened the eyes of many people to the injustices of the world, some of the most important political lessons that came from the band were of a rather more prosaic and personal nature. In his memoir of growing up as a suburban middle-class punk and leaving home to follow The Clash on tour, Martin James reminds us that for all their very human failings, here was a band who were unstintingly generous and humane to their fans.

What emerges from the essays gathered here is the sense that the complex cultural legacy of The Clash has bequeathed to us a great many treasures. Not the least of these is a thirst for political justice, a curiosity about the wider world, a commitment to the possibility of a genuinely multicultural society and a fundamental sense of human decency. Over the last decade or so, there have been various 'moments of danger' that might have prompted us to recall the cultural gifts that we might choose to inherit from the band. The ongoing and seemingly endless era of austerity brings to mind the economic conditions in which The Clash came together to record their incendiary debut album. Moreover, the chauvinism that appears to have been summoned by the Brexit referendum is eerily reminiscent of the climate of racial tension in which the band chose to cover 'Police and Thieves'. In the span of time since the band parted ways, there has perhaps been no point at which The Clash felt quite so relevant to the prevailing political climate as right now. There is, of course – to make what is by now a familiar qualification just once more – a profound risk in acknowledging this. If we issue an invitation to hear The Clash as though they were current artists, we face the danger of compounding the climate of cultural atrophy that deprives such figures of their political force, of adding yet more spectres to those that already haunt popular music, a cultural form that once seemed, wrongly perhaps, the place where the future was under construction, but often now seems capable only of watching itself slowly vanish in the rear view mirror. It is important to note though, as Jacques Derrida reminds us, that the disembodied figure of the spectre not only has ceased to exist but also has yet to exist.[118] This has certain implications for the ways that we might wish to bring to mind a band like The Clash. When we listen in the present to those scores of passionate, funny, angry, melancholy songs we are hearing the 'no longer' that is a set of political ambitions that were defeated with the rise of neoliberalism. We might also, however, be hearing the 'not yet' that is the possibility that these ambitions might still come to pass as the neoliberal project runs aground.[119] It is in that sense that The Clash might just be worth listening to again, and with fresh ears. If we are indeed hearing music from another time – to pluralise that indelible line from 'Spanish Bombs' – then perhaps that time is not the past but the future.

Notes

1 Pat Gilbert, *Passion is a Fashion: The Real Story of The Clash* (London: Aurum Press, 2009), pp. 362–4.
2 Chris Salewicz, *Redemption Song: The Definitive Biography of Joe Strummer* (London: Harper Collins, 2013), p. 237.
3 Marcus Gray, *The Clash: Return of the Last Gang in Town* (London: Helter Skelter, 2001), pp. 237–9.
4 Stuart Bailie, *Trouble Songs: Music and Conflict in Northern Ireland* (Belfast: Bloomfield, 2018), p. 98.
5 Martin McLoone, 'Punk Music in Northern Ireland: The Political Power of "What Might Have Been"', *Irish Studies Review* 12.1 (2004), pp. 29–38.
6 One of the speakers at the conference from which this book derives was

Paul Burgess, formerly of Belfast punk band Ruefrex and now an academic at University College Cork. When asked for his thoughts on the 'riot' he was supposed to have witnessed that evening, Burgess responded: 'By the standards of the time, it was only a two out of ten.'
7. Bailie, *Trouble Songs*, p. 96.
8. Sean Campbell and Gerry Smyth, 'From Shellshock Rock to Ceasefire Sounds: Popular Music', in Colin Coulter and Michael Murray (eds), *Northern Ireland after the Troubles: A Society in Transition* (Manchester: Manchester University Press, 2008), pp. 232–52; Gavin Martin, 'Joe Strummer is Dead: Long live the Clash', *Counterpunch*, 24 December 2002, https://www.counterpunch.org/2002/12/24/strummer-is-dead-long-live-the-clash/ (accessed 12 August 2017); McLoone, 'Punk Rock in Northern Ireland', pp. 29–31; Sean O'Neill and Guy Trelford, *It Makes You Want To Spit! The Definitive Guide to Punk in Northern Ireland* (Dublin: Reekus Music, 2003).
9. *Good Vibrations* (dir. Lisa Barros D'Sa and Glenn Leyburn, 2013). The depiction of punk as an alternative space that allowed young people to transcend the sectarian divide in Northern Ireland was given a contemporary airing in John T. Davis's indelible 1979 documentary *Shellshock Rock*.
10. Bailie, *Trouble Songs*, pp. 100–2.
11. Gilbert, *Passion is a Fashion*, p. 161.
12. Alex Ogg, 'Saint Joe: An Apostate Writes', in Barry J. Faulk and Brady Harrison (eds), *Punk Rock Warlord: The Life and Work of Joe Strummer* (Farnham: Ashgate, 2014), pp. 65–78.
13. Gray, *Return of the Last Gang in Town*, p. 246.
14. Kieran Cashell, 'More Relevance Than Spotlight and Applause: Billy Bragg in the British Folk Tradition', in Ian Peddie (ed.), *Popular Music and Human Rights Volume I: British and American Music* (Farnham: Ashgate, 2011), pp. 5–25; Matthew Worley, 'Revolution Rock? Joe Strummer and the British Left in the Early Days of Punk', in Faulk and Harrison (eds), *Punk Rock Warlord*, pp. 81–92.
15. Figures such as Tony Parsons and Billy Bragg in particular spring to mind here. See Gray, *Return of the Last Gang in Town*, p. 162; Irene Morra, *Britishness, Popular Music, and National Identity: The Making of Modern Britain* (London: Routledge, 2014), p. 174.
16. Samuel Cohen and James Peacock, 'Introduction: The Transnational Clash', in Samuel Cohen and James Peacock (eds), *The Clash Takes on the World: Transnational Perspectives on the Only Band that Matters* (London: Bloomsbury, 2017), pp. 1–25 (p. 5).
17. Salewicz, *Redemption Song*, p. 338.
18. Xan Brooks, '*Three Billboards* Director Martin McDonagh: "Little girls don't have a James Dean to emulate"', *The Guardian*, 11 January 2018, https://www.theguardian.com/film/2018/jan/11/three-billboards-director-martin-mcdonagh-little-girls-dont-have-a-marlon-brando-or-james-dean-to-emulate (accessed 25 February 2018).
19. Cohen and Peacock (eds), *The Clash Takes on the World*; Faulk and Harrison (eds), *Punk Rock Warlord*.

20 Gray, *Return of the Last Gang in Town*, pp. 209–10.
21 Dave Laing, *One Chord Wonders: Power and Meaning in Punk Rock* (Oakland, CA: PM Press, 2015), p. 110.
22 Ibid., p. 114.
23 Ogg, 'Saint Joe', p. 76.
24 Gilbert, *Passion is a Fashion*, p. 224.
25 Simon Frith, *Performing Rites: On the Value of Popular Music* (Oxford: Oxford University Press, 1996), p. 50.
26 Jacques Attali, *Noise: The Political Economy of Music* (Manchester: Manchester University Press, 1985), p. 5.
27 Ibid., p. 11.
28 David Harvey, *A Brief History of Neoliberalism* (Oxford: Oxford University Press, 2005), p. 27.
29 Stuart Hall, 'The Great Moving Right Show', in *Selected Political Writings: The Great Moving Right Show and Other Essays*, ed. Sally Davison, David Featherstone, Michael Rustin and Bill Schwarz (London: Lawrence and Wishart, 2017), pp. 172–86; Jeremy Tranmer, 'The Creation of an Anti-Fascist Icon: Joe Strummer and Rock Against Racism', in Faulk and Harrison (eds), *Punk Rock Warlord*, pp. 93–108.
30 Andrew Gamble, *The Free Economy and the Strong State: The Politics of Thatcherism* (Basingstoke: Palgrave, 1994), p. 105.
31 Ibid., p. 96.
32 Harvey, *A Brief History of Neoliberalism*, pp. 57–8.
33 Gamble, *The Free Economy and the Strong State*, pp. 101–2.
34 Hall, 'The Great Moving Right Show', pp. 173–4.
35 Gilbert, *Passion is a Fashion*, p. 139.
36 Gray, *Return of the Last Gang in Town*, p. 232.
37 Jon Savage, *England's Dreaming: Sex Pistols and Punk Rock* (London: Faber and Faber, 1991), p. 330.
38 Ibid., p. 233.
39 The first three quotes in this paragraph are from 'Remote Control', the final one from 'White Riot'.
40 Gray, *Return of the Last Gang in Town*, p. 150.
41 Savage, *England's Dreaming*, p. 234.
42 Gilbert, *Passion is a Fashion*, pp. 101–4.
43 Savage, *England's Dreaming*, p. 242.
44 Worley, 'Revolution Rock?'
45 Salewicz, *Redemption Song*, pp. 191–3.
46 Gray, *Return of the Last Gang in Town*, pp. 271–3.
47 Samuel Cohen and James Peacock, 'Conclusion: The Only Band that Matters', in Cohen and Peacock (eds), *The Clash Takes on the World*, pp. 243–55.
48 Samuel Cohen, 'Washington Bullets: The Clash and Vietnam', in Cohen and Peacock (eds), *The Clash Takes on the World*, pp. 131–46.
49 Savage, *England's Dreaming*, p. 519.
50 Gilbert, *Passion is a Fashion*, p. 25.
51 Worley, 'Revolution Rock?', p. 91.

52 Ibid., p. 185.
53 Gray, *Return of the Last Gang in Town*, pp. 277–83.
54 Savage, *England's Dreaming*, p. 540.
55 Gamble, *The Free Economy and the Strong State*, p. 36.
56 Ibid., p. 108.
57 The reference here is, of course, to the track 'Guns of Brixton' which appears on *London Calling*. The first writing credit for bassist Paul Simonon, the song offers a premonition of the violence soon to consume that part of the capital.
58 Gamble, *The Free Economy and the Strong State*, p. 117.
59 Cashell, 'More Relevance Than Spotlight and Applause', pp. 6–7.
60 Gilbert, *Passion is a Fashion*, p. 227.
61 Laing, *One Chord Wonders*, p. 53.
62 Johnny Green and Garry Barker, *A Riot of Our Own: Night and Day with The Clash* (London: Indigo, 1997), pp. 161–2.
63 Gilbert, *Passion is a Fashion*, pp. 260–1.
64 Walidah Imarisha, 'Culture Clash: The Impact of Hip Hop Culture and Aesthetics on The Clash', in Faulk and Harrison (eds), *Punk Rock Warlord*, pp. 147–64.
65 Cohen, 'Washington Bullets: The Clash and Vietnam', p. 134.
66 Ibid., p. 137.
67 Tranmer, 'The Creation of an Anti-Fascist Icon', pp. 93–108.
68 Salewicz, *Redemption Song*, pp. 315–19.
69 Tim Satchwell and Joe Streno, *Combat Ready: The Clash* (London: Stay-Free Publishing, 2016).
70 Gilbert, *Passion is a Fashion*, p. 321.
71 Kevin C. Dunn, '"Know Your Rights": Punk Rock, Globalization, and Human Rights', in Peddie (ed.), *Popular Music and Human Rights Volume I*, pp. 27–38.
72 Salewicz, *Redemption Song*, pp. 326–7.
73 The Shea Stadium gigs had in fact been sold out before The Clash were added to the bill and hence no one there had deliberately paid to see the band. Nonetheless, the hugely enthusiastic reception that they received underscores that The Clash appeared at that moment to have crossed over to a mass – that is, white, male, rock – audience in the United States. Gilbert, *Passion is a Fashion*, pp. 325–7.
74 Ibid., p. 317.
75 Gray, *Return of the Last Gang in Town*, pp. 382–3. The pair would collaborate on future recordings for Mick Jones's band Big Audio Dynamite but would never again write together as members of The Clash.
76 Mark Andersen and Ralph Heibutzki, *We are The Clash: Reagan, Thatcher, and the Last Stand of a Band that Mattered* (New York: Akashic Books, 2018).
77 Salewicz, *Redemption Song*, p. 160.
78 Savage, *England's Dreaming*, p. 575.
79 Gray, *Return of the Last Gang in Town*, p. 385.
80 Savage, *England's Dreaming*, p. 541.

81 Antonino D'Ambrosio (ed.), *Let Fury Have the Hour: Joe Strummer, Punk, and the Movement That Shook the World* (New York: Nation Books, 2012).
82 Theodor Adorno, *The Culture Industry: Selected Essays on Mass Culture*, ed. J. M. Bernstein (London: Routledge, 1991).
83 Ogg, 'Saint Joe', pp. 68–70.
84 Ian Maleney, 'The Day The Clash and Punk Turned Trinity into a War Zone', *Irish Times*, 21 October 2017, https://www.irishtimes.com/culture/music/the-day-the-clash-and-punk-turned-trinity-into-a-war-zone-1.3255049 (accessed 21 October 2017).
85 Fredric Jameson, *Postmodernism, or, the Cultural Logic of Late Capitalism* (Durham, NC: Duke University Press, 1991).
86 Ibid., pp. 17–23.
87 Mark Fisher, *Ghosts of My Life: Writings on Depression, Hauntology and Lost Futures* (Alresford: Zero Books, 2014), p. 9.
88 Ibid., p. 10.
89 Ibid., p. 7.
90 This description comes from philosopher Simon Critchley. See Andrew Gallix, 'Rummaging in the Ashes: An Interview with Simon Critchley', in Richard Cabut and Andrew Gallix, *Punk is Dead: Modernity Killed Every Night* (Alresford: Zero Books), pp. 28–40 (p. 38).
91 Cabut and Gallix, *Punk is Dead*, p. 12.
92 Savage, *England's Dreaming*, p. 278.
93 Dick Hebdige, *Subculture: The Meaning of Style* (London: Routledge, 1979), p. 69.
94 The former iconoclast's promotion of Country Life butter, which trades very explicitly on Lydon's long-accomplished status as a slightly errant national treasure, can be viewed here: https://www.youtube.com/watch?v=7mSE-Iy_tFY (accessed 12 February 2018).
95 Owen Hatherley, *The Ministry of Nostalgia* (London: Verso, 2016).
96 Sean O'Hagan, 'Has it really come to this – punk as heritage culture?', *The Observer*, 20 March 2016, https://www.theguardian.com/commentisfree/2016/mar/20/punk-london-spirit-joe-corre-burn-clothes-sex-pistols (accessed 12 February 2018).
97 Savage, *England's Dreaming*, pp. 241–2.
98 The timeless locker room japes of the English sporting icons have been preserved for future generations here: https://www.youtube.com/watch?v=Xf-4Gbqyni4 (accessed 13 February 2018).
99 Cohen and Peacock, 'Introduction: The Transnational Clash', p. 5.
100 Gilbert, *Passion is a Fashion*, p. 130.
101 Sean Egan, *The Clash: The Only Band That Mattered* (London: Rowman and Littlefield, 2015), p. 77.
102 Gray, *Return of the Last Gang in Town*, p. 342.
103 Justin S. Wadlow, '"I am so bored with the USA": Joe Strummer and the Promised Land', in Faulk and Harrison (eds), *Punk Rock Warlord*, pp. 123–46.
104 Gray, *Return of the Last Gang in Town*, p. 381.
105 Edward A. Shannon, '"Don't Call Me Woody": The Punk Compassion and

Folk Rebellion of Joe Strummer and Woody Guthrie', in Faulk and Harrison (eds), *Punk Rock Warlord*, pp. 13–24.
106 This a paraphrase of the comments made by Joe Strummer to the *New Musical Express* journalist Miles in an interview that appeared in the magazine on 11 December 1976. Gilbert, *Passion is a Fashion*, p. 127.
107 Megan Gibson, 'The Clash's "London Calling" Makes for a Bizarre 2012 Olympics Ad', *Time Newsfeed*, 3 August 2011, http://newsfeed.time.com/2011/08/03/the-clashs-london-calling-makes-for-a-bizarre-2012-olympics-ad/ (accessed 12 February 2018).
108 The track 'The Heritage Rock Revolution' appears on Haines's classic 2006 album *Off My Rocker at the Art School Bop* (Degenerate Music).
109 Gallix, 'Rummaging in the Ashes', p. 39.
110 Gray, *Return of the Last Gang in Town*, pp. 439–40.
111 Salewicz, *Redemption Song*, p. 338.
112 Savage, *England's Dreaming*, p. 296.
113 Enzo Traverso, *Left-Wing Melancholia: Marxism, History, and Memory* (New York: Columbia University Press, 2016), pp. 45–8.
114 Walter Benjamin, 'An Outsider Makes his Mark', in *Selected Writings Volume 2, Part 1: 1927–1930*, ed. Michael W. Jennings, Howard Eiland and Gary Smith (Cambridge, MA: Harvard University Press, 1999), p. 310.
115 Walter Benjamin, 'Theses on the Philosophy of History', in *Illuminations*, ed. Hannah Arendt (London: Fontana, 1992), pp. 245–55.
116 For further examination of this metaphor, see Kieran Cashell's essay in this volume.
117 D'Ambrosio, *Let Fury Have the Hour*, p. xxxv.
118 Jacques Derrida, *Specters of Marx: The State of the Debt, the Work of Mourning and the New International*, trans. Peggy Kamuf (London: Routledge, 1994).
119 The distinction/conjunction between the 'no longer' and the 'not yet' in the figure of the spectre appears in the work of Martin Hägglund and informs Mark Fisher's insights into the exhaustion and potential of contemporary popular culture. Fisher, *Ghosts of My Life*, pp. 18–19.

PART I
'No Elvis, Beatles or the Rolling Stones': The Clash, the politics of pop and the neoliberal conjuncture

1

The Clash, revolution and reverse

Jason Toynbee

The career of The Clash coincided with the most intense moment of economic crisis and political struggle in Britain since the Second World War. As The Clash formed in 1976, a wave of strikes hit the UK, and hours lost in industrial disputes reached an all-time high.[1] The British working class, confident and militant, was asserting its collective power. Yet by the time their third album, *London Calling*, was released at the end of 1979, Margaret Thatcher's Tories had come to power on a platform of trade union repression and economic 'reform' in the interest of capitalism. The Clash played out their last years as efforts to push back Thatcherism climaxed (with the 1984 miners' strike) and then subsided. By the time the final version of the band broke up in late 1985, neoliberalism was firmly ensconced in the UK.

I think I've always been aware of this convergence between hard politics (what Francis Mulhern calls 'politics proper')[2] and the path of The Clash, the most overtly political of the major punk rock bands. In the late 1970s and early 1980s, if you were young, on the left and probably white too, you tended to have some sense that The Clash represented *The Struggle*. They recounted it through song, acted it out on stage, and testified to it in interviews. In the early days I was enthusiastic about this, but less so later on when Joe Strummer's pronouncements often seemed naive and out of tune with the times. I'd also stopped listening to the band.

Then in the 1990s I became an academic just as the critique of 'authenticity' in rock was emerging in the new field of popular music studies. The Clash looked like a pretty good example of what was wrong with the whole tradition of authentic expression in rock: they seemed deluded by their own mythology and too earnest by half. Still, it was hard to argue with their extraordinary music, which remained anchored in popular forms, from rock'n'roll to reggae to disco. This made them a difficult band to categorise.

Now, with the benefit of another twenty years of history (first the entrenchment of neoliberalism and then, after 2008, systemic crisis), I look back and wonder whether my earliest assessment of the band was so far off target after all. Perhaps they did encapsulate the spirit of struggle, and their 'authenticity' was valid, necessary even. That at least is the rather tentative thesis I start with in this chapter. My aim is to sharpen it up and test it as we go, using a Marxist approach to culture and history. And because the 'base and superstructure' model is so important in this approach, I want to start by saying something about it.

Base, superstructure and The Clash

According to Marx, 'relations of production constitute the economic structure of society, the real basis on which rises a legal and political superstructure and to which correspond definite forms of social consciousness. The mode of production of material life conditions the general process of social, political and intellectual life.'[3] But if the economic base does indeed 'condition' the various dimensions of the superstructure, the big question is of what precisely does such conditioning consist? Since the 1960s much effort has been exerted on this problem. A key issue has been how to avoid *reductionism*, in other words the idea that superstructure, including its cultural dimension, is a mere effect of the economy and can be simply explained by it.[4] The problem is that such a notion leads to a pessimistic dead end: all music produced in a capitalist economy encapsulates the homogenising logic of the commodity, as Adorno suggested, or it simply represents capitalist interests through some kind of system-supporting 'message'. Many attacks on popular music presume a crude base–superstructure model along these lines. Yet such a model fails to account for even the most nakedly commercial pop music which, against all critical expectations, can cross the threshold into unhinged beauty. In the case of an act such as The Clash, whose music was explicitly anti-capitalist (even while being a commercial product of the capitalist cultural industries), the reductionist model of base and superstructure makes no sense at all.

The way forward must surely be to loosen the tie, and allow that music making, as with all aspects of the superstructure, emerges indirectly from the economic base. As a result, it develops distinctive modes and traditions. And within these, musicians have a good deal of shaping power of their own. What's more, music as a superstructural phenomenon can act 'backwards' down upon the base. So, the music industry has to respond to new movements, genres and ideas generated by musicians and fans. In other words, if the base sets the general conditions – commodity form, profitability, relations of workers, including musicians, to the means of production – nevertheless music making has a degree of autonomy about it. It seems to me that The Clash exemplified this autonomy very well. They pushed it to the limit and in so doing challenged not only the music industry, but the capitalist system as a whole.

As well as pointing to the complex and emergent nature of music as superstructure, we need to open out the concept of the economic base. It is not inert, a merely mechanical object. As Raymond Williams reminds us, the base consists in the activity of people. It is a process. And as Roy Bhaskar emphasises, just as much as superstructure, it depends upon thinking and ideas. In other words, under capitalism the base consists in practices of going to work, of buying and selling shares, of developing new technologies and so on. What then distinguishes it as the base is the fact that such activities 1) have a material end, and 2) are organised in a specifically capitalist way, involving the exploitation of labour to extract surplus value (including 'profit') via the production of commodities for exchange. Together these forces and relations of production constrain the kind of culture, laws and state which exist in a capitalist society. One other point. It is wrong to identify base and superstructure with particular institutions. Music production, for example, belongs to base as much as superstructure. So, The Clash were not just musicians, but cultural workers employed in a cultural industry, and as such their working lives were strongly shaped by its economic imperatives. In the case of culture, then, superstructure is 'nested' within the base, a circumstance that yields a very direct and close relation of force from the latter to the former, but also feedback in the other direction. The result is a paradoxically strong/weak form of autonomy for musicians.

Crisis and the long 1968

In all the advanced capitalist countries for twenty-five years after the Second World War there was an unprecedented period of economic growth, leading to high rates of employment and continuous wage increases. What's more, labour's share of wealth grew at the expense of capital. These developments reflected the renewed power of organised labour. It was manifested in unionisation, welfarism and intervention in the economy by the state; also the willingness of corporations to enter into long-term agreements with unions about wages and conditions. At the same time, higher education was expanding, and feeding into a new fraction of technical and knowledge workers.[5] By the mid-1960s, however, this apparently benign regime was starting to break down. Inflation encouraged increasing militancy among workers across western Europe as they pushed to keep their wages ahead of consumer price increases. 'Wild cat' strikes (in other words unofficial strikes, not endorsed by trade unions) then added to the pressure not only on employers but also governments struggling to manage their national economies.[6] At root here was a declining rate of profit, whose causes are argued over by Marxist as much as mainstream economists.[7] There is, unfortunately, no space to examine the debate here.

More importantly for the present argument, these developments at the base (a growing crisis in the relations of production) were matched by the emergence of what later came to be called 'new social movements' (NSMs).[8] Student mobilisations for reform of education and against the Vietnam War, the black power movement in the United States, and a new wave of feminism; these and other forms of protest seemed to depart from traditional left politics in significant ways. For one thing, their demands were not economic for the most part, going beyond a concern with wages and working conditions. Rather they encompassed issues of identity and recognition. There was also an emphasis on new forms of organisation with direct democracy via councils and assemblies, and direct action in the shape of occupations and teach-ins, for example.

In much of the history and theorisation of NSMs a sharp break has been posed between NSMs and the traditional left. This was not just at the level of demands and organisation but also in terms of social structure. Where the traditional labour movement was essentially working class, NSM theorists pointed to the middle-class or mixed nature of the new movements. They simply did not belong to the grand narrative of Marxist class struggle with its pitched battle between labour and capital. However, along with a new generation of Marxist scholars, I would argue that the notion of a sharp break between NSMs and the labour movement in the 1960s and 1970s is wide of the mark.[9] Partly this is a matter of continuity. The 'new' phenomenon was not actually so new. In fact, parallel kinds of social movement go back to the early days of the fight against capitalism in the nineteenth century.[10] But the relationship between the two phenomena is also key. NSMs, and indeed less specifically political cultures of resistance such as rock and soul music, were not so much radically distinct from the intensifying class struggle of the period as *emergent from it*.

In terms of base and superstructure we might say that there was a high degree of articulation between the crisis at the base and new kinds of protest and cultural expression. This is surely what might be expected at a time of systemic conflict as in the 1960s and 1970s. The relatively stable setting of conditions upwards from base to superstructure was undermined, and new refractions of the revolt against the capitalist order manifested themselves. Still, the thread that united all the movements from labour militancy to the new feminism was resistance to post-war capitalist domination. Across a range of social relations, control and deference, or 'knowing one's place', were breaking down.[11] It is difficult to be precise about the specific kind and direction of causes here, but they were surely multiple and included agitation by one group of insurgents of another, for example students inspired by workers; formation of new class fractions such as a young, technically educated middle class; and resistance to old forms of authoritarianism, for instance legally enshrined racial domination in the United States. The key point is that underlying all these specific kinds of destabilisation was the breakdown of the post-war economic settlement with its promise of continuously improving wages and conditions. In effect, the crisis of profit at the base animated both newer and older kinds of social struggle. As Gerd-Rainer Horn suggests, this upheaval pivoted on the revolutionary year of 1968 when workers and students rose up from Paris to Mexico City.[12] In fact, though, it lasted more than twenty years, the same twenty years in which a profound transformation in the sound and meaning of Anglo-American popular music took place.

The Clash and punk and rock

Later writers, as much as participants in the subculture, have tended to read punk as a revolt against 1960s rock and its legacy: the 'dinosaurs' such as the Rolling Stones, Pink Floyd and Led Zeppelin. More historically informed accounts take into account the 'bleak' urban background of late 1970s New York or London. But by and large this is a story of internal revolution within the larger formation of rock music. I want to argue that such an interpretation is flawed. In fact, there is strong continuity between the music of the mid-1960s and that of ten or fifteen years later. The most obvious point to make is that punk used the same instruments in the same combinations as the 'beat groups'. In the UK, these groups had attempted to copy black American 'rhythm and blues' recordings using a basic instrumental line-up of bass, guitar(s) and drums, sometimes augmented with keyboards. But without the full range of brass and string instruments, the specific skills of African-American musicians, or the sophisticated recording and arranging techniques available in US studios, the beat groups translated the sounds and songs they were trying to copy into a stripped down, local idiom.[13] Quite quickly, the British groups – notably The Beatles – began to write their own material, becoming, in effect, autonomous writing, performing and recording units.[14]

This idiom and form of production then spread back to the USA where it rapidly evolved as part of a largely Anglo-American musical network and market. From the outset the new music was made by and for young people. By the second half of the 1960s, however, it was becoming associated with the emerging counterculture. Amorphous in its organisation and goals, the counterculture was less explicitly political than other new social movements of the period. Nevertheless, it did encapsulate a significantly new set of values that were to have a lasting influence on rock and pop music. These values included a bohemian emphasis on individual free expression, the rejection of bourgeois manners, an interest in drug-induced psychical experiences and enthusiasm for new collective 'lifestyles' – communal living and so on. Contradictions between the first and last of these (individualism and collectivism) ultimately undermined the counterculture as a political movement. But the key point for the present argument is that its values and practices persisted in punk. In other words, there was continuity not only in musical materials, but also social-cultural values across the infamous divide of 1976.

Joe Strummer's own life story exemplifies this. The middle-class son of a nurse and a diplomat, Strummer was a public school (private school in US terminology) drop-out who completed his education by dropping out one more time, from the Central School of Art and Design in London. By the early 1970s he had moved to Newport, Wales, where he hung out at, though he did not attend, the town's art college. Here he began playing in a band. On returning to the capital he moved into a squat while forming a new group. Critically, the West London squatting scene in which he was now immersed encompassed a range of activities and lifestyles from anarchist politics to rock music making. Strummer's training as a musician and his political education were thus classically countercultural. Mick Jones came from a working-class background, but he too (along with the other members of The Clash) went through the transition from youth to adulthood in the bohemian, countercultural milieu of Britain in the late 1960s and early 1970s. This was the world in which punk was formed.

The commonplace notion of 1976 as a punk 'year zero' actually becomes easier to understand with this in mind. In effect, punk was a declaration of renewal, excessive in its claims precisely because its music and politics represented an attempt to extend and deepen the radical rock project that had first emerged a decade earlier. However, the political climate in Britain had changed in important ways by 1976, and labour insurgency and the new social movements were reaching a crossroads. Intensification of industrial conflict that year brought a wave of strikes across public and private sectors of the economy. This militancy of the working class played a large part in bringing down income inequality to its lowest point in UK history.[15]

Despite these substantial material gains, in an important sense struggle against the constraints of capitalism as a system had stalled. At the level of national politics, an increasingly right-wing Labour government was pursuing a contradictory policy of addressing rising unemployment by introducing training and job-creation schemes, while at the same trying to reduce inflation by cutting public spending and pushing down wages, especially in the public sector where it had direct control of the pay roll. In March 1976 James Callaghan took over as Prime Minister after the resignation of Harold Wilson. As Donald Sassoon calls it, Callaghan was 'a shrewd but visionless product of conservative Labourism'.[16] His appointment reinforced the obvious point that the forward march of Labour, both as a radical movement and a governing party, had halted. The widespread sense of suspended political animation and broken promises that followed is precisely the context of the emerging British punk scene. Dreams of a better world were fading even while rock dinosaurs still lumbered across the musical plains. Punk raged against this situation.

What then marked out The Clash; what was their particular contribution to punk insurrection? In the first place, I'd say it was the very didacticism of their music/politics. There is an extraordinary directness about Clash lyrics. Their much-discussed social realism (and reference to the banality of everyday life) is starkly concrete. Places are named, people identified, and metaphor is eschewed in favour of bluntness. 'Career Opportunities' on the first album lists all the non-opportunities (army, airforce, tea-making, police ...) that confront working-class youth, as opposed – we immediately understand – to the government's promises about training and job creation. Meanwhile, according to 'Garageland', 'things are hotting up in the West End' where, in the offices of predatory record companies, contracts are imposed on once countercultural musicians. They sell out in return for new suits and boots. On 'White Riot' the notion of riot as a political tactic is extended from black young people to white youth. Never mind the naivety of such a politics. What I'm trying to draw attention to here is the didactic nature of The Clash's political lyrics, their directness. This is then anchored in musical style – uptempo, declaimed vocals, stripped down backbeat, references to 1950s rock'n'roll, and gestures towards duple march-time. All are signifiers of musical urgency that effectively double the political urgency of the meaning of the words. Early on at least this was shocking. The Clash, like other punk groups, had a powerful agitprop effect because they broke the convention of 'artistry' (from Dylan to prog) that had enveloped rock. Punk bludgeoned, but in so doing it punched through the veil of ideology.

Here I take issue with a certain revisionist approach in popular music studies that refuses this kind of political reading. Peter Wicke, for instance, argues that:

> it is pure romanticism to explain punk rock as the musical means of expression of the young unemployed. They did indeed place rock music in a specific cultural context of use, but this context was determined not by their political consciousness but by the structures of the everyday life they lived. Within this context music [...] again followed the characteristic dynamics of a commercially organised mass music.[17]

It is worth noting in response that punk's constituency extended well beyond the young unemployed. Notionally, it took in working-class youth as a whole, though actually, as we have seen, punk was much more like the preceding rock culture, in that it was a bohemian coalition straddling middle- and working-class youth. The key point, though, is that none of this undermined punk's (albeit naive) politics of resistance and identification with a dominated working class. There is a similar problem with Wicke's suggestion that punk's embeddedness in commerce nailed the lid on the coffin of its politics. In fact, bands knew very well, and constantly criticised, the exploitation of punk by the music industry. Witness, for instance, the critique of a song such as 'Garageland'. There were also the 'DIY' practices of some punks – independent micro-labels and shops, musicians' collectives, distribution by bicycle and so on. These enabled a degree of autonomy, if only for relatively marginal and small-scale music making.[18]

Overall, then, we can say that there were deep contradictions in punk's dual position as an anti-systemic movement and a genre of popular music. For groups such as The Clash, signed to major labels, such contradictions would become overwhelming over time. But, initially at least, punk bands had significant room for manoeuvre that derived from their social role as music makers. As we saw in the discussion of base and superstructure earlier, the particular slot occupied by cultural producers whereby they are granted a good deal of control over their creativity yields an unusual degree of autonomy, far exceeding that of most workers. And it is these conditions that then enabled the new political consciousness of punk subculture, a sense of progress stalled, to be articulated in the music of bands such as The Clash.

Attack as the best form of defence: The Clash at the dawn of neoliberalism

For all that, punk quickly lost its way. The problem was not selling out or commercial manipulation so much as semiotic exhaustion. All popular music genres have relatively poor codes; in other words, their simple rules are only capable of generating a limited array of musical works. As a result, musical communities (consisting of both makers and listeners) become 'analytically competent' rather quickly. This competence brings with it awareness of predictability and boredom. According to Franco Fabbri, once this situation has been reached, change and renewal may then occur via transgression of generic codes.[19] Such was the process through which punk had developed in the first place. It was, in part at least, a response to the growing predictability of established rock. Paradoxically, though, the very simplicity of punk's coding and materials, which, as we saw, yielded its shock effect, meant that by the same token predictability set in quite quickly.

We can hear this on the second Clash album, *Give 'Em Enough Rope*, released in November 1978 in the UK, where there is a good deal of continuity with the first album. Overseen by US producer Sandy Pearlman, the sound is sharper, harder and more polished than on previous recordings. But in terms of structure and approach, the songs follow that mode of didactic urgency which characterised the earlier material. The track listing gives a strong hint of this: 'Safe European Home', 'English Civil War', 'Tommy Gun', 'Julie's Been Working for the Drug Squad', 'Last Gang in Town', 'Guns on the Roof', 'Drug-Stabbing Time', 'Stay Free', 'Cheapskates', 'All the Young Punks…'.

What we have here is more agitprop, urban social realism and boy-gang bonding songs. The best tracks, such as 'Tommy Gun', are great pop tunes in which strong melodies and hooks rub up against lyrical grit and punk sonority. The re-versioning of the American Civil War song 'When Johnny Comes Marching Home' in 'English Civil War' is wonderfully effective, with its dystopian vision of an ultra-right-wing 'new party army' (a reference to the National Front, no doubt) rampaging through London. Generally, though, *Give 'Em Enough Rope* continues with the repertoire of stylistic elements developed by the band over its first two years of existence. If semiotic exhaustion has not quite set in yet, it is surely imminent.

At this difficult moment around two years into the emergence of punk and the career of The Clash, the political situation in the UK was reaching crisis point. The so-called 'winter of discontent' of 1978/79 involved large-scale strikes by public-sector unions which were supported by the federation of British unions, the Trades Union Congress (TUC). On the other side, the Labour government of James Callaghan was now set firmly on a policy of holding down public-sector wages. In effect, an open civil war had erupted within the labour movement. Under a previous agreement ('the Social Contract'), the TUC with its constituent unions had agreed to cap their demands for wage increases. And in fact inflation had fallen from 27 per cent to single figures. But now 'mutualism' was abandoned. The government insisted on a maximum of 5 per cent pay increases, even while motor manufacturer Ford was agreeing to a 17 per cent deal in response to strikes across its UK plants. As public-sector unions representing many low-paid workers who had received below-inflation settlements over the previous two years began a series of strikes (health service workers, gravediggers, fire fighters, railway workers), Labour's wage policy looked to be in ruins. In the run-up to the General Election on 3 May 1979, party leader Margaret Thatcher reversed the Conservatives' previous (relatively) conciliatory policy towards the unions. With a campaign slogan of 'Labour Isn't Working', and using images of the previous winter's strikes, the Conservatives won the election on an anti-trade-union ticket.[20] As we now know, the first neoliberal government in an advanced capitalist country had been elected.

A few days later, The Clash began jamming, writing and rehearsing the material for what would become their third studio album, *London Calling*. This followed twelve months or so of writers' block for Strummer and Jones, and the sacking of manager Bernie Rhodes. The Clash had occupied a wasteland of uncertainty. Now, though, they were concentrating on working together as a band again, with Paul Simonon and Topper Headon very much part of the creative unit, playing covers and trying out new ideas in an intense and sustained regime of work. By August they were recording, this time with British producer Guy Stevens. Stevens had worked with soul acts in the 1960s as well as British psychedelic rock bands. His open yet sometimes bizarrely interventionist approach seemed to suit the rejuvenated Clash.[21]

London Calling is an extraordinary piece of work. Significantly, the band continue to use punk materials: Strummer's declaimed vocals, staccato rhythm guitar and the other stylistic elements we noted earlier. But now 'punk' becomes a metanarrative, a means of framing a series of other musical codes. Notably, there are references to rock'n'roll, ska, contemporary reggae, Phil Spector's Wall of Sound and soul music. Saxophones make an appearance, even disco drumming and octave bass (on 'Lost in the Supermarket'). Yet this is far from mere eclecticism or pastiche. The references are synthesised, pulled into an almost integrated whole. That 'almost' matters. Crucially, there is enough distance between musical voices to generate *frisson*, perhaps a degree of Brechtian alienation. Where previously The Clash had used the blunt instrument of univocal punk aggression, now there is polyphony. Something like Bakhtin's much discussed dialogism is in play here. The distinct voices and echoes of other musical styles 'interanimate' one another, drawing attention to the citation that's going on.[22]

One aspect of this is Joe Strummer's singing. He manages to maintain the 'Strummer' inflection, simultaneously hoarse and adenoidal. Yet he is now employing it in diverse ways: more interpolation with everyday speech, whispering, an approximation of crooning, falsetto passages, even word-swallowing self-parody. In addition, beyond his own singing and playing, Jones has a key role in writing, conceiving and arranging the collage that is *London Calling*. Headon's drumming is crucial too. He comes into his own as a super-adept drummer who can move in and out of diverse styles through the medium of sticks and skins. Meanwhile Simonon, a tyro in 1976, has become an extremely competent bass player, well able to work across the various idioms that are deployed on the album.

What about the politics? The point, I think, is that the message of popular resistance and dystopian critique developed in the earlier material is actually amplified with the new musical approach. Where previously punk directness 'doubled' the urgency of the lyrics, the shifting musical landscape of *London Calling* underlines the politics in a different way. It is a function of that 'almost' integration of elements, whereby the juxtaposition of styles draws attention to semantic content. A constantly shifting, rippling musical fabric seems to unstitch the words, foregrounding their enunciation and thereby their meaning.

The opening and title track, 'London Calling', sets the agenda. Certainly, it points towards the future, namely a dystopian scenario of social conflict.

Yet at one and the same time, the song is portraying the situation in Britain *now* in 1979, after the election of the most right-wing and combative government in living memory. More than that, it is a call to arms to resist:

London calling to the faraway towns
Now war is declared and battle come down

If indeed 'the ice age is coming, the sun is zooming in', nevertheless it seems by the last verse that catastrophe can be averted. Strummer, in the guise of narrator, looks back and observes, 'yes, I was there, too/ an' you know what they said? Well, some of it was true!' After all, then, he has survived. No foolhardy confidence here. This is a sober assessment of political possibility in desperate times. Against the odds we can, we will, win.

In 'Working for the Clampdown' the scenario is again one of intensifying repression. As with the album as a whole, context is everything here. And once again, Thatcher's arrival in Downing Street is conjured up. Before the election Strummer had written a personal manifesto for the weekly music paper *New Musical Express* calling for the reunification of Ireland and criticising Conservative policies.[23] Now as the band worked long hours in the studio the political backdrop was gloomy and repressive. As bad as the Labour government might have seemed, Thatcher and her cabinet were of a different order, with their programme of austerity and their assault on organised labour. This surely is the step change in British politics, the clampdown, to which the song refers. In the song, though, the resistance wins decisively through an act of will, by letting 'fury have the hour' and being prepared to 'kick over the wall' causing 'government's [*sic*] to fall'.

Reversal

Base and superstructure exist by dint of their relations, as Raymond Williams emphasises. The former sets limits to, and exerts pressures on, the latter. Here Williams is critical of older formulations in which base is conceived as controlling or prefiguring superstructure.[24] Quite simply, any conception of base determining superstructure in a direct or inflexible way does violence to the complexity and change that are the stuff of concrete history. As I argued earlier, what makes more sense is a kind of loose-tight notion of base–superstructure, one that among other things allows for the way that an activity such as music making is part of *both* levels. Contradictions but also opportunities for political action follow, as we saw in the activity of The Clash.

But the question also arises of history and temporal coincidence, or lag, between changes at the base and in the superstructure.[25] This question is posed most sharply during periods of systemic crisis as in the 1960s and

1970s. So, the rapid emergence of the counterculture in the mid-1960s coincided almost exactly with the moment when the first fissures began to tear apart the post-war economic order. There is a sense here that shifts in culture and the rise of new social movements almost anticipated crisis in the base, namely the end of the long boom and renewed industrial conflict. In contrast, at the start of the 1980s, as capitalist order was reimposed, cultural and political resistance persisted for several more years. Here, then, superstructural developments – specifically political culture and action – had a certain impetus that carried over into the newly hostile environment. In the UK, the turning point was the miners' strike of 1984 when, despite a desperately hard-fought struggle, the miners were defeated by Thatcher's Tory government (mining was a publicly owned industry in the UK). As new anti-trade-union legislation was introduced in the wake of the strike, so too it seemed popular music was taking a turn away from the innovation of punk and post-punk[26] towards the conformity of the New Pop. All the while capitalism at the base was rapidly developing in significantly new ways, adapting to the crisis of profitability through the shaking out of manufacturing jobs in the old industrialised regions and the export of these jobs to factories in industrialising countries in parts of what had previously been the 'Third World'. Along with this, and particularly in the UK, came the growth of financial services, banking and so on.[27]

Clearly, then, the inauguration of neoliberalism was contested. Relations of force were exerted between culture, politics and economy in contradictory ways. Sometimes, superstructural developments at the level of law and the state seemed to be ahead of developments in relations of production. Yet the 'old' political and cultural resistance also persisted beyond the insurrectionary moment of the late 1970s into the new era.

What light can the later career of The Clash throw on this transitional moment? According to the standard account, *London Calling* represents something like a high point in the musical career of The Clash. Its conjoint aesthetic-political power was never to be repeated. In 1981 Joe Strummer was keen to emphasise that 'we're getting a lot more political in our old age. As I get older my politics are clarifying themselves, becoming more pointed. More potent...'[28] It seems, then, that the political will of the band was undiminished after *London Calling*. What had changed, though, were the conditions of musical creativity that might enable expression of those politics.

First, a caveat; it is simply not the case that the albums and performances tell a simple story of decline. In fact, on *Sandinista!* (1980) and *Combat Rock* (1982) the music was changing in significant new ways. True, the first of these suffered from an acute lack of editing. The band took the demands of CBS and their own management for concision simply as unwarranted interference.[29] In the end, The Clash got what they wanted – a budget triple album – but the result was a sprawling concoction with too much weak material spread across the six vinyl sides. That said, there were brilliant moments too.

'The Magnificent Seven', for instance, was a very early, but highly successful appropriation of hip hop in a rock context. The vocal phrasing has a strong kinship with hip hop, as Joe Strummer declaims over a quasi-disco bass line played by Norman Watt-Roy of The Blockheads. This is still a *Strummer* voice though: hoarse, urgent, English. Far from yielding pastiche, what we get is savage parody as, through the aperture between punk and rap, Strummer zooms in on a series of scenes from everyday life under capitalism. Ever a critic of The Clash on the grounds of their faux-authenticity and musical naivety, Simon Reynolds does not approve. He cites a 'sardonic allusion [by post-punk group Scritti Politti] to The Clash's idea of themselves as "The Magnificent Seven"'.[30] I think this is a misreading. Nowhere in the track is there any identification of the band with that romantic gang of brigands. Rather, the Magnificent Seven appear to be nothing less than the working class itself – abused, exploited, misled but ultimately unbowed. The rhyme – 'You're fretting, you're sweating/ But did you notice, you ain't getting' – holds the key. There's also a reference to Marx and Engels at the 'seven eleven'. Strummer is now critiquing the system from a clearly socialist perspective, though with his usual mix of directness and often surrealist wit.

Still, if The Clash were capable of producing great new music at the start of the 1980s, there was also a strong sense that as a creative and performing unit the band had begun to encounter serious problems. For one thing, they were falling out with each other. Already during the New York recording sessions for *Sandinista!* observers noted increasing tension between Jones and Strummer.[31] And by 1981 Topper Headon was descending into heroin addiction.[32] Of course, heavy drug use and the transformation of creative intimacy into distrust and rivalry are perennial problems found in rock bands. But there was another factor that made these issues much harder to cope with: a contradiction between the group's professed radicalism and the actuality of being a major label act.

Earlier we examined how 'loose-tight' base–superstructure relations in the cultural sector allow for a degree of creative, and potentially political, autonomy for musicians. So it was for the early Clash. But the commercial logic of rock, as in all the winner-takes-all markets for cultural products, is the maximisation of audiences.[33] Key here is the vast US market. CBS/Epic were clear about this, and they supported and promoted ever larger tours across the US as the band began to establish themselves there. Strummer, and I think Jones and Simonon too, were happy to go along with this in part at least because the goal of selling more records and playing to larger concert audiences was about something more than commerce. Just as with radical parties and social movements, so with The Clash, to effect change one has to take one's message to the largest possible number of people. However, the stardom that followed then took them away from their audiences: gigs were less intimate celebrations of collectivity, more huge spectacles of commodification. In general terms, we might say that the band were falling in line with the established protocols of rock commerce. Fame also exacerbated stress and personal tensions. For Headon, addiction followed by expulsion from the band had much to do with the corrosive effects of celebrity. So too the fall-out between Strummer and Jones that led to the latter's firing in 1983. These contradictions of politics and commerce had been latent in the band's early career. But in the period after *London Calling* they increasingly, and destructively, made themselves manifest.

This makes the return to form of *Combat Rock* (1982) all the more remarkable an achievement. As well as two great pop punk anthems in 'Should I Stay or Should I Go' and 'Rock the Casbah' there is some of the most accomplished agitprop yet from the band. For instance, the opening track 'Know Your Rights' unmercifully lashes the bourgeois pretensions of the 'rule of law'. On the other hand, the politics of 'Red Angel Dragnet', co-written and declaimed by Paul Simonon, are more oblique. Apparently a hymn to the uniformed vigilantes, or 'volunteer cops', who were patrolling the lawless streets of New York at that time, the track is, we finally realise, a critique. Having invoked Travis Bickle (the De Niro anti-hero from Scorsese's *Taxi Driver*) as prophet of the Red Angels, only a few lines later Simonon asks 'What is the dream?/ I'll tell it/ To live like they do in the movies.' In other words, overcoming the violence of the neoliberal city through popular justice is as much a fantasy as any Hollywood film. The key point is that the later Clash held to the band's original radical project. What they could not overcome, though, were the accumulating contradictions generated by claims for political authenticity on the one hand and the fact of rock stardom on the other.

Meanwhile, other, larger contradictions generated by neoliberalism at a world historical level put the final boot in, as it were. Here the sharp swing to the right in the UK and US, in other words the struggle for control of the state and the commanding heights of the economy, made any cultural expression of anti-capitalist politics much more problematic than it had been a few years earlier. Most importantly, the 'authoritarian populist' governments[34] of Thatcher and Reagan were now using supply-side economic policy to generate unemployment and the export of manufacturing jobs. One after another, strikes were defeated and anti-union laws enacted to take the strike weapon out of workers' hands. When defeat is overlaid upon defeat in this way, the political force of cultural expression is severely curtailed. Tone and mood become liable to anachronism. What was once righteous determination to fight now looks like bombast. Even the post-punk avant-garde was suffering from that contradiction.

But whereas the post-punk bands either left the scene or reinvented themselves, with *Cut the Crap* in 1985 the rump of The Clash (Strummer and Simonon) stumbled into a chasm between political claim and political reality. The attempt at renewal through a return to punk fundamentals yielded little of musical interest, and ultimately the demand to *cut the crap* was simply an embarrassment. I don't mean to suggest that resistance had become futile, an all-too-easy conclusion to reach with the benefit of hindsight. But it *was* surely the case that sloganising from stage or studio could have little purchase now. Rather, any renewal of struggle would need to be, in the first place, a properly political response to neoliberalism and its brutal ordering of the material conditions of life. More than thirty years later such a response is only just starting to come in fits and starts.

Reckoning

So what to conclude about The Clash-in-their-time, that short but momentous bout from the last gasp of the extended revolution of 1968 to the inauguration of neoliberal capitalism? First, in their role as cultural workers The Clash were exemplary activists. They took on the task of representing the downtrodden and showing up the capitalist system as both oppressive and dishonest. Second, as music makers they developed a rich palette that enabled the renewal of elements of punk musical style to powerful aesthetic effect. Third, their artistic achievements, as writers and performers, depended on an understanding by audiences that they were authentic in their commitment to politics – that they 'meant it'. Fourth, the career of the band showed the possibilities, but also the limitations of cultural activism.

Marx's major insight about base and superstructure (developed by later writers) was that while capitalism is indeed a system, it is not monolithic. Culture emerges from, rather than being strictly determined by, the economy. And particularly in times of crisis, opportunities for resistance in the cultural sphere open up: in the late 1970s crisis enabled The Clash to fly. Still, by definition cultural workers are political auxiliaries, and they can only serve the fight for emancipation in a subordinate role. When crisis is succeeded by the re-establishment of capitalist class power, all the contradictions of political art intensify, so that even a group with the energy and determination of The Clash cannot transcend the difficulties they encounter. In sum, their short career demonstrates the power of music to move and shake the world, even if this is to a great extent a dependent power.

Notes

1 Douglas A. Hibbs Jr, 'On the Political Economy of Long-Run Trends in Strike Activity', *British Journal of Political Science* 8 (1978), pp. 153–75.
2 Francis Mulhern, *Culture/Metaculture* (London: Routledge, 2000).

3 Karl Marx, 'A Contribution to the Critique of Political Economy: Part One Preface', in John F. Sitton (ed.), *Marx Today: Selected Works and Recent Debates* (New York: Palgrave Macmillan, 2010), p. 92.
4 Roy Bhaskar, *The Possibility of Naturalism: A Philosophical Critique of the Contemporary Human Sciences* (London: Routledge, 1998), pp. 65–7; Raymond Williams, 'Base and Superstructure in Marxist Cultural Theory', *New Left Review* I.82 (1973), pp. 3–16.
5 Eric Hobsbawm, *Age of Extremes: The Short Twentieth Century, 1914–1991* (London: Abacus, 1995), pp. 295–8.
6 Donald Sassoon, *One Hundred Years of Socialism: The West European Left in the Twentieth Century* (London: I.B. Tauris), pp. 357–82.
7 Michael Roberts, *The Great Recession: Profit Cycles, Economic Crisis – a Marxist View* (London: Lulu Press, 2009).
8 J. L. Cohen, 'Strategy or Identity: New Theoretical Paradigms and Contemporary Social Movements', *Social Research* 52 (1985), pp. 663–716.
9 Colin Barker, Laurence Cox, John Krinsky and Alf Gunvald Nilsen, 'Marxism and Social Movements: An Introduction', in Colin Barker, Laurence Cox, John Krinsky and Alf Gunvald Nilsen (eds), *Marxism and Social Movements* (Leiden: Brill, 2013), pp. 1–40.
10 Paul D'Anieri, Claire Ernst and Elizabeth Kier, 'New Social Movements in Historical Perspective', *Comparative Politics* 22.4 (1990), pp. 445–58.
11 Anti-colonial and national liberation struggles in the global south preceded yet also paralleled these developments in the advanced capitalist countries.
12 Gerd-Rainer Horn, *The Spirit of '68: Rebellion in Western Europe and North America, 1956–1976* (Oxford: Oxford University Press, 2007).
13 Allan F. Moore, *Rock: The Primary Text – Developing a Musicology of Rock*, 2nd edn (Abingdon: Routledge, 2016).
14 Jason Toynbee, 'Fingers to the Bone or Spaced Out on Creativity? Labour Process and Ideology in the Production of Pop', in Andrew Beck (ed.), *Cultural Work: Understanding the Cultural Industries* (London: Routledge, 2002), pp. 39–55.
15 Stephen P. Jenkins, 'The Income Distribution in the UK: A Picture of Advantage and Disadvantage', CASE Paper 186 (Centre for Analysis of Social Exclusion, London School of Economics, 2015), Fig. 4, p. 11.
16 Sassoon, *One Hundred Years of Socialism*, p. 498.
17 Peter Wicke, *Rock Music: Culture, Aesthetics and Sociology* (Cambridge: Cambridge University Press, 1990), p. 147.
18 David Hesmondhalgh, 'Indie: The Institutional Politics and Aesthetics of a Popular Music Genre', *Cultural Studies* 13.1 (1999), pp. 34–61.
19 Franco Fabbri, 'A Theory of Musical Genres: Two Applications', in David Horn and Philip Tagg (eds), *Popular Music Perspectives* (Göteborg and Exeter: International Association for the Study of Popular Music, 1982), pp. 52–81.
20 Sassoon, *One Hundred Years of Socialism*, pp. 497–509.
21 Chris Salewicz, *Redemption Song: The Definitive Biography of Joe Strummer* (London: Harper Collins, 2006).

22 M. M. Bakhtin, 'Discourse in the Novel', in *The Dialogic Imagination* (Austin, TX: University of Texas Press, 1981), pp. 269–422.
23 Pat Long, *The History of the NME: High Times and Low Lives at the World's Most Famous Music Magazine* (London: Portico, 2012).
24 Williams, 'Base and Superstructure', p. 4.
25 As Williams (ibid., pp. 4–5) notes, articulating temporal sequence, lag and so on in relations between base and superstructure has actually been the longest standing way of overcoming the tendency to crudely reduce superstructure to base.
26 On post-punk and its political significance, see David Wilkinson, *Post-punk, Politics and Pleasure in Britain* (Basingstoke: Palgrave Macmillan, 2016).
27 David Harvey, *A Brief History of Neoliberalism* (Oxford: Oxford University Press, 2005).
28 Paul Du Noyer, 'Interview with Joe Strummer', *New Musical Express*, 3 January 1981.
29 Pat Gilbert, *Passion is a Fashion: The Real Story of The Clash* (London: Aurum Press, 2009), p. 281.
30 Simon Reynolds, *Rip it Up and Start Again: Postpunk 1978–1984* (London: Faber and Faber, 2005 [Kindle edition]), location 4077.
31 Gilbert, *Passion is a Fashion*, p. 279.
32 Ibid., p. 288.
33 Richard E. Caves, *Creative Industries: Contracts Between Art and Commerce* (Cambridge MA: Harvard University Press, 2000), pp. 73–83.
34 Stuart Hall, 'Gramsci and Us', *Marxism Today*, June 1987, pp. 16–21.

2
The Clash and musical artistry: against the corporate voice

Caroline Coon

This chapter had its origins in a keynote address delivered at a conference devoted to The Clash held in Belfast in June 2014.

What Colin Coulter could not have known when he invited me to give this keynote talk[1] was how important for the construction of my political thought about change, conflict and peace Belfast has always been – as Belfast surely was for The Clash.

As a youth in the 1960s, I was engaged in how to do politics in my art and also in direct political action on the street. We confronted an ever more tooled-up and militaristic police force whose tactics, we believed, were honed on the streets of Belfast. Making political change via democratic, peaceful means is a long, painstaking slog. Which is why, as a youth, violent political action – the acting out of political frustration – was potentially seductive. Although I rejected political violence as practised by, say, the Weatherman Underground in the USA, Release[2] lawyers defended the Angry Brigade. Then one of my younger brothers became an environmentalist. He worked on getting a private member's bill through parliament to stop an oil pipeline destroying beautiful Welsh countryside. The bill failed and, frustrated, my younger brother announced to me that he was considering blowing up the pipeline and that he was going to Belfast to 'talk to some people'. I waved him off from my front door on Friday 3 March 1972, and welcomed him home again on the following Monday. My brother's political orientation was changed forever. I was lucky, my brother was lucky. On Saturday 4 March 1972 my brother had been in Belfast, close enough to the Abercorn restaurant bombing to see the blood, death and devastation it caused.

Four years later, I witnessed Joe Strummer and The Clash being youthfully seduced by the politics of Baader Meinhof/The Red Army Faction and the Italian Red Brigades and Leila Khaled and … only later, as they realised the danger of moral short cuts that can lead people to the wrong place, to regret some such youthful endorsements. Joe Strummer and The Clash chose to do their politics with and through the artistry of their music.

Oh, but let me pause here, before I get into my talk, to make a gender point: I had to laugh a few weeks ago when men in the tennis world spluttered in consternation when it was rumoured and then confirmed that Andy Murray might employ, oh horror, a woman tennis coach: Amelie Mauresmo. These quotidian 'Women Keep Out!' and 'everyday sexism' messages are what Virginia Woolf called 'a closed shop tactic'. They are sexism acted out in what Mary Douglas might have described as informal to formal rituals through which power – always male power – is kept purified and contained.

I talked at length to Joe Strummer about what he would have to confront with me, a woman, as manager. I had witnessed the vicious homoerotic jealousy that male journalists used to attack any women who got close to musicians, and how they condemned musicians who allowed women to be more than sex objects – we groupies, slags and whores, boilers, bitches and sluts! Women like Yoko Ono and Linda McCartney and Courtney Love, who were and are, lest we forget, women artists with intellectual agency.

I was fully aware of the sexism that The Clash would have to act out in order to keep popular, be 'one of the lads' and stay friends with gate-keeping, white, male journalists in the male-dominated corporate music industry. In 1976 The Clash were living and working in a very misogynist rock environment, a toxic place for women where sexual harassment and rape were our industrial hazards. In my life, I have seen six generations of boys and young men try not to be sexist. I have witnessed how difficult it is for young men to practise equality as they are socialised, inducted, bullied and groomed into culture by older men determined to maintain a rigid but fragile, orthodox, patriarchal, heterosexual masculine construct in a male-dominated status quo.

It goes to The Clash's credit, and mine, and it says a lot about The Clash's latent feminism, that 1) I had the guts to offer my skill set to The Clash as manager to keep the band together and 2) The Clash's imperative to keep together nullified their fear of female contamination and male ridicule.

Artistry

It was Professor Jacqueline Springer who first intimated that I could use the word 'artistry' in a talk I gave to her students at Syracuse University (London) in 2014. I was amazed that it was again legitimate to use the word in an academic context because, although artistry has ruled my life, I have witnessed how, over the last forty years or so, the skills of artistry have been denigrated or even despised.

If it were not for the artistry of The Clash we would not be here at this conference. So, this is going to be a story from my own experience, my subject angle, of how I was able to recognise The Clash's exceptional popular music talent – and how I saw a fashionable contempt for inspirational heights of artistry develop, especially in the corporate media, and why this endangers young people's creative abilities.

I define artistry as *effortlessness.* The effortlessness of artistry is acquired through the thousands of hours needed to achieve great skill. When I first saw The Clash in rehearsal, before their first public performance, it was their exceptional musical talent and the ambitious potential of their artistry that jolted me and penetrated my heart. It is untrue, a myth, that the musicians that I consciously wrote about as the punk movement in the summer of 1976 were unskilled or musically unambitious or playing 'dumb'. Of the musicians in the first British 'punk' groups I mentioned in the various strands of my punk narrative – the Sex Pistols, The Clash and The Damned – most of them were as musically accomplished and ambitious as it is possible for teenagers to be. Others, like Johnny Rotten and Paul Simonon, were culturally educated and aware art students.

What I saw and heard in these young musicians was what I had been schooled to recognise, understand – and to aspire to – since I was a child. What I heard musicians like The Clash say was: 'From the time I was a small kid...' To acquire great skill as an artist it is usually considered necessary to begin as a child. The great artists who taught me as a child were the superstars of their times, who had wowed audiences all over the world, who had learned their skills as children from other great artists.

At the Russian Ballet School I went to aged five, the feats of artistry that my teachers had achieved were captured in framed photographs on the walls. If we children worked hard we would be able to perform such feats of artistic expression in many years to come. At first we were taught to copy the technique of our teachers, copy repeatedly until what we learned in copying became second nature, instinctive ... at which point we became free to innovate. This is a classic teaching method that respects the sacred nature of learning and is the best way to train and nurture exceptional talent. This was training, an apprenticeship, with the acute knowledge that only 1 per cent of us would be exceptional enough to make it 'to the top'. The reward for those of us who did not become the very best was honesty to oneself, the honesty of hard work which can reward and feed into self-esteem and human well-being. And, of course, training in the acquisition of skill in one field can be transferred to any other.

Picture this: in a studio, children and teenagers are sweating, groaning, falling ... and a teacher is egging us on, criticising, demanding and praising! How I loved these teachers who showed me how powerful art – music, dancing, writing – could be. We held our teachers in awe. We respected the *authority* of their experience.

And there was something else special about my teachers. I mean, from the age of five I was being taught by Russian women and men. And what were Russians doing in the depths of the English countryside? Well, my teachers were exiles, refugees, and, to use a familiar word, immigrants. Nadine Nicolaeva-Legat, who founded the Legat School of Ballet in Kent (1939), had been the prima ballerina of the Imperial and State theatres of Moscow and St Petersburg. She had, with many of her colleagues, escaped one of the various stages of the Russian Revolution.

My teachers escaped to England because the art they wanted to perform – the dance, the stage set painting and costume design, the music, the literature – was considered so dangerous and subversive of the society in which they wanted to perform it that it was banned. My teachers and their colleagues, such as Stravinsky, Diaghilev, Nijinsky, Léon Bakst and Natalia Goncharova, often threatened with imprisonment, fled to the West in order to live freely as the exceptional artists they worked hard to be. It was as a child that I learned that art often collides with the status interests of those in power. In fact, the more powerful they are – the Stalins, the Hitlers, the Maos – the more afraid they are of youthful artistic expression.

But before I sound a little too smug about 'freedom in the West', I have to remind myself that it was only comparatively recently that formal censorship of the arts was abolished in the United Kingdom. Until I was 23 – in 1968 – a royal functionary called the Lord Chamberlain had the statutory authority to *prohibit* the performance of plays when he was of the opinion that 'it is fitting for the preservation of good manners, decorum or of the public peace so to do'. The first London performance of the musical *Hair* – that exuberant, or 'shocking', expression of 1960s youth rebellion turned into popular theatre in which my flatmate had a part – was delayed until this censorship was abolished under the Theatres Act 1968. In 1971 I was a witness for the defence in the OZ magazine obscenity trial. The state objected to a cartoon of Rupert Bear with an erect penis. And in 1977 I was a witness for the defence in the Sex Pistols indecency trial. The state objected to the word 'bollocks'.[3]

Children trained like I was are being trained to enter an elite. 'Elite'. I am not afraid of this word. The elite status that superstars and great artists like The Clash achieve is earned through dedication and hard work. You might think that the elite artists who trained me in the classical tradition were too snobbish to have anything to do with popular culture. Think again! Thousands of children like me, although taught to be elite in skills, are also taught to value *the art of the people*, folk art and song. I don't know if any of you are ballet fans or if you have seen the ballet *La Fille Mal Gardée* (1960)? But one of the highlights of this ballet is a clog dance choreographed by Frederick Ashton. He was inspired by the folk dancers, or as we might say today, the *street dancers*, the clog-wearing millworkers of Lancashire.

In fact, there was hardly a piece of music or a physical movement that I was taught as a child that was not rooted in popular culture. The melodies that we danced to, and the dances that we incorporated into the refinements of our artistry, were often folk songs, folk melodies and folk dances. We were taught how heroes such as Ralph Vaughan Williams, Percy Grainger and Cecil Sharp feared that folk art and music were becoming extinct. Because the oral tradition through which folk art and music survived was being undermined by increased literacy, printed music and twentieth-century technology, they were determined to collect and preserve it, this rich cultural heritage of rural and urban working people. There has ever been a flow of popular culture into high art and high art into popular culture, a circular current of fertilisation and renewal. Popular/folk culture and high art depend on each other.

Now, before my talk enters the adult world of *performance*, let us remember those teenagers practising for hours in their bedrooms with posters of their pop idols on their walls, or the children like me in elite ballet training. We have finished our class. We are sitting exhausted on changing room benches. Yes, there I am, wincing in pain, but proudly. I have worked so hard that blood has turned my pink satin point shoes red. My toes are bleeding.

Performance

Performance. Just mentioning the word can make me nervous because performance needs an audience and an audience, whether many or singular, has the power to judge, to cry Success! or Failure! And how do performers get an audience? We have to advertise. And this is where artists, whatever they are performing – be it music, dance, writing, art – have to step out of their private bubble to negotiate with the public and confront commerce and advertising, most of which is mediated through the corporate power of the press.

Let me give you just two instances of my experience of corporate press power, red in tooth and claw.

In 1976, on one of the cusps of social change heralded by the musical artistry of what I named the punk rock movement, I was writing the singles column for *Melody Maker*. Independent record companies would send me records and I often made one my Single of the Week. One day, *Melody Maker*'s editor called me: 'Do not', he ordered, 'review any more of these independent singles!' I was astonished. 'Why not?' I gasped. I think the editor was astonished in turn by my naivety. Patiently he explained to me that corporate record labels like EMI and Sony were complaining. They took out advertising in *Melody Maker*. Lots of it! And, of course, the independents did not. I learned that the music, or all the art we read about in corporate media, is largely dependent on who is buying the advertising.

The *Melody Maker* editor held weekly meetings where it was decided what to put in the paper, what musicians to single out for attention, what each journalist would write and so on. At one of the first editorial meetings I attended, newly released albums were being handed out for review. Holding up the unheard, pre-release third album of a very famous band the editor said: 'Here you are – it's time we gave this band a bad review.' Until that moment I believed media reviews were critical but honest appraisals of artistry. I had to learn that a dishonest agenda in relation to prime producers of art is common practice across all corporate media.

This is why artists – musicians – have such a fraught, needy, love–hate relationship with the corporate media. We need it to broadcast our existence but we know the corporate voice has the power to make or break us. Older, experienced artists have to teach the young:

1 to understand that many *critics of art* can be envious and jealous of those with the talent and skill to be *makers of art*, and
2 that it is always wise to be very flattering and nice to critics and journalists in the corporate media.

Corporate media has power because of its mass appeal. We buy into corporate media for information and news, sure. But we also demand that corporate media feeds our desire for vicarious thrills. Thrill sells! Catastrophe, floods and pestilence, violence, scandal, shock, disgust, crime! To thrill us into buying their product, the corporate voice is hysterical, hyperbolic and catastrophising – in corporate media humanity is always doomed! And most perniciously, we buy into corporate media's monstering and demonising of people who we flatter ourselves are not like us. Corporate media relies on our very human but base nature, the mass appeal of hatred of others: posh politicians, trade unionists, foreigners ... female body parts ... celebrities ... like The Clash. The rock'n'roll editor who demanded that 'bad' album review surely knew his readership well, and how emotionally rewarded or thrilled they would be to read about a group of famous musicians being brought down.

We cannot banish or magic away corporate media in democracy. But we can learn how to read it. We can learn its agenda. We can learn how to talk to it and be in it, or not be in it. Every branded paper or magazine caters to a particular group with its own particular class of hatreds, its own particular whipping post people, who are most often the powerless.

A powerless group that corporate media has had the most impunity to attack is young people. When teenagers like me were leaving school in the 1960s, we were entering a working world where everything for the rich and the powerful in Empire, Church and state was falling apart. 1968 became the Year of the Young Rebels from London to San Francisco via New York, Prague, Paris and Berlin. We attacked adults for their hypocrisy and warmongering. We demonstrated. And, of course, state police forces were deployed against us, as was corporate media.

Over the years I have learned that this powerless versus power confrontation is a generational necessity. Every generation has to fight, and will have to fight, against new manifestations of oppressive power. We can look back at youth protest movements of the past – beatniks, hippies, punks, rastas, acid house, rave and hip hop – we can compare and contrast the protests of today – the Occupy Movement, Slut Walk, the Arab Spring – and predict youth protests of the future.

Generations of young people have thrown, and always will throw, their bodies into the civil rights fray, the Rights Revolution. Unfortunately, bodies are flesh. Our bodies can be controlled, battered and imprisoned. But our minds cannot be imprisoned. Nothing infuriates power more than its inability to control the human mind. Power is especially provoked by human minds that create music. Which is why oppressed people always and ingeniously turn to folk song, to popular song, to give voice to their plight. Wasn't it amazing to see a tyrant like Vladimir Putin so terrified of a Pussy Riot song? Or how in Iran, Khamenei's theocracy imprisoned youths for dancing to Pharrell Williams singing 'Happy'?

Each new youth rebel generation looks back to how oppressed peoples of the past got their voices heard. In the 1970s punks often relied on 1960s rebel reggae. In the 1960s we found the folk and popular songs of Paul Robeson, Joan Baez, Woody Guthrie ... Popular songs are morale-boosting for the powerless precisely because protest-wrapped-in-melody can be wafted sinuously and subtly over the heads of Establishment power brokers and their weaponry.

The corporate voice demands that we believe that young people are apathetic! Today when I read *youth blaming* and *youth bashing* in corporate media I can afford a laugh. When corporate media disparages youth as disengaged I know they are wrong. Because decades of politically engaged youth rebellion has made civil society progressively more humane. Terrible things are happening, but believe me, the world is a better place than it was when I was born. Revolutions to oust tyrants are usually savage. Rebellion happens in stages. Nevertheless people *en masse*, often uplifted and comforted by youth's popular songs, have proved that diversity, plurality and tolerance, gender equality and education, democracy and free speech are the best solutions for the well-being of all humanity.

Let me take a breath here ... I imagine a tide of *buts* coming towards me! Yes, of course, there are BUTs ... zero hour contracts, criminal banks, escalating financial inequalities, religious fascists, tax avoidance ...

Skill, rigour, discipline

The BUT I want to focus on for the last part of my talk is what happened to the reputation of skill, technique and artistry in the process of this progressive change. After the World Wars, it was not only authority wielded by the rich, the Church and the state that needed to be cut down. All authority was characterised as an attribute of privilege. All 'privilege' became suspect. Anything elite had to be abused. The authority of Every Person was a threat. The authority of parents ... The authority of teachers ...

When I left the environment where teachers had so brilliantly and authoritatively taught me the skills I needed to develop artistry, I entered the 1960s workplace of further education. And I got a shock. My teachers at the Central School of Art were advocating an anti-skill attitude to art. Skill and technique were considered authoritative and elitist. Instead, *spontaneity* and *improvisation* were the way forward.

So afraid were many of my white male teachers of appearing skilled and therefore elite and somehow not proudly working class that they stopped calling themselves artists. It became *de rigueur* to call oneself 'a painter' – this sounded almost as macho as being able to call oneself 'a coal miner'. Radical white male students in my art class demanded and got Central to abolish life drawing class. I came to college one day to discover that it was impossible to work because 'radical' students had barricaded shut the door to the workroom. This improvisational, anti-skill, anti-elite ethos spread across all the arts.

While declines in deference to power and authority are obviously essential to democratic development, it is also anti-democratic to dumb democracy down. The million-selling popular song that for me most characterised this perverse anti-democratic trend was Pink Floyd's 'The Wall' from the eponymous album (1979). The band gets choirs of school children to sing 'We don't need no education, We don't need no thought control. Hey, teacher, leave them kids alone.'

What most worried me about the fall of authority was how it appeared to be bringing artistry down and this would silence those who most needed creativity to express themselves, the better to break down the walls of exclusion and rise out of oppression. There has always been peer-to-peer transfer of skill in folk art – but ambitious exponents of folk art or popular art always search out masters up the hierarchy of artistry from whom to learn.

I reject the idea – amplified by the corporate voice – that popular culture is without skill or that the heights of artistry are only for posh people. Natural talent is classless. However, most teenagers in all popular counter-culture movements have to start off doing it themselves, making their art with limited means. For me, the relative lack of skills in teenage punk bands I wrote about in 1976 was an expected phase of youth artistic development: the lack of skill was not a principle.

I understood Mark Perry – Mark P – when he announced in the first punk fanzine *Sniffin' Glue* (1976) that 'anyone can do it' and I understood when the *Sideburns* fanzine offered the famous advice: 'This is a chord, This is another, [...] Now form a band.' This brave rhetoric was partly infused with popular anti-artistry and anti-elitism. It was partly ingratiating rhetoric to curry favour with his underprivileged peer group, his readers. I understood it when some young people, newly identifying themselves as punks and taking up instruments for the first time, sneered 'I don't want to be a musician!' I understood this as protective bravado.

Not for a minute did I think it cute or 'right on!' to flatter or encourage such low expectations. In fact, it dismayed me when all too soon this bravado cover for novices appeared to set into a philistine punk dogma. Because without skill, or the ambition to develop skill, thwarted and frustrated young people are more likely to give up rather than persist to achieve their potential. Anti-artistry or anti-skill dogma – a false egalitarianism – cannot sustain a group of musicians for long and could partly explain why so many punk bands broke up after one or two years. Disdain for the kinds of skill, rigour, discipline, the sustained application and artistic knowledge that The Clash represent, and which made them inspirational international superstars, feeds into the social stasis that blights the lives of deprived young people. Contempt for elite artistry and the authority of teachers fails us all, but it especially fails the most deprived.

I understood Mark P, with all his energy and youthful enterprise, when he railed with bathos against The Clash for *selling out*. But I think to take this sell out rhetoric at face value is to misunderstand how counterculture spreads, develops and makes for progressive change in dominant culture. The 'punk died the day The Clash signed to CBS' myth – it is a myth since the evidence proves exactly the opposite to be true – smacks to me of envy, a thrilling put-down punishment of the band for their exceptional talent. To put The Clash on a restricted DIY musical pedestal, constrained by rules, is to demean them and the aspirations of their artistry. Brilliant musicians should not have to waste time pressing their own records in a shed while restricting themselves to four chords when what they passionately want to do is write conscious lyrics and perform wide-ranging music as best they can for as many people as possible.

To avoid any misunderstanding, let me say clearly that I appreciate how all kinds of music making, at every level, is crucial for civil life and the greater common good. Everyone could have a musical instrument or music-making software at home. We can appreciate all music, ordinary part-time and amateur music making, our friends making music, making bad to good noises according to taste and all those who are in local bands. As Professor David Hesmondhalgh so brilliantly explains, music making is essential to human flourishing, social cohesion and spiritual well-being. What I think we ignore at our peril is the agency of stardom. I think we should guard against contempt for the exceptional few, the elite, who have the natural talent and the character to do the work necessary to rise to the top.

The teenagers I corralled into the punk movement, with all its complex and different groupings – the musicians and their fans – were determined to be creative, to use popular music and art to express their despair at a society not offering them employment, career opportunities or a future. Disparagement rained down from every quarter. The old rock establishment, never so challenged, allied with corporate media to fall upon this new youth movement and its music with whipping post glee. 'Filth and Fury!' headlines converged with music industry put-downs.

If young people are to oppose and outwit the power of the corporate voice, then they surely need skill and artistry. In fact, what I witnessed happen was as interesting as it was very smart. I witnessed those relatively skilled musicians who were actually *doing it* up on stage – the Sex Pistols, The Clash, The Damned, The Jam – begin to protect themselves with an egalitarian *front*. Their apparently cavalier attitude to musicianship and artistry was pure bluff and guile. For those novice but aspiring musicians who got up on stage for the first time, never having sung or played a note before, like Johnny Rotten and Siouxsie Sioux, their plight without technique came as a shock. They quickly realised that they needed skill if they were to finesse their originality and fulfil their creative ambitions. After a few consecutive performances both Johnny and Siouxsie lost their voices. They couldn't talk let alone sing! To continue they had to have singing lessons – in secret – to acquire the technical skill needed to preserve and develop their vocal cords.

Technical skills – artistry – whether in 'low' or 'high' art are what performers fall back on to overcome stage fright and nerves. The disciplined skills of artistry are needed to persevere and keep going when courage and inspiration dry up. Those who do not figure this out do not survive long as musicians or in any other art form. Behind closed doors – out of sight – all the punk musicians who are world famous icons practised for hours. In order to appear 'the same as' and 'equal to' their fans, the increasingly skilled punk musicians worked hard to deny that they worked hard for the artistry that made them elite and famous.

It has been interesting to watch the industrial growth of academic interest in *punk ideology*, *punk core values* and *a punk ethic*, the anti-consumerist theory that, as Colin Coulter says, leads academics to 'devote considerable attention to a great many other, arguably less important, bands' than The Clash. The point is, do any of the bands that say they practise a so-called punk, no-skills-needed, four-chord, DIY ideology have enough talent to be troubled by superstardom? Unapologetically, I agree with David Laing when he says that 'the example of The Clash in developing a dialectic of political comment within the rock mainstream should not be underestimated'.

Perhaps you all know the speech that the great American writer William Faulkner made when he accepted his Nobel prize for literature? He talked about his creativity: 'a life's work in the agony and sweat of the human spirit'. The young counterculture rebels I interviewed in the 1970s brimmed with human spirit. Many of those who survived did so precisely because they acquired great skill and sweated and agonised for their artistry and their music. The Clash practically lived in their rehearsal room. Their life was an increasingly skilled, hardworking day after day routine of eat, sleep, write, practise, perform; eat, sleep, write, practice, perform ... As manager of The Clash I saw what fans did not see. I witnessed what 'right-on' journalists and many leftist academics, keen to perpetuate the no-skill-do-it-yourself punk dogma, do not write about.

Picture this – but for the shock cancellation of their performance in 1977 this might have happened in Belfast: The Clash have just finished performing a 90-minute set. As the band come off stage we clear a path through fans so that they can stagger to their dressing room. Roadies guard the door. No one is let in. Inside the band are utterly exhausted, they cannot speak. Mick, Paul and Topper are silent, panting for breath, pouring with sweat. Joe Strummer is flat out on the floor, ashen faced, his arms flung out. And I notice, once again, that the plasters meant to protect his guitar-playing fingers are shredded and soaked with blood. Joe Strummer's fingers are raw and bleeding.

Afterword

At the end of my talk, the first comment made to me was: 'I didn't expect that from you!' David Hesmondhalgh made one of the last. He said: 'But the question is, how do we prevent young people being daunted by elite skills?'

I took this to be a rhetorical question addressed not to me but to the audience, mostly made up of academics already teaching and students who would soon enter the academy and become teachers. The comment/question pleased me because I confidently thought it meant that Hesmondhalgh had understood the central argument around which my talk was structured and that I had proved my point: The Clash so obviously exemplified youth *not* daunted by the elite skills of musicians they revered as teenagers. Had I believed that Hesmondhalgh's 'question' was addressed specifically to me I would have added to my reply about the pedagogical function of education: 'If teachers do not know how to prevent youth being daunted by exceptional skills then they should not be teaching.'

The challenge my talk posed, and that needs answering, is: Why have academics been so steadfastly invested in a leftist belief that successful bands of the punk movement couldn't play more than four chords and disdained musical ambition and elite skills of musicianship?

If we paid attention to what now-famous musicians of the punk movement like The Clash have actually said about the origins of their teenage musical ambitions, then the roll call of the greatest skilled musicians in the world that they were inspired by, learned from and desired to become would be endless. Recently a host of managers, musicians and recording engineers, including Bernie Rhodes, Tony James, Terry Chimes, Steve Levine and Mick Jones, yet again, across BBC airwaves, have had to denounce the 'punk musicians couldn't play' myth.[4]

In 2013 Mick Jones explained his musical ambition to Daniel Rachel:

> It was quite amazing how we progressed from this punk band to something altogether different. It was mind-blowing. It was always about much more than just the end of the street. We weren't parochial in any way. Even from the start you can tell that. We came out of punk, but we became something of our own.[5]

As The Clash became something of their own, as well as fan praise they were increasingly policed by journalists – academics were soon to follow – sniffing out a so-called betrayal of 'punk ideology' and with some righteous, anti-capitalist agenda. This naive, and hypocritical, response to The Clash's ambition, elite talents and status made the band increasingly defensive. How young people, singly and in groups, respond to attacks and criticism is not for discussion here, but in The Clash's case it was necessary to put up a 'strong' outward appearance, a carapace that was increasingly macho and militaristic.

The Clash 'gang' was served and protected by trusted roadies. As a gang they were fortified by, and revelled in, a hyperbolic 'straight' masculinity expressed in words and style, which when facing outwards did indeed appear sexist. Men such as road manager Johnny Green could be relied on to burnish and collude with the band's orthodox, gun-toting, hard man image. In November 1977 Siouxsie and the Banshees supported The Clash in Manchester. After the Belle Vue show Green was asked to take the band to the station. 'I tried to talk to [Siouxsie] – I was charged up by the show and everything that had happened: the riot, the music, the response. I didn't get a word of reply. I dropped her at the station and didn't even get a "thank you". What an old bag.'[6] A narrative like this from Green, the everyday and much-approved slagging of professional women who are not male-pleasing enough, played into the late 1970s backlash against feminism that was rampant in all areas.

The Clash's outward-facing sexism was strictly ordained in the predominantly masculine context of their work environment. Furthermore, sexist rhetoric – disparaging women to other men – bonded them to other men and was part of their tactic to be 'like' their male fans, 'equal' to male gatekeeping journalists and, as in regard to women, compliant rule-followers of the powerful corporate men on whom their careers depended. While, due to their international popularity, they were facing the realities of commerce and warding off accusations of 'disappointing' and 'letting down' their male fans for failing to be anti-consumption and adequately socialist, I certainly thought it was too much to ask that these young men, exceptionally and uniquely for the time, would also stand up against the so far indelibly patriarchal world as full-time feminists.

Women, women like me, we had to live – and still have to live – with a double standard. When men like The Clash faced inwards, faced us, we were able to feel like their equals as colleagues, friends and lovers. What we had to put up with, take, suck up and rise above was what happened behind our backs. Oh, the name-calling and the sexualised, take-down, 'killer' humiliations! We knew, and had to tolerate the fact – if, that is, we were to continue having careers in the public workspace – that when men, even our closest men friends and colleagues, were with other men, they were not likely to have the valour to stand up against misogyny. When journalists, such as Marcus Gray,[7] make superficial criticisms of The Clash for being sexist they are certainly pots calling the kettle black. (Thank you to the many men who have understood what misogyny is and are with women trying to stamp it out.)

Often I am asked these days what it was like for me to work within a 'predominantly masculine context'. My answer is usually: where do you think I or any other women, whatever colour or class, could work that was not a predominantly masculine context? The context of patriarchal entitlement and misogyny was, and still is, inescapable. While we women were, and are, changing the world, we have to live in it. The tactics I used/use to enact my own liberation strategy are too complex and diverse to go into here.[8]

In my talk, when I mentioned the brave, sexist-defying choice The Clash made to have me as manager, it was the inward-facing, proto-feminist band that I wanted to draw attention to. I'd like to add a little about what I witnessed when The Clash related to young women other than me. Take a closer look, past the imposed patriarchal frame. The fact is, all the young women I interviewed in 1976, because they had just formed or were about to form bands, had personal and professional connections to The Clash. Mick, Joe and Paul seemed to run a School for Teaching Chords to Young Women. Creative, innovative women freely intermingled with, and added to, the music-making ideas and style of The Clash. The creative transactions mitigated sexism. As the band themselves have noted, Ellen Foley, Pearl Harbour, Wendy James, Chrissie Hynde and Viv Albertine are among the women musicians who documentary makers, journalists and academics usually exclude as *artists in their own right* from their hyper-macho versions of The Clash.

Even as these young women were trying to extricate themselves from subordination in normative heterosexual relationships, they were relating to male musicians as creative collaborators. In the late 1970s, because of feminist campaigning advances, I witnessed a collegiate, fluid interaction between women and men that had not been experienced before. So commonsensical and normal was this gender mixing in our working lives that I could understand how possible it was for young women of the punk generation to believe all the old sexist boundaries and prohibitions were irrelevant.

When I did my first formal interview with The Slits I asked about 'female gender'. Ari groaned. Viv warned me off. 'We're just not interested in questions about Women's Liberation. There's loads of people who think rock is basically a male idiom, but bollocks! You either think chauvinism is shit or you don't. We think it's shit.'[9]

But, alas, it *was* 'loads of people' that women were up against. The Slits were not to know that in 1972 the feminist Marion Fudger had helped organise a 'Women in Rock' conference at *Melody Maker* to discuss how women could be taken seriously as artists in an industry that stereotyped and polarised us as either rock whores or folksong virgins.[10] I thought the cover of the first Slits album creatively telling in its portrayal of these young women as newly born, liberated creatures rising out of primeval mud. But I was not surprised when Richard Williams, then editor of *Melody Maker*, said to me: 'I don't know why they bother to be naked – they are all so ugly.' Yes, not only did misogyny deafen the MEN-ONLY rock establishment, it blinded them, too.

When Dorian Lynskey can opine, in 2010, that 'the burgeoning women's movement was ill served by protest music' by women musicians, but then mention Gloria Gaynor's 'colossal "I Will Survive"', we can only scream with laughter. When he then attempts to diminish the liberationist intent of this song by adding '[d]espite being widely embraced as a feminist battle cry, [it] had its roots in more personal concerns',[11] we can only hope a critic who still cannot recognise the personal as political will go to hell!

Because young punk women had little experience of the adult world, they were yet another generation unaware of women's largely hidden historical political struggle. They had no idea how *thick* and high the sociopolitical wall was that was blocking their way. They had yet to comprehend what an armoury of anti-sexist resources and skills they would need to deploy in future.

Punk women's iteration of 'good little girls' refusal and their boisterous, loud and assertive manners combined with gender-busting dress codes and style helped women break free from passive femininity.[12] Shocking punk women changed the public face of women for all time. But I witnessed these young women's carefree 'fuck you' or 'Oh Bondage! Up Yours!'[13] optimism with apprehension. I knew, only too well, how soon, outside their circle of friends, they were likely to confront corporate forces, male impunity and privilege – often enforced by violence[14] – that would exclude them, sabotage their careers and bring to their attention how few rights to bodily integrity and self-determination they actually had.

Given the harsh economic conditions in the late 1970s, Mark P's anger at the unchecked exploitative evil of the corporate world was understandable. I empathised with his dream of a non-capitalist economic model. But my experience of founding and running a civil rights organisation in the 1960s, that had to be 'free' at the point of need, made me question anti-capitalist rhetoric and the practical reality of 'alternative' communistic economic models.

Many who write about the punk era, because it was *their* coming of age moment, tend to characterise 1976 as a Year Zero. But it was the well-established 'hippie' counterculture network of voluntary organisations, small independent record companies, magazines and consumer outlets that punk generation entrepreneurs and activists overlaid and tapped into. Small market entities catering to era-specific cultural needs and accoutrements have always flourished outside the structures of corporate industries. Tools, materials and technology may change but successive generations of youth have always started out doing it for themselves with few and crude recourses. In 1976 a traditional sociopolitical, generational, countercultural manifestation was, post hoc, particularised and branded 'DIY' and 'indie'.

Joe Strummer, as the hippy 101er John 'Woody' Mellor, was signed to the independent Chiswick Records when he had his hit single 'Keys to Your Heart' (1976). He surely knew that musicians are as likely to be ripped off by independent as corporate companies. The Cartel – the independent record distribution network set up in 1980 – collapsed after eight years.

Mark P's genuine disappointment at The Clash's 'failure' – the realisation that punk fans and society would not be saved by worshipped punk gods – was partly an acting out of masculine angst, and partly displaced fury at Labour Party politicians failing to tackle recession and unemployment. Of course fans like Mark P desired The Clash to do more than rail against capitalism. But, hey, if leftist politicians, Marxist theoreticians and trade unions have failed since 1917 to establish successful, enduring, alternative models to corporate capitalism anywhere in the world, then it was a bit rich to expect a socialist 'infrastructure outside of the corporate music business' to be created by a group of musicians barely out of their teens!

The fact that The Clash could not fulfil anti-capitalist expectations distressed Joe Strummer greatly. Instead, I witnessed The Clash pay attention to, care for and be exceptionally available to their fans – they played 'for free' in support of numerous causes wherever in the world they toured. Instead, The Clash wrote the magnificent music that supported and inspired all those whose political activism confronted capitalist exploitation. Instead, as fair capitalists, The Clash struggled with CBS to produce affordable products.

Perhaps it is the past fifty years of academic reverence for leftist theoreticians who endlessly propose unworkable economic models that has shaped hatred of capital[15] and has created consumers who think it acceptable not to pay for what they consume, the twenty-first-century version of piracy that is making it difficult for musicians today to 'make a living'? It is an eternal solipsistic pessimism that wants to destroy the old, complain about nostalgia and rebuke artists for not creating anything 'genuinely original'. This is a species of cultural blindness and ignorance.

On the cusp of every generational change, be it progressive or repressive – in my lifetime every step forward has provoked a ferocious backlash – people have pilfered from the past. This is what the past is for! It is telling of meaning and intent to hear which popular songs of the past are adopted by new subcultures as they wait for contemporary songs to be written of and by their own.[16] When The Clash's deep curiosity and knowledge of the world's cultural heritage enabled them to plunder the past and interpret The Crickets' 1960 hit 'I Fought the Law' for the punk era, we had a pointed indication of their irony and intent.

How urgently we need fighting popular songs to raise our spirits today! In the midst of another oppressive cycle, with backlash, human-rights-threatening, extreme right-wing politicians currying favour and garnering votes among those most hurt by wicked inequality and capitalist fraud, we will be playing The Clash and ... write your own inspirational play list of rage and protest songs of the past and ... expect an eruption of songs written by this era's outraged and angry youth and ... by the way, what *did* you expect of me?

Notes

1. This chapter was conceived as the first of three performance essays, the further two being 'Against the Corporate Voice: the Price and Cost of Protest in The Clash Era and Beyond' (the economics and funding of social innovation and activism. Who pays?) and 'Against the Corporate Voice: Young Women in The Clash Era and Who Said "I am not a feminist, but..."' (the 1970s backlash against feminism and its impact on young women musicians). The original text of the keynote has been revised slightly and appended with an afterword addressing some of the issues that arose during the discussion prompted by the talk.
2. Release was 'founded by young people for young people' in 1967 by Caroline Coon and Rufus Harris. Essentially, we dealt with one of the 1960s most urgent social problems – the arrest and imprisonment of young people accused of violating the Dangerous Drugs Act of 1965. After our 24-hour emergency telephone number was published, not only did we deal with civil rights matters but we quickly became the 'welfare branch of the alternative society', advising on all manner of problems including running away from home, homelessness, psychological distress and pregnancy. When *The Release Report on Drug Offenders and the Law* by Caroline Coon and Rufus Harris was published by Sphere Books in 1969 the police and government tried to ban it. See Helene Curtis and Mimi Sanderson, *The Unsung Sixties: Memories of Social Innovation* (London: Whiting and Birch, 2004), pp. 189–90. http://www.release.org.uk/
3. The prosecution failed because the defence established that 'bollocks' was a venerable word in the English language.
4. For the fortieth anniversary of the release of the first Clash album, 11 April 2017, on BBC Radio 6 Music and BBC Radio 5Live.

5 Daniel Rachel, *Isle of Noises: Conversations with Great British Songwriters* (London: Picador, 2014), pp. 171–3.
6 Johnny Green and Garry Barker, *A Riot of Our Own: Night and Day with The Clash* (London: Indigo, 1997).
7 Marcus Gray, *Last Gang in Town: The Story and Myth of The Clash* (London: Fourth Estate, 1995).
8 See, for instance, Caroline Coon, *Laid Bare – Diary – 1983–1984* (London: Cunst Art, 2017).
9 This interview was for *Melody Maker* in June 1977 and was later published in Caroline Coon, *1988: The New Wave Punk Rock Explosion* (Orbach & Chambers, 1977; repr. London: Omnibus Press, 1982), pp. 102–14.
10 Sue Steward and Sheryl Garratt, *Signed, Sealed and Delivered: True Life Stories of Women in Pop* (London: Pluto Press, 1984).
11 Dorian Lynskey, *33 Revolutions Per Minute: A History of Protest Songs* (London: Faber and Faber, 2010), pp. 225, 373.
12 Alice Echols, *Daring To Be Bad: Radical Feminism in America 1967–1975* (Minneapolis, MN: University of Minnesota Press, 1989).
13 'Oh Bondage Up Yours', the debut single of Poly Styrene and X-Ray Spex, September 1977, Virgin.
14 When Helen Reddington researched *The Lost Women of Rock Music: Female Musicians of the Punk Era* (Aldershot: Ashgate, 2007), she learned that a significant percentage of the women she interviewed had been sexually assaulted and/or raped.
15 François Furet, *The Passing of an Illusion: The Idea of Communism in the Twentieth Century* (Chicago: University of Chicago Press, 1999).
16 See Caroline Coon, 'Preface', in William Osgerby (ed.), *Subcultures, Popular Music and Social Change* (Newcastle: Cambridge Scholars Publishing, 2014).

3

'Up in heaven (not only here)': The Clash, left melancholia and the politics of redemption

Colin Coulter

In his accomplished biography of The Clash, journalist Pat Gilbert seeks to capture that singular, compelling energy so central to the enduring appeal of the band. The 'word that summed up The Clash's approach to their art better than any other', Gilbert asserts, was 'passion'.[1] This particular attribute of the London four-piece was exemplified most dramatically in their legendary stage performances. Fans often recount seeing the group in concert as a moment of personal epiphany, the point when the scales fell from their eyes and they began to see the world anew.[2] In the age of digital reproduction, there is an abundance of evidence to bear out these fervent first-hand testimonies. The online footage of The Clash live at the Elizabethan Ballroom, Belle Vue, Manchester in November 1977, for instance, captures the band at their early, incendiary best.[3] Amid all the frenetic energy bounded by the venue's low ceiling and tiny stage, the eye of the viewer is inexorably drawn to the possessed figure of Joe Strummer. The iconic front man delivers the words of the unnervingly predatory tale of urban psychosis 'What's My Name' as though his very life depends upon it. Wide-eyed and bathed in sweat, Strummer declaims the unsettling lyrics to an enraptured audience and barks obscenities at the camera positioned stage right before stumbling over the microphone stand and careering backwards into the drum riser where he lies momentarily obscured from view as the song comes to an abrupt end. Even four decades on – perhaps *especially* four decades on – the footage of The Clash performing the songs that comprise their debut album is utterly exhilarating.[4]

There are, then, considerable grounds for Gilbert's claim that 'passion' was central to the purpose and power of The Clash. While this familiar representation of the band may well be true it is, at best, only partially so. The work of The Clash was certainly marked by a tangible *passion*, but it was also, and often at the same time, defined by an indelible *pathos*. The songs that Joe Strummer and Mick Jones wrote together return time and again to rail against the multiple injustices of global capitalism and to declare that, perhaps, another world is possible. Almost in the same breath, however, the tracks that the band recorded give voice to the sense that the iniquities of a planet scarred by war and poverty are likely to endure, that the future might just be written after all and that what lies ahead is unlikely to be any better than what has come before.[5] The songbook of The Clash is marked by a palpable air of pessimism, a quality that is best captured perhaps in the notion of 'left melancholia', to which we will return at some length at a later stage. In the discussion that follows, we will examine this sense of political fatalism across the span of the illustrious songwriting partnership of Strummer and Jones and provide a particularly close reading of the track that perhaps illustrates that trait better than any other, the timeless elegy for the wretched of the earth that is 'Straight to Hell'. While the mood of despondency that defines much of the work of The Clash might be expected to diminish its political significance or valence, the opposite is in fact the case. It is, as we will illustrate later, precisely the 'left melancholia' of the band's back catalogue that is the source of their radical political influence, that identifies them as the authors of 'protest songs'[6] with a genuinely profound and enduring power. The sense of pessimism that pervades The Clash songbook might be attributed in part, of course, to the increasingly bleak domestic and global political environment in which the band were operating. It also owes a great deal to the very particular back story of the group's charismatic and controversial front man and it is to that autobiographical detail that we turn our attention next.

'We had a hedge back home in the suburbs'

In April 1977 The Clash released their eponymous debut album to widespread critical acclaim. The glowing reviews garnered by the record almost invariably underscored its 'authenticity' as a cultural document of the time. The social realist broadsides that comprise *The Clash* were held to have captured the sclerosis and menace of a contemporary Britain in the throes of an escalating economic and political crisis. On hearing the album, renowned fanzine writer Mark P(erry) dispensed with his own recent, vehement criticism of the band. The fourteen tracks gathered together on *The Clash*, Perry insisted, were 'like a mirror' that 'reflects all the shit' and 'shows us the truth'.[7] While the lyrics that feature on the band's debut album trade heavily in bleak images of tower blocks and motorway flyovers, the author of these lines grew up in a setting far removed from those potent emblems of urban decay. It would soon emerge that The Clash front man Joe Strummer had in fact been born John Graham Mellor in Ankara during a spell when his father, a career civil servant in the Foreign Office, was located in the Turkish capital. After further stints in comparably glamorous settings such as Cairo and Mexico City, the Mellors had returned to England for a time, where their two sons were enrolled in private school. These autobiographical snippets inevitably became ready ammunition for journalists keen to dismiss as fraudulent the radical political pronouncements of The Clash.[8] Critics of the band were quick to point out the disparity between the 'everyman' persona constructed by Joe Strummer and his real background as the public schoolboy John Mellor.[9] In their memoir of the punk era, Julie Burchill and Tony Parsons, for instance, suggest that the distinctive, drawling, adenoidal speaking voice of The Clash front man was one that had required 'de-elocution' lessons.[10] This vein of inverted snobbery was exemplified in reviews of the 1980 hit single 'Bankrobber'. Journalists were wont to point out that the opening line of the track – 'My daddy was a bankrobber' – did not in fact square with the autobiography of the artist who had written it. Taking the quest for literalism to absurd lengths, the review that appeared in *Sounds*, for example, snidely informed readers: 'Actually, John Mellor's daddy was a Second Secretary of Information at the Foreign Office.'[11]

The sneers that journalists often directed towards Joe Strummer were perhaps an understandable response to the revisions and evasions in which the singer often engaged, not least during the early days of The Clash.[12] It might be said, however, that the dismissal of the front man as merely a former public school boy masquerading as a man of the people fails to acknowledge fully the complex and, in some senses, rather troubled nature of his background. While the Mellors returned home for a period when their two sons were young, a new posting in Tehran meant that the family did not settle in England. In view not least of the volatile political context that awaited in Iran, Ron and Anna Mellor decided that their children should remain in boarding school on the outskirts of London. From the age of nine, John Mellor would have almost no contact with his parents, seeing them only during the summer holidays when the Foreign Office would pay for him and his brother David to travel to various locations overseas.[13]

These peculiar family arrangements inevitably had a formative influence on the youngster who would in time become Joe Strummer. On various occasions, the singer would, understandably, express his hurt and anger that he had been 'abandoned' by his parents.[14] As someone deprived of a real home at an early age it is hardly surprising that throughout his life Joe Strummer seemed unable or unwilling to settle anywhere. From the moment that he left school, the singer lived a peripatetic existence, moving between a sequence of temporary abodes, primarily in the London squatting scene. Even when The Clash began to experience mainstream commercial success, the band's front man seemed content to have no place to call home, carting his meagre possessions from place to place in a sequence of plastic bags.[15] This sense of rootlessness was perhaps the source of his abiding attraction to 'outsiders' and would find clear echoes in his presentation of self.[16] As someone who had no real home from an early age, it was understandable that John Mellor would find it even more difficult than most other young people to arrive at a stable understanding of who or what he was. This critical ontological lack would, as so often the case with the truly gifted, become the site of his creativity, given form in his artwork, his cartoons and, most importantly, his songs. It would also become the space of a recurrent personal reinvention. Over the years, Mellor shed his skin several times, cutting out from his life many erstwhile friends and becoming someone else entirely.[17] Some of the most crucial of these reinventions were marked by sudden name changes. As a young man entering art college, Mellor adopted a new alias in homage to the great dustbowl protest singer Woody Guthrie.[18] In time, the moniker 'Woody Mellor' was deemed to have served its purpose and abandoned in favour of 'Joe Strummer', a name that gestured self-deprecatingly towards what he saw as his limited technique as a guitarist while simultaneously burnishing his credentials as a 'blokey' man of the people ('This is Joe public speaking').[19]

It is certainly tempting to see the various personae fashioned by the young man who would become Joe Strummer as an attempt to protect or perhaps reconstruct a self that had been quite profoundly damaged.[20] Those who spent time in the company of the singer speak of a personality more conflicted than most. Here was an individual who was exceptionally and effortlessly charismatic, whose humour, energy and generosity routinely drew people towards him. While often the centre of attention, he was also a solitary individual who appeared to exist at the edge of the frame of other people's lives.[21] Those who were, on the face of it at least, close to Strummer often admit to not feeling genuinely close to him at all, that he was someone that they never quite got to know. It is said with some frequency that there was a certain 'sadness' about the man.[22] A principal source of that sorrow is widely believed to be a tragedy that befell the Mellor family in the summer of 1970. A few weeks before John Mellor was due to begin art college he discovered that his elder brother David, an introverted personality who had dabbled with the occult and fascist politics, had taken his own life.[23] This tragic event understandably had a traumatic and lasting effect on the young man who would soon reinvent himself as Joe Strummer. While the singer only rarely talked about the suicide of his elder brother, its impact is clearly discernible in his artistic life. Running through the compositions that Strummer wrote with Mick Jones there is a very palpable sense of the 'sadness' that those close to him often discerned in the front man. It is this thread of melancholia not least that gives the songbook of The Clash such a remarkable charge – both personal and political – even after all these years.

'But I just wanna stay in the garage all night'

In the eyes of many fans, The Clash were – indeed are – an affirmation of the power of popular music to be a force for progressive political change. The songs that the group committed to vinyl brought a range of injustices both at home and abroad to an audience that might otherwise have remained oblivious. Moreover, the passionate lyrics that Joe Strummer wedded to Mick Jones's timeless arrangements articulated the hope that a better world might just at some stage heave into view. If the future really is unwritten, then perhaps there is a chance that we might get to make our own history after all. The sense of political optimism that attended the band was given its most explicit form in their famously belligerent stage performances. These moments of 'impassioned communion'[24] at times almost appeared to be forms of political praxis in themselves, a radical quality captured well by Dave Laing in his memorable description of The Clash in concert as being 'like a unit of partisans charged with some crucial beachhead'.[25] It is little wonder then that so many of those who saw the band live were inspired to become involved in a range of progressive cultural and political causes.

The construction of The Clash as the advocates and maybe even the agents of some radical political alternative is the one that holds sway in how the band are remembered. While the group certainly articulated a sense of political optimism, they also gave voice to other rather different, and often less acknowledged, sentiments. There is in the work of The Clash a certain sense of pessimism or fatalism that is perhaps understated in representations of the group. This thread of 'left melancholia' certainly becomes more pronounced as their career proceeds, but it is there from the very outset. The band's debut album offers a withering critique of a British society in the mid-1970s where the state is profoundly racist and power is in the hands 'of the people rich enough to buy it'. The tone here is one of incandescent rage that gives rise to a radical, if admittedly inchoate, political agenda. Listeners to *The Clash* are at various stages encouraged to resist US imperialism ('I'm So Bored with the USA'), incited to reject wage labour ('Career Opportunities') and exhorted to forge a multicultural alliance with black youths willing to resist state repression with physical force ('White Riot'). While this mood of political belligerence runs through the album from the very outset it is, significantly perhaps, foreclosed by the track that concludes the record.

One of the first gigs that The Clash ever played – at the Screen on the Green in London in August 1976 – drew a stinging review from *NME* journalist Charles Shaar Murray, who insisted that they were 'the sort of garage band that should be speedily returned to the garage, preferably with the motor still running'.[26] This early denunciation prompted Joe Strummer to write 'Garageland', a defence of the *do-it-yourself* ethic and *lo-fi* aesthetic that were central to the founding ideals of the punk movement. The tone of the lyrics that feature here is ostensibly one of spirited defiance. While the culture industries are exercising all their wiles to seduce the bands that punk spawned ('Meanwhile things are hotting up in the West End alright'), the intention of our faithful narrator is to resist the lure of Mammon ('I don't want to go to where the rich are going'). This mood of pugnaciousness ('We're a garage band, We come from garageland') is, however, undercut both by the despondency of Strummer's delivery and by what Kieran Cashell elsewhere in this volume terms the song's 'haunting harmonica sub-frequencies'. The despondent and haunted nature of the track is, of course, entirely appropriate when it is viewed in its wider context. While 'Garageland' articulates an ambition to remain beyond the reach of the mainstream culture industries, most people hearing it for the first time will have encountered it as the closing track of an album brought out by a major record corporation.[27] In that sense, the release of *The Clash* might be considered to mark the first of several political reversals that the band would experience over the course of their career. With its elegiac tone, 'Garageland' captures that sense of defeat and introduces a thread of melancholia that would become ever more pronounced in the years to come.

While the back catalogue of The Clash is replete with songs mapping a range of injustices across the globe, there are relatively few that deal with the politics of the personal. A memorable exception to this rule comes in the form of 'Lost in the Supermarket', a track that stands out even in the stellar company of the other eighteen that comprise the album widely regarded as the band's creative peak, *London Calling*.[28] In one of his most autobiographical lyrics, Strummer sketches out what is, in part, a familiar leftist critique of the spiritual emptiness of late capitalism.[29] While the wares of the culture industries promise instant and eternal happiness, these blandishments prove time and again to be hollow. The narrator of the song has sought refuge in commodities – he has seen 'all the programmes', 'saved coupons from packets of tea' and purchased that 'giant hit discotheque album' – but none of these ever seem to ease the pain. He remains 'lost in the supermarket' and 'can no longer shop happily'. In this lyric, we are reminded that the person who would become Joe Strummer was prone to feelings of alienation in the precise sense that the young Marx draws out in the *Paris Manuscripts*,[30] that he was, in other words, someone who simply did not feel *at home* in the world. While this sense of estrangement reflects the quintessential emptiness of a social order premised on the commodity form, it also owes its origins to matters that are rather more autobiographical. In a relatively rare gesture towards his own troubled upbringing, Strummer suggests that he 'wasn't born so much as [he] fell out'. Growing up in a 'hedge back home in the suburbs', his principal memory seems to have been hearing 'the people who live on the ceiling' who would 'scream and fight most scarily'. Against this backdrop, it is perhaps fitting that when the band came to record 'Lost in the Supermarket', the track would feature their other principal vocalist. It is rather apt, in other words, that the person who wrote those words about not being able to find any sense or value for themselves in the world would be unable to commit them to vinyl. The vocal duties here are passed to Jones, whose reedy delivery lends the song a suitably plaintive air. Strummer's presence is an appropriately spectral one, consigned to a distant reiteration of the chorus towards the end of the track. While the delivery of The Clash front man often had a certain haunted quality, he rarely sounded quite so vulnerable or lost as in this particular moment.

By the time The Clash came to record their fourth studio album, the band had long since dispensed with the *lo-fi* manifesto issued in 'Garageland'. The thirty-six tracks that feature on *Sandinista!* showcase a dizzying array of musical styles. The sheer ambition of the music that appears on the album is mirrored in the words that were written to accompany it. Across the six sides of vinyl that comprise *Sandinista!* we encounter some of the finest and most elaborate lyrics that Joe Strummer ever crafted. Among the most compelling of these is a clutch of songs that dramatise the inequalities that bedevil both the band's native land and their newly adopted home on the other side of the Atlantic. The genuinely epic lyrics of 'Something About England' begin with what will become a recurrent motif of a chance encounter with a hapless vagrant. The opening narrative sees Mick Jones stumbling upon an 'old man' 'propped inside' a 'dirty overcoat' 'at the foot of the pillar of the road'. Invited to explain the 'gloom' of what was by now the early Thatcher era, the transient, voiced by Joe Strummer, insists that the ills that afflict English society are endemic and long-standing – 'you really think it's all new', he scoffs – before proceeding to offer an overview of a century blighted by poverty and war. The old man was shipped out during the Second World War and was among 'the few' who returned to limp around Piccadilly and Leicester Square, a sequence accompanied by a suitably disconsolate, ghostly rendition of a popular tune from a previous global conflagration, 'It's a Long Way to Tipperary'. While those who survived the slaughter were promised a land fit for heroes, this bold promise would never be realised. The society to which *the Greatest Generation* returned was one marked by familiar class distinctions – 'there was masters an' servants an' servants an' dogs' – that would prove deeply resistant to change. While those who had served King and Country were promised a better future, they would continue to endure multiple privations, not least in the guise of substandard housing ('the architects could not care').

This theme would take centre stage in another critical track that appears on *Sandinista!* Propelled by Mickey Gallagher's Hammond organ, 'Up in Heaven (Not Only Here)' sets a jaunty tempo at odds with the dystopian lyrics of the song.[31] Mick Jones on lead vocals decries the bleak realities of the 'crumbling' tower blocks in which the veterans of the Second World War were required to live. The lifts are broken and are now used as public conveniences. Every home is like a 'cage, it's like captivity'. When the wind hits the building it tilts and 'one day it will surely fall to the ground'. While the residents of the tower blocks endure lives of utter 'misery', this has little consequence for those who designed the estates but were never required to live there, the 'bourgeois clerks who bear no guilt'. This sequence of indictments was written almost forty years ago, but has a very real and precise resonance in the present day. A short distance from the Westway – the elevated urban motorway in west London forever synonymous with The Clash – stand the blackened remains of Grenfell Tower. When we return to listen to 'Up in Heaven (Not Only Here)' with its condemnation of 'crumbling blocks' and heedless 'bourgeois clerks' it is impossible not to think of that most dramatic incidence of architectural incompetence and civic neglect, one that cost the lives of seventy-two people in the summer of 2017.

The mournful historical panorama of 'Something About England' finds a transatlantic double in another of the more memorable tracks to appear on The Clash's famously uneven triple album. When the band were recording *Sandinista!* in New York, Strummer was staying in the renowned Iroquois hotel.[32] Returning home late one night, the singer crossed paths with an elderly homeless man looking for some change. That chance encounter would prompt Strummer to write what Cohen and Peacock have described as a 'melancholic deconstruction of the "American dream"'.[33] In 'Broadway', the lyricist once more casts a street vagrant as the narrator of a compelling, sweeping social history. Emerging out of the night, the homeless man confides that he was born 'into misery, in the back of a truck' and it would seem that his luck has failed to turn ever since. He has often gone hungry and 'worked for breakfast'. All around him in New York are the trappings of an easy wealth that at times appear alluring. The vagrant is especially drawn to the prospect of driving 'one of those cars' that transport the glitterati between the city's various glamorous night spots. In pursuit of this 'better' life, he has tried his hand at boxing and in his time in the ring he 'took those right hooks'. It is implied, however, that the 'American dream' is not only unattainable but not worth attaining. In an enigmatic sequence in the middle of the song, the narrator has an apparent change of heart, but for no obvious reason. It simply all felt 'different one morning, maybe it was the rain'.

'Broadway' contains some of the most affecting and Delphic lyrics that Joe Strummer wrote over the course of his career. What the song showcases with particular clarity is a very specific, and often unacknowledged, quality of the singer's voice. Perhaps the predominant conception that exists of Strummer is that of the impassioned front man declaiming all that is wrong with the world. While his voice certainly lent itself to full-blooded rage, it was also suited perfectly to a certain form of melancholia. Think, for instance, of that inexplicably moving throwaway comment on 'The Call Up' when he discloses 'maybe I wanna see the wheat fields over Kiev and down to the sea'. Or take more or less any line from 'Leopardskin Limousines', the heart-breaking lament for a doomed extramarital tryst that illuminates the debut solo album *Earthquake Weather*. While there are many moments that illustrate the particular quality of melancholia in Joe Strummer's voice, there are few quite as haunting or powerful as those on 'Broadway'. When the singer confides that 'suddenly I noticed that it weren't quite the same', it feels not only that the dreams of one individual have died, but that those of an entire society are about to suffer the same fate.

'There ain't no asylum here'

The final album by The Clash to feature the songwriting partnership of Joe Strummer and Mick Jones, *Combat Rock*, begins in what might be considered characteristically bellicose fashion. The opening track and lead single 'Know Your Rights' marks how elementary civil liberties are eliminated in the face of power and wealth, while the following number – the hypnotic, neglected gem 'Car Jamming' – rages at the fate of the first of several casualties of the Vietnam War that appear on the album. The mood of belligerence that opens *Combat Rock* soon dissipates, however, and the passion of that opening pair of tracks gives way to an increasingly pervasive air of pathos. While this tone of abjection is to the fore on tracks such as 'Sean Flynn', 'Ghetto Defendant' and 'Death is the Star', it finds its apogee in the song that closes side one of the record but which, with its air of abject finality, should perhaps have drawn the curtain down on the entire album.

Of all the songs that The Clash recorded together, 'Straight to Hell' represents perhaps the band's finest hour. Opened by Mick Jones's distinctive D major guitar signature and sustained by drummer Topper Headon's queasily insistent 'bossa nova beat',[34] the song offers the listener a panorama of the wretched of the earth. In his 'heartfelt' lyrics,[35] Joe Strummer begins with a snapshot of those British 'railhead towns' devastated by the closure of 'steel mills' that were the first to have their state subsidies revoked when Margaret Thatcher came to power.[36] As recession takes hold, the opportunities that once existed have frozen like 'winter ice', not least for those migrants drawn to the country by the promise of a better life who remain capable only of speaking 'King's English in quotation'. In the following verse, we are transported – not for the first time on *Combat Rock* – to south-east Asia where we find the offspring of an American soldier and a Vietnamese mother brandishing a photo of her parents as proof of paternity.[37] The Amerasian child pleads to be taken to the United States but is informed by her father that there is no place for her there, that her blood 'ain't Coca Cola, it's rice'. Perhaps the callous indifference of the US serviceman will prove to be a blessing in disguise. The depiction of American society that features in the penultimate verse of the song is after all distinctly hellish.

Discarding his habitual love of Americana, Strummer portrays the United States as consumed by 'junkie-dom', a place where the dispossessed ease their pain with the sedative procaine and remain mindful of the 'volatile molatov' seeking to clear their slums for more lucrative developments.

The 'post-colonial melancholia'[38] of 'Straight to Hell' provides a compelling and epic travelogue around a planet deformed then, as it is now, by inequality and injustice. It becomes clear, however, that Strummer's intention here is not merely to document specific instances of poverty, war and displacement but rather to acknowledge their connections within a prevailing social order that is genuinely systemic. In the final verse of the song, Strummer underlines that the moments of injustice we have just encountered are not aberrations but rather the norm, that they can, and indeed do, happen 'anywhere', on 'any frontier', in 'any hemisphere'. The tone in which these global iniquities are documented is one not of anger bur rather of pure resignation. There is simply no prospect of asylum or of justice in this world. King Solomon, after all, 'he never lived round here'. The only option that remains is to go 'straight to hell, boys'.

If we are to understand the abject tone of 'Straight to Hell' we need to acknowledge the manner in which it documents – or, more precisely, immediately prefigures – a certain historical moment. The final days of the 'classic' line-up of The Clash coincided with the ascent of the neoliberal project towards power. When the band went into the studio to record *Combat Rock* not only was Thatcher in Downing Street but Ronald Reagan had recently taken up residence in the White House. It was never inevitable that the policies advocated by these close ideological allies would become hegemonic. For most of her first term, for instance, it seemed unlikely that Thatcher would survive to serve another let alone a third.[39] An imperial skirmish in the south Atlantic – at its height in the week that *Combat Rock* hit the shops – would, however, transform the context of British politics. On a tide of patriotic fervour generated by reclaiming the Falklands, Thatcher was returned to power in June 1983 with a greatly enhanced parliamentary majority. In the course of this second term, the sheer ambition of Thatcherism would become apparent, with the Conservatives introducing a series of neoliberal strategies that would leave British society transformed and traumatised and that would in time become the blueprint for other countries across the globe.[40] While Thatcher may well have survived the perilous political terrain of the early 1980s, the same cannot be said of The Clash. Within weeks of her second electoral triumph, it was announced that Mick Jones had been sacked from the band due to musical differences both literal and metaphorical, sundering one of the most fruitful songwriting partnerships in the history of popular music.

The specific historical context in which 'Straight to Hell' was written was, then, that of the emergent neoliberal conjuncture. At the moment the track was recorded, those political forces responsible for the misery and injustice documented in the song were in the ascendant and moving towards what only in hindsight looks like their inevitable triumph. In the song's lyrics, there is no sense that such a calamity might be avoided. In its refusal to even conceive of a different outcome, 'Straight to Hell' might be said to prefigure the ultimate victory of neoliberalism, an ideological project that from the outset insisted that 'there is no alternative'. While it may seem counter-intuitive at first, it is, as we shall see later, precisely this sense of despondency that makes the track an especially powerful and enduring song of social protest.

But if that is really so, then we have a problem. The venerable tradition of radical songwriting is conventionally understood as drawing on what Ian Peddie has termed the 'resisting muse'.[41] Songs of social protest, in other words, are those that seek to mobilise resistance, to brush against the grain of history. At first glance, it is hard to see how a track such as 'Straight to Hell' might accord with such a definition. The tone of the song is after all not one of resistance but of resignation. If we look again from a different angle, however, it will become apparent that not only is 'Straight to Hell' a protest song, it is an especially potent and durable one. It is so, moreover, not in spite of its utter despondency but rather precisely because of it. In order to understand how that might be so we need to consider the nature of that disposition towards the world sometimes termed 'left melancholia'.

'I don't believe in books but I read them all the time'

In a provocative essay published in 1999, Wendy Brown sought to diagnose the malaise afflicting a Left still reeling from the 'constellation of defeats'[42] that littered the late twentieth century. Brown draws our attention to a condition that she refers to as 'left melancholy', a concept derived from Walter Benjamin but which in her deployment owes rather more to Sigmund Freud. In his famous essay on mourning and melancholia, Freud characterises the latter as arising from a refusal to let go of a love object that results over time in an escalating loathing of the self. It is precisely this mode of pathology, Brown suggests, that afflicts the contemporary Left. The inability of leftists to relinquish those modes of thought and deed that no longer have any purchase on the present has served to foreclose the field of political possibility. Incapable of recognising the potential of new forms of cultural theory and political practice, the Left has come to represent a deeply 'conservative force', blind to the transformative power of more contemporary ways of being in, and thinking about, the world.[43]

Among the sharpest responses to this withering depiction of the contemporary Left is the work of Jodi Dean. In her book *The Communist Horizon*,

Dean points out, correctly, that Brown's thesis is premised on an entirely 'misleading' representation of the work of Walter Benjamin.[44] The notion of 'left-wing melancholy' appeared initially in a brief literary review that Benjamin published in 1931, and was developed further in an essay entitled 'The Author as Producer' that appeared three years later.[45] In both of these works, the object of his ire is not, as Brown suggests, those on the Left who are unwilling to relinquish their former ideals but rather those who do so with alacrity. The specific focus for Benjamin in these essays is the 'hacks' of the New Objectivity movement who throw progressive shapes but in reality are merely complicit in the assimilation of revolutionary energies into the existing order of things. His critique is remarkably close, in other words, to that often directed towards The Clash by detractors who revel in turning the classic line 'turning rebellion into money' – from '(White Man) In Hammersmith Palais' – back on the band.

While Dean shares with Brown the conviction that there exists a debilitating 'left-wing melancholy', she uses the concept in the original sense intended by Benjamin.[46] The essential shortcoming of the Left, Dean contests, is not that it has been unprepared to let go of its erstwhile ideals but rather that it has been willing to do so only too readily. This capitulation has led leftists into a sequence of 'melancholy practices' intended to shield them from the guilt that arises from having abandoned the revolutionary project. Dean suggests, rather pointedly, that this 'left melancholia' finds form in precisely the modes of political thought and practice that Brown seems to advocate. It assumes the guise, that is, of that 'incessant activity' characteristic of the contemporary Left that appears progressive but in actuality leads merely to the 'sublimation of goals and responsibilities into the branching, fragmented practices of micropolitics, self-care, and issue awareness'.[47] However, these once-dominant modes of politics are, Dean suggests, in the process of decline. There are growing signs that the Left 'has worked or is working through its melancholia' and has begun once more to conceive of the possibility of real social transformation.[48]

The depiction of 'left melancholia' that we find in *The Communist Horizon* is one that accords rather better with the realities of contemporary political culture, not least because it adheres more closely to the original meaning that Benjamin intended for the concept. What is perhaps missing from Dean's account is an acknowledgement of the potential of melancholia as a source and form of progressive politics. While Benjamin coined 'left-wing melancholy' as a term of abuse he was, it should be remembered, an exemplary exponent of precisely that political disposition. In his writings on Baudelaire, for instance, Benjamin makes the case that it is 'images of the melancholy' that 'kindle the spiritual' and ensure that 'our gaze is fixed on the ideal'.[49] That the writer was drawn time and again to the notion of melancholia was the outcome not merely of an autobiographical accident – that he was 'born under the sign of Saturn' – but also a profound epistemological commitment. As Enzo Traverso notes, while Benjamin's devotion to 'an empathic and mournful exploration of the world reduced to a field of ruins' might appear a kind of fatalism, it was in fact a form of revolutionary practice.[50] Benjamin contends that the purpose and promise of the 'tenacious self-absorption' of melancholia is that 'it embraces dead objects in its contemplation, in order to redeem them'.[51] The role of the writer in this enterprise is the critical one of 'ragpicker', the person who collects 'rags of speech and verbal scraps', images of the dead and tales of the vanquished.[52] The revolutionary potential of these relics only becomes apparent in those periods when radical social transformation seems possible, when we can conceive of making that 'leap in the open air of history'[53] that marks the revolutionary project. In these 'moments of danger', Benjamin suggests, the living must recognise the tributes of the ragpicker, 'seize hold of a memory' that will enable them not merely to reinvent the future but to redeem the past.[54] This revolutionary energy exercises a 'retroactive force' that 'will constantly call in question every victory, past and present, of the rulers'.[55] It heralds that long-awaited moment of redemption when 'by dint of a secret heliotropism the past strives to turn toward that sun which is rising in the sky of history'.

The beguiling blend of the material and the messianic that threads the work of Walter Benjamin intimates a way in which we might return to listen to 'Straight to Hell' as though for the very first time. His writings suggest that perhaps the mood of abjection that pervades such a song is precisely the source of its political power, that its heartfelt lyrics are among those 'rags of speech and verbal scraps' garnered in the midst of one political crisis that must be reclaimed and repurposed by future generations in the midst of their own. It is to this particular act of reclamation that we turn our attention next.

'You really think it's all new'

Although one of the finest songs in the back catalogue of The Clash, 'Straight to Hell' is far from the band's most famous. The track is certainly less well known than, say, the almost always hilariously misplaced 'London Calling' or that hardy perennial of bar room karaoke, 'Should I Stay or Should I Go?'. Insofar as 'Straight to Hell' enjoys any widespread public recognition, it does so primarily because of its association with another song that borrows explicitly from it. Since the mid-2000s, Mathangi 'Maya' Arulpragasam has produced music that splices together a giddy diversity of contemporary urban and global styles. The songs that she records under the stage name M.I.A. often draw heavily on the singer's personal experience of violence and displacement. The daughter of a senior figure in the Tamil insurgency, M.I.A was forced to flee her native Sri Lanka as a child and spent periods of her life in London, Madras and New York.[56] This peripatetic autobiography provides the backdrop to songs that often deal with the plight of migrants and refugees. In view of these preoccupations, it was always likely that M.I.A. would be drawn to the heartsore ballad that is 'Straight to Hell'. Released in February 2008, 'Paper Planes' would become an international hit on the back of its appearance in the global box office success *Slumdog Millionaire*. The song borrows the distinctive guitar signature from 'Straight to Hell' and, like its predecessor, seeks to animate the lives of those displaced by conflict and injustice. There, however, the similarity between the two tracks ends. Where the tone of The Clash song is utterly despondent, that of M.I.A.'s repurposing of the track is entirely joyous. The migrants who feature in her song are creative and resourceful, manufacturing 'in a second if you wait' the bogus visas – the *paper planes* of the title – that render all national borders porous. There is a sense of mischief and romance here that Joe Strummer would surely have loved. The refugees we meet are not only surviving but prospering, making a living from various illegal trades with a certain 'swagger' and with a hint of violence that appears entirely comical – most notably, the 'irresistible gun-shot/ gun-cock/ cash-register-ker-ching hook'[57] of the chorus. While the characters who populate 'Straight to Hell' appear the wretched of the earth, those who feature in 'Paper Planes' seem almost certain to inherit it. At first glance at least, it would be difficult to imagine a pair of connected songs that are so disconnected in their sense of political possibility.

The palpable differences between 'Straight to Hell' and 'Paper Planes' are, predictably, often interpreted as an expression of critical distance. This interpretation tends to centre upon the dramatically contrasting biographies of the people who wrote the lyrics of the two songs: the attempt by the son of a British diplomat to capture the plight of those enduring displacement by war is held to have drawn a stinging rebuke from the daughter of a Third World insurgent whose formative years were spent among the displaced. In his account of 'Paper Planes', the journalist Ben Thompson, for instance, suggests that the song reverses the monologue that usually flows from the developed to the underdeveloped world and in doing so 'turns globalization inside out'.[58] An academic version of this reading appears in the work of Cohen and Peacock who suggest that the M.I.A hit represents 'an act of sedition or revolt' aimed at a song tainted by its 'occasionally hamfisted attempts to speak "for" migrants'.[59] While these interpretations solemnly observe the conventions of contemporary debates on the perils of 'cultural appropriation', they do not, alas, capture the spirit of the song that they are attempting to describe. If 'Paper Planes' really does harbour some hostility towards 'Straight to Hell', it is simply *inaudible* when we actually listen to the song. The joyous and mischievous tone that defines the M.I.A. track suggests that it has in fact a deeply sympathetic relationship to The Clash number from which it draws. This sympathy becomes apparent once we listen to both songs again, this time through the ears of Walter Benjamin.

'Straight to Hell' was, as we saw earlier, recorded at a time when the balance of historical forces was moving, seemingly inexorably, in favour of the neoliberal project. While the sense of melancholy with which the track maps this process might initially make it an unlikely candidate for the status of 'protest song', it is, however, precisely that quality that makes it such a compelling one. According to Benjamin, melancholia is a wellspring of creativity, curating and recounting stories with a 'germinative power' that only becomes apparent in those sequences of history when the field of political possibility suddenly broadens.[60] It was precisely one of these 'moments of danger' that gave birth to the M.I.A. track under consideration here. Recorded in the summer of 2007, 'Paper Planes' calls to mind more than any other song the period when the crisis long since latent within the global financial system finally came to a head. As a sequence of previously impregnable corporations went to the wall, it seemed for a time that there was the serious prospect of genuinely radical political change. If we are to grasp the revolutionary potential of such moments, Benjamin insists, we must seize those images from the past that flash up before us. And in sampling 'Straight to Hell', that is, precisely, what 'Paper Planes' does. It matters little that the M.I.A track is neither an exact copy nor an homage. The intention of the revolutionary moment, Benjamin insists, is not to repeat history but rather to bring it to a halt. And, for the purposes of the discussion here at least, it does not matter overly if in fact the author of 'Paper Planes' does turn out to have had a problem with a former public school boy attempting to summon the refugee experience. The precise motivations that led to 'Straight to Hell' being recalled are rather less important than the sheer fact of its recollection.

For Benjamin, it is these acts of remembrance that actualise the radical potential of the melancholy cultural artefacts of the past. As the era of neoliberalism appeared to enter the period of its twilight,[61] 'Paper Planes', with telling symmetry, invoked a song that perhaps more than any other captured its moment of triumph a quarter of a century earlier. In sampling 'Straight to Hell', M.I.A unleashes the radical energy that was always present within the melancholia of the track. A song that seems unable to conceive of the possibility of a better world suddenly becomes one imagining such a world already under construction. 'Paper Planes' should not then be heard as a rejection of 'Straight to Hell' but rather as the moment of its redemption. This peculiar sympathy between two classic songs recorded by very different artists at very different times reminds us of something that Walter Benjamin would have known better possibly than any other cultural commentator. It was perhaps only when we had been condemned straight to hell that we could begin to conceive of the possibility of storming heaven once more.

Notes

1. Pat Gilbert, *Passion is a Fashion: The Real Story of The Clash* (London: Aurum Press, 2004), p. 126.
2. Matthew Worley, 'Revolution Rock? Joe Strummer, and the British Left in the Early Days of Punk', in Barry J. Faulk and Brady Harrison (eds), *Punk Rock Warlord: The Life and Work of Joe Strummer* (Farnham: Ashgate, 2014), p. 92.
3. The footage can be viewed at: https://www.youtube.com/watch?v=hvVQMOjTnxE (accessed 12 July 2017).
4. Antonino D'Ambrosio (ed.), *Let Fury Have the Hour: Joe Strummer, Punk, and the Movement That Shook the World* (New York: Nation Books, 2012), p. xxiv.
5. The phrase 'the future is unwritten' appears on the sleeve of the single 'Know Your Rights' and would provide the subtitle to Julien Temple's posthumous documentary about Joe Strummer.
6. D'Ambrosio, *Let Fury Have the Hour*, p. 4.
7. Randal Doane, *Stealing all Transmissions: A Secret History of The Clash* (Oakland, CA: PM Press, 2014), p. 42.
8. Worley, 'Revolution Rock?', p. 89.
9. Barry J. Faulk and Brady Harrison, 'Introduction: John Woody Joe Mellor Strummer: The Many Lives, Travails and Sundry Shortcomings of a Punk Rock Warlord', in Faulk and Harrison (eds), *Punk Rock Warlord*, p. 2.
10. Marcus Gray, *The Clash: Return of the Last Gang in Town* (London: Helter Skelter, 2001), p. 162.
11. Sean Egan, *The Clash: The Only Band That Mattered* (London: Rowman and Littlefield, 2015), p. 78.
12. Alex Ogg, 'Saint Joe: An Apostate Writes', in Faulk and Harrison (eds), *Punk Rock Warlord*, pp. 76–7.
13. Gray, *Return of the Last Gang in Town*, pp. 80–1; Chris Salewicz, *Redemption Song: The Definitive Biography of Joe Strummer* (London: Harper Collins, 2006), pp. 40–68.
14. Gray, *Return of the Last Gang in Town*, pp. 80–1.
15. Salewicz, *Redemption Song*, p. 352.
16. Edward A. Shannon, '"Don't Call Me Woody": The Punk Compassion and Folk Rebellion of Joe Strummer and Woody Guthrie', in Faulk and Harrison (eds), *Punk Rock Warlord*, pp. 20–1.
17. Gray, *Return of the Last Gang in Town*, pp. 101–2.
18. Gilbert, *Passion is a Fashion*, pp. 14–15; Shannon, 'Don't Call Me Woody', p. 14.
19. Ogg, 'Saint Joe', p. 73.
20. Gray, *Return of the Last Gang in Town*, pp. 228–9.
21. Ibid., pp. 93, 323.
22. Gilbert, *Passion is a Fashion*, p. 8.
23. Ibid., pp. 14–15.
24. Gray, *Return of the Last Gang in Town*, p. 429.

25 Dave Laing, *One Chord Wonders: Power and Meaning in Punk Rock* (Oakland, CA: PM Press, 2015), p. 110.
26 Salewicz, *Redemption Song*, pp. 170–1.
27 Jon Savage, *England's Dreaming: Sex Pistols and Punk Rock* (London: Faber and Faber, 1991), pp. 399–405.
28 Gilbert, *Passion is a Fashion*, p. 259.
29 Gray, *Return of the Last Gang in Town*, pp. 80–1.
30 Karl Marx, 'Economic and Philosophical Manuscripts', in *Karl Marx: Selected Writings*, ed. David McLellan (Oxford: Oxford University Press, 1977), pp. 83–121.
31 Gray, *Return of the Last Gang in Town*, p. 341.
32 Gilbert, *Passion is a Fashion*, p. 276.
33 Samuel Cohen and James Peacock, 'Introduction: The Transnational Clash', in Samuel Cohen and James Peacock (eds), *The Clash Takes on the World: Transnational Perspectives on the Only Band that Matters* (London: Bloomsbury, 2017), p. 9.
34 Salewicz, *Redemption Song*, p. 323.
35 Chris Barsanti, 'Mystery Train: "Joe Strummer" on Screen', in Faulk and Harrison (eds), *Punk Rock Warlord*, p. 169.
36 Andrew Gamble, *The Free Economy and the Strong State: The Politics of Thatcherism* (Basingstoke: Palgrave, 1994), p. 109.
37 The sex of the child is not specified in the song, but feminine pronouns are used here to avoid a clutter of gender binaries.
38 Gilbert, *Passion is a Fashion*, p. 320.
39 Gamble, *The Free Economy and the Strong State*, p. 119.
40 Kieran Cashell, 'More Relevance Than Spotlight and Applause: Billy Bragg in the British Folk Tradition', in Ian Peddie (ed.), *Popular Music and Human Rights Volume I: British and American Music* (Farnham: Ashgate, 2011), p. 16.
41 Ian Peddie, *The Resisting Muse: Popular Music and Social Protest* (Farnham: Ashgate, 2006).
42 Enzo Traverso, *Left-Wing Melancholia: Marxism, History, and Memory* (New York: Columbia University Press, 2016), p. 22.
43 Wendy Brown, 'Resisting Left Melancholy', *Boundary 2* 26.3 (1999), pp. 19–27.
44 Jodi Dean, *The Communist Horizon* (London: Verso, 2012), p. 158.
45 Walter Benjamin, 'Left-Wing Melancholy (On Erich Kästner's New Book of Poems)' (1931), *Screen* 15.2 (1974), pp. 28–32; Walter Benjamin, 'The Author as Producer' (1934), in Walter Benjamin, *Understanding Brecht* (London: Verso, 1998).
46 Dean, *The Communist Horizon*, p. 175.
47 Ibid., p. 174.
48 Ibid., p. 174.
49 Walter Benjamin, *Essays on Charles Baudelaire* (Cambridge, MA: Harvard University Press, 2006), p. 29.
50 Traverso, *Left-Wing Melancholia*, p. 47.
51 Walter Benjamin, *The Origin of German Tragic Drama* (London: Verso, 2009), p. 157.

52 Walter Benjamin, 'An Outsider Makes his Mark', in *Selected Writings, Volume 2, Part 1: 1927–1930*, ed. Michael W. Jennings, Howard Eiland and Gary Smith (Cambridge, MA: Harvard University Press, 1999), p. 310.
53 Walter Benjamin, 'Theses on the Philosophy of History', in *Illuminations*, ed. Hannah Arendt (London: Fontana, 1992), p. 253.
54 Ibid., p. 247.
55 Ibid., p. 246.
56 Randeep Ramesh, 'MIA Accused of Supporting Terrorism by Speaking out for Tamil Tigers', *The Guardian*, 11 February 2009, https://www.theguardian.com/music/2009/feb/11/mia-sri-lanka-tamil-tigers (accessed 12 July 2017).
57 Ben Thompson, 'MIA's Paper Planes Turns Globalisation Inside Out', *The Guardian*, 16 June 2011, https://www.theguardian.com/music/2011/jun/16/mia-paper-planes (accessed 12 July 2017).
58 Ibid.
59 Samuel Cohen and James Peacock, 'Conclusion: The Only Band that Matters', in Cohen and Peacock (eds), *The Clash Takes on the World*, p. 253.
60 Walter Benjamin, 'The Storyteller: Reflections on the Life of Nikolai Leskov', in Arendt (ed.), *Illuminations*, p. 90.
61 Laurence Cox and Alf Gunvald Nilsen, *We Make Our Own History: Marxism and Social Movements in the Twilight of Neoliberalism* (London: Pluto, 2014).

PART II

'Back in the garage with my bullshit detector': The Clash and the cultural politics of punk

4
'Are you going backwards, Or are you going forwards?' – England past and England future in 1970s punk

Ruth Adams

Ranking Roger: The Clash did so much. They set the trend for others to come through. Anarchy was to destroy the old but you've got to make sure you build a good new thing. Their records were like the anarchist rebuilding.[1]

This chapter examines the ways in which the cosmopolitan and political approach of The Clash could be regarded as progressive and forward looking. Specifically, it will focus on the engagement with reggae by the band (and the punk subculture more broadly), and make the case that this helped them to move forward, creatively and politically. The Clash imagined a multicultural, postcolonial future and actively sought to make it manifest, in their music and also through their engagement with the Rock Against Racism movement. Their continuing influence on popular music in the UK is evident. A comparison is made with the Sex Pistols, in terms of how each band reflected and represented images of English national identity, both its past and its possible future(s). I will argue that, broadly speaking, these two groups could be said to constitute the 'Janus-face' of English punk, as the Sex Pistols were more inward looking and focused on England's cultural and political past. However, I will consider too the factors that complicate and problematise such a dichotomous distinction.

The Sex Pistols and 'English heritage'[2]

While the Sex Pistols were regarded as uniquely shocking and like nothing ever seen before by their contemporaries, they might also be framed as the ghosts of England past. They and those around them who helped create their image – manager Malcolm McLaren, graphic designer Jamie Reid and fashion designer Vivienne Westwood – collected, magpie-like, disparate aspects of English history and culture. Through a process of what Dick Hebdige has identified as 'bricolage', these bits and pieces were brought together in a chaotic, uneasy admixture to form a new milieu. Union flags, royal portraits, cups of tea, 'penny dreadfuls', caricatures by Gillray and Cruikshank were all incorporated. McLaren used Dickensian imagery in constructing the band's image, describing them as his 'little Artful Dodgers', and casting himself as Fagin. Johnny Rotten built his stage persona from a combination of the Victorian street urchin, Shakespeare's (or, more specifically, Olivier's) Richard III, and old man Albert Steptoe.[3] In Julien Temple's 1999 retrospective of the Pistols' story, *The Filth and the Fury*, the band are presented as the inheritors of the English music hall tradition – the heirs to the crowns of Arthur Askey and Max Wall, operating outside the 'legitimate theatre' and characterised by clownish outfits, silly walks, smutty jokes and cocking a snook at the Establishment. The band, it is stressed, were working in the tradition of English, working-class culture, a point neatly illustrated by Steve Jones's contribution to punk style, the knotted hanky, that improvised staple of the British seaside holiday. The Pistols, then, might be characterised as agents of English heritage, albeit unconventional and unlikely ones. In this respect, they were absolutely of their time, given that the 1970s was when the 'heritage industry' – from visits to 'stately homes' to the immense popularity of Laura Ashley – became a firmly established element of national life. Christopher Brooker has claimed that 'never before in history had there been an age so distrustful of the present, so fearful of the future, so enamoured of the past. Therein lay the significance of the Seventies.'[4] This is not to imply that the Pistols were reactionary, far from it. Their furious *détournement* of the conventional tropes of British history provided the disillusioned and disenfranchised with vivid weapons to attack the complacent jingoism that characterised the 1977 Jubilee celebrations; celebrations that seemed, as Jon Savage suggests, like 'an elaborate covering of the social cracks – with fading Coronation wallpaper'.[5] Unlike the mainstream heritage industry, the Pistols were trafficking in history, not merely wallowing in nostalgia.

Hate and war

For all its offensive republicanism, 'God Save the Queen' expressed a desire for a new, more positive reframing of Englishness – an England, perhaps, of citizens rather than subjects. As Lydon protested: 'You don't write "God Save the Queen" because you hate the English race, you write a song like that because you love them and you're fed up with them being mistreated.' He even went so far as to say, 'We declared war on England without meaning to.'[6] The metaphor of war was an apt one because, as Mark Sinker argues:

'No Future' was never a threat; it was a promise. It was – it is – a moral fact, a fundamental conundrum: how to behave in the last days, when authority is ended. Life during wartime; how to live happily and decently when this is as good as things may ever get.[7]

It was apt too because at the time the Second World War still loomed extremely large in nominally post-war British society. This dominance of history (and a historical victory) was, for many punks, a problem, both because it was used to justify a pervasive jingoistic complacency, and as a stick to beat the younger generations; hence the deployment of the swastika as the ultimate offensive symbolic weapon. However, as Patrick Wright suggests:

> Abject and manipulative as it undoubtedly is, the public glorification of war can express the real counterpoint which the experience of war has provided to the routinised, constrained and empty experience of much modern everyday life. In war [...] personal actions can count in a different way, routine can have a greater sense of meaning and necessity, and there can be some experience not just of extremity (avant-garde pleasure), but also of purpose. In this undoubtedly limited respect war can indeed be recollected as both more meaningful than normal everyday life and also as a purification.[8]

Given that a major complaint of punk was a persistent boredom, it seems feasible that they were, to some extent, 'envious' of the extreme experiences of the older generations. Joe Queenan suggests that The Clash single 'London Calling' 'captures the punks' desperate, somewhat theatrical yearning to fight the kind of pitched battle their parents had fought 30 years earlier. That is, to participate in a battle that might lead to something more lethal than a head butt.'[9] Punk can thus be understood as a form of symbolic war that could facilitate a sense of purpose, and explains too the covetous attitudes towards the militant stances of some black communities and cultures in Britain. Denied a war of their own, punks might still aspire to 'a riot of their own'. Accordingly, Hebdige suggests that reggae 'attracted those punks who wished to give tangible form to their alienation. It carried the necessary conviction, the political bite, so obviously missing in most contemporary white music.'[10] Hebdige argues that, paradoxically, it was in the 'exclusiveness of Black West Indian style, in the virtual impossibility of authentic white identification, that reggae's attraction for the punks was strongest'.[11] Reggae and Rastafarianism seemed to make no concessions to white audiences, they were defiantly alien and 'other' and, as such, manifested a 'foreign body which implicitly threatened mainstream British culture from within'.[12] This was appealing to punks who wished to explicitly threaten mainstream British culture from within.

Punky reggae party

Writing in 1979, Hebdige argued that while defining itself in relation to black West Indian culture gave punk a distinct, and arguably subaltern, white 'ethnicity', this identity, while readily comprehensible and usefully oppositional in the short term, was ultimately a parochial dead-end. This was a white 'ethnicity' that was 'centred, however iconoclastically, on traditional notions of Britishness [...] It was "local". It emanated from the recognizable locales of Britain's inner cities. It spoke in city accents [...] They were bound to a Britain which had no foreseeable future.'[13] It was this, argues Hebdige, that 'gave punk its curiously petrified quality, its paralysed look [...] the punk subculture, forever arrested [...] is incapable of renewal, trapped, as it is, within its own history, imprisoned within its own irreducible antinomies'.[14] The nihilistic stance that declared that there could be 'No Future' was inherently self-limiting, and the explosive avant-gardism of the Sex Pistols was not made to last.

However, I would argue that the enthusiasm for reggae demonstrated by The Clash and others in the punk scene, rather than trapping them in a fossilised white ethnicity, produced a lively dialectic between black and white cultures that allowed them to move beyond the limitations of the subculture and to articulate creatively a new future. White youths, like their black counterparts, 'could place themselves through reggae "beyond the pale" in an imagined elsewhere'.[15] As Hebdige observes, although

> the frantic, bug-eyed style of punk was totally at odds with reggae's slow, moody beat, there were obvious similarities between the two types of music. The punks talked about Britain's crisis in much the same way as roots reggae artists dwelt on the decline of Babylon. Both punk and reggae in Britain were rooted in the city and in city experience.[16]

By the time of the Notting Hill carnival riots of the summer of 1976, reggae was, as Marcus Gray observes, increasingly recognised as 'some of the most vital music currently being made' and potentially 'a cultural blueprint for the development [...] of punk'.[17] Paul Gilroy suggests that

> The street carnival, with its bass heavy sound systems pumping out the new militant 'rockers' beat of reggae as the half bricks and bottles flew overhead, demonstrated to the punks the fundamental continuity of cultural expression with political action. The two were inextricably interwoven into a dense and uncompromising statement of black dissent which was a source of envy and of inspiration to a fledgling punk sensibility. This envy and its creative consequences were spelled out by the Clash in their song 'White Riot', described by one writer as the after-effect 'of

being caught in the racial no-man's land between charging police and angry black youth at the Notting Hill Carnival riots of 1976'.[18]

Within a week of the Notting Hill riot, The Clash had added to their set the song '1977', with its echoes of reggae vocal trio Culture's 'Two Sevens Clash', which references an apocalyptic prophecy by black nationalist Marcus Garvey.[19] Reggae was added to The Clash live experience by tour DJs Don Letts and Barry 'Scratchy' Myers. Jamaican politics and culture were also in evidence on the cover of 'White Riot', which featured a photo of Joe Strummer, Mick Jones and Paul Simonon with their hands up against a wall, a pastiche of the cover of Joe Gibbs and the Professionals' *State of Emergency* album. Stencilled on Strummer's boiler suit were the phrases 'Heavy Manners' and 'Heavy Duty Discipline', a reference to Jamaican Prime Minister Michael Manley's draconian law enforcement strategies, suggesting both solidarity with the Rastafarians and that the UK too was in the grip of an oppressive state apparatus. As Pat Gilbert argues, their 'identification with the West Indian community was passionate and genuine' and their 'profound, exuberant MacInnes-esque affection for Anglo-Caribbean culture was obvious'.[20]

The Clash took this connection further and expressed 'their hostility to both racist nationalism and nationalist racism in [...] records which recast reggae music in their own idiom'.[21] In doing so, they can be contrasted to the 'emphatically white' rock of the Sex Pistols.[22] The decision to play reggae was not one taken lightly by The Clash, however, and their initial reluctance was certainly influenced by the position taken at the time by Rotten, which was that white people playing reggae was a form of cultural imperialism. Simonon remembers that '[w]e had an early song called "Dig a Hole"', '[i]t went, "Dig some reggae but don't play any"'.[23] Earlier examples of white reggae were not encouraging. Eric Clapton had a hit in 1974 with a watered-down version of the Bob Marley song 'I Shot the Sheriff', but any notion that he had any sympathy for the plight of black people was rather disabused by his racist rant at a Birmingham concert in 1976, a rant that was the impulse for the formation of Rock Against Racism. However, a cover of Junior Murvin's 'Police and Thieves' was added to The Clash's otherwise too short debut album. Gray records that 'Joe agonized a while about the cultural exploitation issue, before eventually coming to the conclusion that The Clash's version was an honest attempt to meet an inspirational music genre and its attendant culture halfway.'[24] Mykaell Riley from the British reggae band Steel Pulse recalls that

> We knew punks were into reggae because they were turning up at the gigs, but for punk to embrace reggae it was taking a risk and going against what traditional pop musicians did. Then the Clash did 'Police and Thieves' and that confirmed there was an audience; before that they

were just another punk band. But it was a duality: where on one hand we were saying 'great', some were saying, 'they killed the fucking song'. But it brought attention back to Junior Murvin and confirmed that reggae had value.[25]

In the context of the album, 'Police and Thieves' made a neat counterpoint to 'White Riot', 'spelling out the band's empathy with black Jamaican and inner city British youth [...] making it clear that "White Riot" was not racist or separatist, but envious'.[26] On later releases, as well as cover versions, The Clash began to incorporate reggae sounds and sentiments into their own songs, such as 'Rudie Can't Fail' and 'Guns of Brixton' on their third album, *London Calling*.

The band's enthusiasm for reggae appeared, to some extent, to be reciprocated. After journalist and Island Record employee Vivien Goldman played *The Clash* to Bob Marley and Lee 'Scratch' Perry, and explained what the band were about, they responded with 'Punky Reggae Party' in 1977. This song posited an imaginary shindig at which the Wailers and the Maytals would make 'a joyful sound' alongside The Damned, The Jam, The Clash and Dr Feelgood, and at which 'boring old farts' would not be welcome. Punk and reggae were united, suggested the song's lyrics, by the fact that both were 'Rejected by society, Treated with impunity [and] Protected by their dignity.'[27] However, it would be misleading to suggest that the relationship between punk, reggae and black culture in general was an unproblematic rapprochement and mutual appreciation society. David Hinds, the singer from Steel Pulse, states that although 'we did appreciate the fact they were respecting us as a people',

> we saw [... The Clash] emulating reggae, not coming up with the real thing. My mind couldn't get past the fact they were a white act [...] We felt you can't take the originality from us when it comes to chopping the rhythm guitar and the drums with the right accent. You've got to feel that shit.[28]

In a similar vein, Hebdige has argued that

> given the differences between them, there can be no easy synthesis of the two languages of rock and reggae. The fundamental lack of fit between these two languages (dress, dance, speech, music, drugs, style, history) exposed in the emergence of black ethnicity in reggae, generates a peculiarly unstable dynamic within the punk subculture.[29]

The Clash never found or claimed an easy synthesis between the two; however, I would suggest that ultimately it was the impossibility of authentic white identification with the black experience that vivified rather than dulled their enthusiasm for reggae music and their attempts to incorporate it within their own; these tensions gave the music an edge. For example, Strummer and Simonon's experiences at the Notting Hill carnival shattered any illusions they may have harboured that they were as one with the black victims of police brutality: 'We got searched by policemen looking for bricks, and later on we got searched by Rasta looking for pound notes in our pockets', Strummer told Janet Street-Porter in an interview on ITV's *London Weekend Show*.[30] Similarly disillusioning was a trip to Jamaica that Strummer and Jones took at the end of 1977, in a bid to find some inspiration for their second album. They hoped to make a real connection with the culture that they loved, but were disappointed. Joe later recalled that

> 'We came out of the Pegasus Hotel all togged up in our punk threads. I tell you, we was like two punk tourists on a package tour. Completely naïve. We knew Lee Perry, sort of, but we couldn't find him, so we were on our own.' While walking down to the docks to score some ganja, they were openly called 'white pigs' on the street. 'The only reason they didn't kill us was that they thought we were merchant seamen off the ships.'[31]

Once they had managed to buy some weed, they headed back to their hotel room where they stayed holed up for the remainder of their two-week holiday. Although this was not the inspiration they were hoping for, the experience did prompt the song 'Safe European Home', which Gray describes as a 'bluntly honest account of culture shock, naivety, rejection and fear'.[32]

The Clash song that best encapsulates this sense of alienation and exclusion combined with cultural yearning is '(White Man) In Hammersmith Palais'. The story behind the song is that Joe Strummer, Clash roadie Roadent and DJ Don Letts had gone to a reggae all-nighter at the eponymous Palais in June 1978, hoping to hear some radical 'roots rock rebel' reggae from artists such as Dillinger. They were disappointed both by the rather slick presentation of the music, and the behaviour of some fellow audience members who seemed more bent on petty crime and violence than consciousness expansion. As Jon Savage suggests, this song articulates

> the perennial problem of the kneejerk white approach to black culture, which holds that what is, in fact, pop and highly mediated, is 'authentic', the voice of struggle. The song moves from confusion to despair as Strummer realises that unitary rhetoric pales before the reality of state power. But, like all great pop records, the music subverts the song's lyrical message: at the time Strummer realises the limits of his well-intentioned rhetoric, the group's music is their most full, sympathetic fusion of Punk and Reggae to date, with its dub-like space, the slightly phased hi-hat and the plaintive, melodica-style harmonica.[33]

Moving in this stylistic direction also had the added advantage of freeing the band from the convention that punk songs should be three minutes of stripped down rock guitars, and opened up new creative avenues and opportunities. The introduction of Mikey Dread as a producer in 1980, for example, pushed The Clash towards a heavier dub sound, evident on 'Bankrobber'. This gave The Clash a musical future direction, and produced a progressive, fusion sound.

Punk rock against racism

An engagement with reggae music notwithstanding, the racial politics of the early punk scene were often confused, ambiguous and contradictory, leading to misapprehensions and encouraging some unpleasant and dangerous attitudes on the fringes. Neil Spencer, editor of *NME* in the late 1970s and early 1980s, reflects that

> People don't realise how finely poised things were in punk rock. It could have gone another way quite easily. A lot of those early punks were really racist. This goes back to the irresponsibility of Malcolm McLaren and the whole conundrum of the Jewish rag trade shopkeeper flogging swastikas on the King's Road.[34]

As Savage observes: '[t]o those without a key to Punk's bewildering jumble of signals, its combination of cropped hair, emotive symbols and brutal, harsh music that seemed to eradicate almost every trace of pop's black origins, pointed one way'.[35] The Clash were obliged to state explicitly on more than one occasion that 'White Riot' was not a racist song. Roadent recalls a 1976 gig at Lanchester Polytechnic in Coventry at which the 'students called an emergency general meeting of the union and by order of the committee they decided not to pay these fascists'.[36] Controversy around the song was reanimated when it was released as a single in the spring of 1977, not helped by the ambiguous lyrics. In an interview in *NME* in December 1978, the journalist Miles challenged Strummer on this point, who responded, 'They're not racist! They're not racist at all!', reciting them to prove his point.[37] Unfortunately, suggesting that black people 'don't mind throwing a brick', while defended by Strummer as a 'clumsy attempt' to encourage people to protest, could easily be interpreted as an unhelpful stereotype. Or, as Dotun Adebayo puts it more baldly: 'It was the kind of thing the National Front would say.'[38] Despite Pat Gilbert's assertions that Strummer eschewed 'political correctness' in favour of the 'phrases and images [that] were those of the beat poet reflecting the language of the street', and Johnny Green's claims that 'Joe wanted to challenge people, he wanted to force people to think [...] by] getting people to confront'[39] racist ideas and language, in a climate of racial tension, ignorance and propaganda, the use of terms such as 'kebab Greek', 'wops' and 'Chi man' were perhaps ill-advised.[40] Lines such as 'a black sharp knife never slips' in 'The Last Gang in Town' reinforced a connection in the public imagination between black people and violence in the context of a wider 'moral panic' about mugging.[41]

These ambiguities and issues are illustrated well by the 1978 film *Rude Boy*, a low-budget quasi-documentary about The Clash, told from the perspective of young fan and wannabe roadie, Ray Gange.[42] Although the film is largely celebrated for its live footage of the band, through a combination of factual and fictional scenes it gives a vivid impression of Britain as a powder keg of racial tensions, and a sense of the urgent context in which the Anti-Nazi League and Rock Against Racism (RAR) movements were established and operated. This chimed well with the urgency of punk, which gained momentum at the same time; as Gilroy suggests, punk supplied

> an oppositional language through which RAR anti-racism could speak a truly populist politics. The first issue of *Temporary Hoarding* [RAR's house magazine] made this relationship explicit and asserted the fundamental commitment to music which characterized the early RAR output. 'We want Rebel music, Street music. Music that breaks down peoples' fear of one another. Crisis music. Now music. Music that knows who the real enemy is. Rock against Racism. Love Music Hate Racism.'[43]

The twin values of a hatred of racism and a love of music were sufficient to unite a mixed bag of people in common cause. RAR's audience, suggests Gilroy, 'was conceived not only as consumers of the various youth cultures and styles but as a powerful force for change which, in its diversity, created something more than the simple sum of its constitutive elements'.[44] The growth of the movement coincided too with the emergence of a British reggae scene, and this allowed RAR to programme mixed bills of black and white British bands; most famously the Victoria Park Carnival Against the Nazis in April 1978, when an estimated 80,000 people marched seven miles from Trafalgar Square to watch X-Ray Spex, The Clash and Steel Pulse among others.

The timing was crucial to the success of the movement. As David 'Red' Saunders, the founder of RAR recalls,

> Our chance to do this was because of the punk explosion. It was a cultural awakening. Without punk the intervention of Rock Against Racism would have been tiny. Reaching a white punk audience and involving a British black reggae audience was vital because that was the principle of what we were doing: you're showing a better future; this is how we can be; we can work together; if we can work together we can live together; if we can live together we can work together. We don't have to love each other. We just have to have a realistic situation where we get on.[45]

RAR regarded itself as having a 'didactic educational function',[46] and although its primary focus was to tackle racism in the UK, it also addressed 'broader issues such as British troops in Northern Ireland and international concerns in Zimbabwe and South Africa'.[47] This was an approach shared by The Clash who had diverse political interests and referenced, among others, the Red Army Faction, Brigade [sic] Rosse and the Sandinistas. At times, The Clash's politicking smacked of an adolescent enthusiasm for outlaw glamour rather than a considered and rigorous commitment to revolutionary movements, and they were often accused of sloganeering, but they demonstrated a sincere wish to expand their fans' political horizons. As Robert Howard[48] argues,

> what is politics if it's not sloganeering? You have to chuck these things out there in order to capture people's attention and stimulate their imagination and hopefully lead them into some form of self-knowledge. The Clash were fucking brilliant in terms of dropping little pieces in the ointment that would expand and lead you to amazing places. I hadn't heard of the Sandinistas before the Clash and I went searching and that led me on to all sorts of stuff. Joe Strummer is going to be a far more pivotal, inspirational figure to you as a teenager than some politician.[49]

Like The Clash, RAR worked towards the creation of a better future in part by 'trying to get people to think about things historically'. As Kate Webb, a central RAR committee member, suggests,

> It was asking bands to think reflectively about what they were up to; getting kids who are growing up in a multiracial Britain to think about was there a connection between contemporary racism against their mates at school and the Holocaust. And to see how easily these things can just arise out of ignorance and blindness.[50]

Expressing these ideas primarily through music made them palatable and even exciting for audiences who might otherwise have been turned off by political propagandising. Syd Shelton, a photographer, designer of *Temporary Hoarding* and a key member of the central RAR committee, asserts that

> The theatrical statement of multiculturalism from the stage was our biggest message and that message was self-perpetuating. We were arguing with white people. They were the ones we had to convince to change their ideas. Putting together UK reggae and UK punk was in itself a political statement. We weren't going on stage to preach to people. The theatre of the stage was a political act. That was absolutely central to Rock Against Racism.[51]

RAR helped break down some of the barriers between black and white, reggae and punk, and asserted similarities rather than differences, shared experiences as grounds for shared values and action. Poet Linton Kwesi Johnson recalls:

> I could identify with punk because it was anti-establishment and an expression of disenfranchised youth rebellion and dissatisfaction with the prevailing state of things. This was a period of high unemployment amongst both working-class white youth and black youth. There were grounds for solidarity and that's basically what happened. A lot of the places, the audience was overwhelming white youth, but they were into what we were doing, and into our culture, and into our ideas of rebellion. It was a shared experience and it was wonderful.[52]

These largely white audiences were educated not just about the evils of racism, but about the pleasures of black culture. As Brinsley Forde of Aswad recalls,

> Suddenly a black person wasn't this alien, and it was music that started to break the barriers down. That's what reggae did for punk and what punk did for reggae. You'd done punk gigs. You'd been accepted by the punks and viewed them as people so there wasn't this divide. Music had brought everybody together. That was the most dramatic thing about it. People going, 'But I love this music so these people can't be that bad.'[53]

But there was a separatism here still, within the demographics of both audiences and bands, and the lingering questions of authenticity and power that framed issues of cultural appropriation and mixing. This is flagged up in the film *Rude Boy*, during a testy backstage interchange between Ray Gange and Mick Jones:

Gange: Did you see that black geezer singing 'White Riot'? I thought it was really funny.
Jones: Yeah? What's so funny about it? [...] I wish that more black guys would come to our gigs.
Gange: That's alright, but not to see a lemonade singing White Riot.
Jones: What do you mean, lemonade? There's not enough of them for me.
Gange: It's great to see black geezers, but watching a black geezer sing White Riot, it's like watching a white man chant Rastafari and all these black things.

Indeed, it was quite feasible for a young person to be a fan of The Clash and immune, or even hostile, to the progressive political messages they hoped they were communicating. Due to what Gilroy has described as 'crucial ambiguities in the punk anthems which dealt directly with "race" and sought to make a connection between the position of dispossessed whites and the experience of racism', this music was vulnerable to appropriation by the far right. Gilroy observes that

> The Stranglers' 'I Feel Like a Wog' and the Clash's 'White Man in the [*sic*] Hammersmith Palais' both featured almost continually in the Rock Against Communism chart in *Bulldog*, the paper of the Young National Front. They held the number one and number two positions as late as September 1982.⁵⁴

This tendency is embodied by Ray's skinhead friend Tom in *Rude Boy*. Over a game of pool in an empty youth club, Tom boasts about committing racial violence and becomes enraged by Anti-Nazi League posters on the wall. He tears them down exclaiming 'They don't say they're fucking socialists, do they? [They're trying to ...] brainwash kids [...] They make me fucking sick.' Even in contexts which seem shorn of ambiguity, such as Rock Against Racism concerts, another scene in *Rude Boy* suggests that the perception that this was a worthy, middle-class venture attracting opportunistic followers could alienate sections of the young working-class audience. Gange has a conversation with Topper backstage at the Carnival Against the Nazis:

Gange: Are you going to enjoy this?
Topper nods.
Gange: Really? I think it's such a load of bollocks [...] It's some anti-National Front Communist shit, you know what I mean? [...] Fucking hell, there's going to be about 50 thousand people, it'll be alright. It just seems such a fucking bollocks, don't it? Ooh, Anti-Nazi shit and fucking bollocks.
Topper: Students?
Gange: Fuckers. Yeah, that's it, cause they're at university they never go out, and then all of a sudden, ooh, anti-fascist, let's get in on this lads, all fuck off.

While The Clash were supportive of RAR's values and intentions, they too sought to distance themselves from aspects of the movement's aesthetics, and peddled a line that they had given the venture credibility. 'I'm glad we did the anti-Nazi rally because it was important', said Simonon. 'But it was a bit off-putting with all these hippies wandering about with a giant bucket, going, "Put your money in here!" and shaking it all around. We wanted to make the left seem more glamorous because at the time it was all hippies.'⁵⁵ Watching footage from the event in *Rude Boy* he appears to have a point, as there is a distinct difference in style (and age) between many of the activists running and supporting the event and the punk kids in the crowd. Ultimately, though, for The Clash and RAR it was an event of mutual benefit. The Clash were an attractive, if last-minute, addition to the event's line-up, and got to play their biggest gig to date, producing some thrilling footage for posterity. However, Roger Huddle, an RAR committee member, recalled that 'The Clash all left after their set except for Mick Jones, who stayed to the end.'[56]

That said, The Clash's involvement with RAR continued beyond this landmark event. In 1979, following riots in Southall and the death of Blair Peach, a schoolteacher who sustained fatal head injuries at the hands of the police at an Anti-Nazi League demonstration, John Dennis from RAR recalls that he

> got a call from Joe Strummer out of the blue. He was slightly drunk and was saying, 'The punks are all falling apart. I want to put a gig together with all the big names in punk and record it for an LP to sell to support RAR. Can you book Hyde Park?'[57]

Impetus came too from Pete Townshend of The Who, resulting in the 'Southall Kids Are Innocent' benefit gigs and an *RAR's Greatest Hits* record. Syd Shelton recalls that

> We hired the Rainbow in Finsbury Park for two nights and booked the Pop Group, the Ruts, the Clash, Misty, Aswad, Bongo Danny and the Enchanters, and the Members to raise money for all the legal fees for all those arrested in Southall and to buy new gear for People Unite.[58]

Red Saunders recalled with fondness the

> solidarity, the enthusiasm, the buzz: it was of those young people. It was their music, their three-chord stuff, their lyrics. These were extraordinary times [...] RAR was about the culture and energy of that moment. We were dedicated to the spirit of the time. It was a short window of punk and reggae.[59]

That short window was already starting to close, however. John Dennis reflects that 'The Clash were fantastic but punk was moving on – tellingly, their expenses for the night were £230 compared to Aswad and the Ruts, who got £60 – and the audience was the blue-jean jacket brigade. It wasn't the RAR audience that we knew.'[60]

Two Tone – looking back to go forward

The Clash helped open up other avenues for the future of multicultural music in Britain, in particular Two Tone, the altogether more joyous fusion of rock and reggae that followed in punk's wake. This embodied the 'hope that the humour, wit and style of working-class kids from Britain's black and white communities could find a common voice [...] that a new, hybrid cultural identity could emerge along with the new music'.[61] The band that kick-started the whole Two Tone movement was The Specials, a mixed-race group from Coventry, the brainchild of Jerry Dammers. The Clash gave The Specials their first big break, inviting them to be the support on their 'Out on Parole' tour in 1978. Dammers relates:

> I couldn't believe I managed to blag our way onto the Clash tour. Some pub rock bands had done reggae but when the Clash did their punk version, although it was less like reggae, it seemed much more raw and credible because it took on board the political message of reggae. That was a musical inspiration when I formed the Specials but I wanted black people involved.[62]

The tour proved to be a baptism of fire for The Specials in more ways than one. Bass player Horace Panter recalls:

> We started the tour as civilians but ended as a combat unit. It was our rock 'n' roll boot camp. We played this infamous gig at Crawley Sports Centre where there were loads of skinheads with Nazi badges and tattoos. The atmosphere was horrible. You could palpably sense this kind of malevolence brewing. That was a wake-up call to us. We weren't just going to be a pop group.[63]

Two Tone was political, but in a different mode to the sloganeering of The Clash. As Hebdige observes, there was 'nothing solemn or evangelical about Two Tone. It offered an alternative to the well-intentioned polemics of some of the more highly educated punk groups, who tended to top the bill at many of the early Rock Against Racism gigs.'[64] Or, as the Madness T-shirt put it more succinctly: 'Fuck Art, Let's Dance'. As Strummer observed:

> A lot of the bands were doing the punk-reggae thing at the time, us included, but they were taking it all very seriously, very rootsy. [The Specials], though, had a really different approach, which was down to a lot of things, but mainly, I think, Terry's voice. He didn't have a reggae voice. He sounded so English, and that was the difference.[65]

Two Tone brought rock and reggae together in a way that harmonised 'the form and the lyrics, the sound and the sense, so that, without being intrusive, the multiracial message could be *inferred* by a broadly sympathetic audience. They were giving shape to a sensibility rather than a political programme.'[66] One of the key ways in which they did this was in the make-up of the bands; unlike the groups involved in RAR,[67] almost all Two Tone bands included black and white members. It was a postcolonial carnival collage that Hebdige describes as 'the Ghost Dance of the British Empire, played out at the moving point where the pre-war Lambeth Walk meets Peter Tosh's Steppin' Razor: culture-clash converted into fun – *Knees Up Mother Brown* with coconuts'.[68] This is not to say that Two Tone lacked serious intent or that it was not sometimes overtly political, but that the 'political objectives of Two Tone were more modest. The targets were more clearly defined: unemployment, the police, and authoritarian government.'[69]

Two Tone co-opted past styles of music and fashion to create an image of a racially harmonious present and future, while their lyrics often acknowledged that the realities of society were far from utopian. Dammers recalls that the band adopted the Rude Boy look after their encounters with right-wing youths on The Clash tour 'in order to get through to those kids and try to make the skinhead revival anti-racist'.[70] They also introduced to their sound the music of the original Rude Boys, ska. Many reggae fans and musicians (including some of The Specials themselves) were bemused and unimpressed by this retromania, regarding it as an entirely backward step.[71] Ska seemed musically and politically unsophisticated compared to contemporary roots and dub reggae, but some, such as Brinsley Forde, began to see the point of it:

> That music was old now. We were making new music [...] But then you have to stop and go 'Wow! It means that people are accepting and listening.' It was all about understanding and tolerance and accepting it may not be how I want to do it. It was the music they loved and the music that I loved; why shouldn't they get the opportunity?[72]

As Ranking Roger argues: 'It was going backwards with a forward message.'[73]

Looking forward

The multicultural music of punk and Two Tone set the pattern for the future as the music, like the language of young London and other British cities, became, in Ben Gidley's phrase, 'irretrievably "creolized"'.[74] The leading edge of UK music draws now not just on rock and reggae, but hip hop and decades of dance music (of both of which The Clash were early champions), and a huge diversity of global music transported by immigrant communities. That The Clash are still a vital part of this contemporary creolised culture is evidenced by the frequency with which they are sampled by black British artists. British Sri Lankan artist M.I.A.'s single 'Paper Planes' samples 'Straight to Hell', and was itself subsequently sampled by T.I. and Jay-Z on 'Swagga Like Us'. Urban pop act Rizzle Kicks and grime MC Lethal Bizzle have sampled The Clash's covers of 'Revolution Rock' and 'Police On My Back' in preference to the original versions. As Les Back observes:

> The modes of expression that are produced possess a kind of triple consciousness that is simultaneously a child of Africa, Asia and Europe. In the language of black vernacular culture, the music has gone *outernational*, simultaneously inside and beyond the nations through which it passes.[75]

The multicultural, postcolonial future that The Clash imagined and actively sought to make manifest in their music has to a large extent come to pass. The UK is not a melting pot paradise by any stretch of the imagination, but its national story is diversified and enriched by myriad voices and styles, and its popular culture fizzes with a hybrid vigour. For all their inescapable whiteness, The Clash played a key role in breaking down boundaries and expediting the *outernationalisation* of British music.

Notes

1 Daniel Rachel, *Walls Come Tumbling Down: The Music and Politics of Rock Against Racism, 2 Tone and Red Wedge* (London: Picador, 2016), p. 64.
2 I develop this analysis at greater length in Ruth Adams, 'The Englishness of English Punk: Sex Pistols, Subcultures, and Nostalgia', *Popular Music and Society* 31.4 (2008), pp. 469–88.
3 A character from the British television situation comedy *Steptoe and Son* (BBC 1962–74) about a pair of London 'rag and bone' men, best summed up by the catchphrase frequently delivered by his exasperated son: 'you dirty old man'.
4 Richard Weight, *Patriots: National Identity in Britain 1940–2000* (London: Pan Macmillan, 2003), p. 544.
5 Jon Savage, *England's Dreaming: Sex Pistols and Punk Rock* (London: Faber and Faber, 1991), p. 352.
6 *The Filth and the Fury* (dir. Julien Temple, 2000).
7 Mark Sinker, 'Concrete, so as to Self-Destruct: The Etiquette of Punk, in Habits, Rules, Values and Dilemmas', in Roger Sabin (ed.), *Punk Rock: So*

What? The Cultural Legacy of Punk (London: Routledge, 1999), pp. 120–39 (p. 133).
8 Patrick Wright, *On Living in an Old Country: The National Past in Contemporary Britain* (London: Verso, 1985), p. 23.
9 Joe Queenan, 'Meltdown Expected', *The Guardian*, 9 August 2007.
10 Dick Hebdige, *Subculture: The Meaning of Style* (London: Routledge, 1979), pp. 63–4.
11 Ibid., p. 64.
12 Ibid., p. 64.
13 Ibid., p. 65.
14 Ibid., pp. 69–70.
15 Ibid., p. 65.
16 Dick Hebdige, *Cut'n'Mix: Culture, Identity and Caribbean Music* (London: Routledge, 1987), p. 96.
17 Marcus Gray, *Last Gang in Town: The Story and Myth of the Clash* (London: Fourth Estate, 1995), pp. 185, 186.
18 Paul Gilroy, *There Ain't No Black in the Union Jack* (London: Routledge, 1992), p. 163.
19 Garvey predicted that there would be chaos on 7 July 1977, when the 'sevens' met. Anecdotal reports suggest that the song created something of a panic in Jamaica, with some businesses and schools shuttering their doors for the day. See 'Culture Leader Joseph Hill Dies in Berlin', *Billboard*, 21 August 2006, http://www.billboard.com/articles/news/57472/culture-leader-joseph-hill-dies-in-berlin (accessed 12 August 2017).
20 Pat Gilbert, *Passion is a Fashion: The Real Story of The Clash* (London: Aurum Press, 2005), p. 135.
21 Gilroy, *There Ain't No Black in the Union Jack*, p. 162.
22 Hebdige, *Subculture*, p. 68.
23 Gilbert, *Passion is a Fashion*, p. 134.
24 Gray, *Last Gang in Town*, p. 285.
25 Rachel, *Walls Come Tumbling Down*, p. 63.
26 Gray, *Last Gang in Town*, p. 285.
27 Lee Perry also produced the Clash single 'Complete Control' in 1977, although this was definitively not a reggae record, and some accounts suggest that the band tweaked Perry's production to tone down the dub echo effects he had introduced.
28 Rachel, *Walls Come Tumbling Down*, p. 63.
29 Hebdige, *Subculture*, p. 70.
30 Gray, *Last Gang in Town*, p. 183.
31 Ibid., p. 322.
32 Ibid., p. 322.
33 Savage, *England's Dreaming*, p. 488.
34 Rachel, *Walls Come Tumbling Down*, p. 24.
35 Savage, *England's Dreaming*, p. 243.
36 Ibid., p. 243.
37 Gilbert, *Passion is a Fashion*, p. 135.
38 Rachel, *Walls Come Tumbling Down*, p. 25.

39 Gilbert, *Passion is a Fashion*, p. 136.
40 These appear in the lyrics of 'Hate and War' and 'Lightning Strikes (Not Once But Twice)'.
41 See Stuart Hall et al., *Policing the Crisis: Mugging, the State and Law and Order* (London: Palgrave Macmillan, 2013).
42 *Rude Boy* (dir. Jack Hazan, David Mingay, 1980).
43 Gilroy, *There Ain't No Black in the Union Jack*, pp. 156–7.
44 Ibid., p. 158.
45 Rachel, *Walls Come Tumbling Down*, p. 18.
46 Ibid., p. 26.
47 Ibid., p. xx.
48 Better known as Dr Robert, lead singer with the Blow Monkeys.
49 Rachel, *Walls Come Tumbling Down*, p. 357.
50 Ibid., p. 26.
51 Ibid., p. 48.
52 Ibid., p. 62.
53 Ibid., p. 68.
54 Gilroy, *There Ain't No Black in the Union Jack*, p. 161.
55 'Flashback: The Clash Rock Against Racism in 1978', *Rolling Stone*, 13 May 2014, http://www.rollingstone.com/music/videos/flashback-the-clash-rock-against-racism-in-1978–20140513 (accessed 1 August 2017).
56 Rachel, *Walls Come Tumbling Down*, p. 143.
57 Ibid., p. 199.
58 Ibid., p. 199.
59 Ibid., p. 203.
60 Ibid., p. 203.
61 Hebdige, *Cut'n'Mix*, p. 109.
62 Rachel, *Walls Come Tumbling Down*, p. 242.
63 Ibid., p. 242.
64 Hebdige, *Cut'n'Mix*, p. 109.
65 Rachel, *Walls Come Tumbling Down*, p. 243.
66 Hebdige, *Cut'n'Mix*, p. 110.
67 With the notable exception of X-Ray Spex.
68 Hebdige, *Cut'n'Mix*, p. 110.
69 Ibid., p. 110.
70 Rachel, *Walls Come Tumbling Down*, p. 243.
71 Horace Panter recalls that 'At first, Lynval [Golding, guitarist and vocalist of The Specials] said, "'It's old-man music. Music must move forward." 2 Tone looked back to go forward.' Ibid., p. 244.
72 Ibid., p. 244.
73 Ibid., p. 243.
74 Ben Gidley, 'Youth Culture and Ethnicity: Emerging Youth Interculture in South London', in Paul Hodkinson and Wolfgang Deicke (eds), *Youth Cultures: Scenes, Subcultures and Tribes* (London: Routledge, 2007), pp. 145–59 (p. 157).
75 Les Back, *New Ethnicities and Urban Culture: Racisms and Multiculture in Young Lives* (London: UCL Press, 1996), p. 185.

5
Retrieving the messianic promise of punk: The Clash in 1977

Kieran Cashell

No future

It is an 'uncanny and slightly depressing' experience to have one's own past 'recuperated' as the subject matter of social history.[1] So Simon Critchley laments the canonisation of past countercultural movements as available historical objects. Endorsing Jon Savage's pioneering exposition of punk culture in *England's Dreaming* as inaugurating the paradigm, Critchley inadvertently recapitulates the narrative's received popular moral when he proclaims that, like many spontaneous emancipatory social movements, punk burned out bathetically: despite its auspicious initiation in the late 1970s as a creative combination of oppositional culture and social agitation, punk terminated 'in a nihilistic stupor of distrust and drug abuse'.[2]

Today, four decades after the event the experience of punk is irretrievably mediated.[3] More depressing than Critchley could have imagined in the late 1990s, this prophylactic process makes something so resistant, anti-mainstream and defiantly nihilistic as punk appear increasingly remote, innocuous and naïve ... yet also weirdly fascinating. If punk culture is now forever submerged in the aspic of media history – screened, its radical momentum embalmed – this has the insidious effect of inoculating its political provocation. Hysterically remediated by the contemporary culture industry, punk is also eviscerated of critique, rendering the 'politics of punk' strangely oxymoronic, ultimately perhaps even incomprehensible to subsequent generations.

In any post-revolutionary society's drive to systemic equilibrium, as Slavoj Žižek observes, all post-traumatic effects of its violent genesis must be eradicated. As oppositional social formations are recuperated to the establishment through institutional assimilation, their transgressive aftershock is inevitably neutralised. Such functional reification, however necessary for the stability of society, also urgently involves finding a consensual way (with the implied threat of state-sanctioned violence in the background) of 'burying the catalysts'.[4] When, in other words, a radical social formation seeks establishment in the aftermath of its originary emancipation, the cataclysmic reagents of its revolutionary emergence are inevitably suppressed:

> New social movements, punk, the New Left – after the victory of democracy, all these impulses suddenly and enigmatically lost ground and more or less vanished from the scene ... punkers [sic], students with their sit-ins, committees for human rights ... literally became invisible the moment the new system established itself – and with it its own myth of origin was likewise extinguished.[5]

But the inaugural articulation of naked protest – that first vocalisation of refusal – should not, Žižek warns, be too expeditiously dismissed as a vacuous exclamation devoid of political content; rather, '[t]his empty form of protest, the NO deprived of concrete content', in its primordial, radically foundational expression, remains *constitutionally significant* precisely because 'it opens up a space into which concrete demands and projects of change can then inscribe themselves'.[6] As an event of clearing, indeed, the a priori 'gesture of rejection' may in fact be 'initially more important than any positive content ...' that may follow it.[7]

In terms of punk culture, this event of 'zero-level'[8] social protest finds expression in the syntagm 'No Future' which Cyrus Shahan has exegeted through Walter Benjamin's controversial text 'The Destructive Character'.[9] Defined by the rejection of positive productivity, the destructive attitude is recognised by commitment to 'one activity ... the erasure of all traces of our times'.[10] Combining apocalyptic and anarchistic qualities in an affirmative 'NO', the destructive ethos is exemplified, Shahan claims, in the songs of The Clash. Referring specifically to 'London's Burning', Shahan argues that the song represents a paradigmatic expression of the primal frustration that turns to the liberation of destructive energies to alleviate the anomie: the cityscape is ablaze, not literally, but with an internal meltdown, 'with *boredom* ... now'.[11] And like several early Clash songs, Strummer's visceral articulation itself sounds inflammatory, incandescent with incitement to physically exorcise this inward rumbling angst. Thus it was with such riotous songs that punk unleashed an internalised energy, tapping into the creativity of violence and redirecting precocious destructive tendencies, via the affirmative negation, into creative dissent. Yet the violence of punk, as Žižek correctly observes, is not violent 'in the sense of killing people'. Rather, punk's activism is perhaps best characterised in ideological terms as 'ultraviolence', disrupting 'public order' by destroying the redundant socio-symbolic shibboleths 'of private and state property'.[12]

Motivated by Benjamin's description of the historian as a 'prophet facing backward',[13] this chapter seeks to retrieve the revolutionary significance of punk precisely as such an emancipatory catalyst. The social historian intentionally turns away from the contemporary period. In his famous parable, Benjamin's harbinger of history is depicted as ensnared in the maelstrom of progress, propelled backwards into the future, facing the accumulating 'catastrophe' of the past.[14] From a similar apocalyptic perspective, the materialist historian casts a clairvoyant eye on the past, divining the 'contours of the future ... in the fading light of the past'.[15] As it sinks out of view, certain epiphenomenal effects are deposited in the past like imagery on a photographic negative awaiting future actualisation.[16] Remaining in abeyance until some unexpected alignment brings them to exposure, these traces are finally developed only in constellation with the present. Thus, Benjamin claims, the latent destiny of the past is retroactively accomplished.

Benjamin is a profoundly dangerous thinker. The radical instability of his thought is often explained by his doubly intransigent commitment to the incommensurable axes of Marxism and Jewish theology: 'I am speaking here about an identity', he once insisted, 'which emerges only from the paradoxical reversal of one into the other.'[17] 'Theological-Political Fragment' (1920–21), an early unfinished attempt to thematise this reciprocal consummation, suggests that 'just as a force, by virtue of the path it is moving along, can augment another force on the opposite path, so the secular order ... promotes the coming of the Messianic Kingdom'.[18] Ultimately, however, it isn't until Benjamin's very last writings that this dramatic tension begins to crystallise into something more coherent and politically powerful. His posthumously published *Über den Begriff der Geschichte* ('On the Concept of History') engages the hypothesis of liberation theology in order to realise the emancipatory political promise of Marxism: 'In the idea of classless society, Marx secularised the idea of messianic time.'[19] This short text, 'the most radical, pathbreaking and seminal doctrine of revolutionary thought since Marx's *Theses on Feuerbach*',[20] represents Benjamin at his most dangerous and apocalyptic: using theological thinking to liberate the powerful dormant emancipatory forces embedded in historical materialism, he writes: 'political action, however destructive, reveals itself as messianic'.[21] On the other hand, in this secular context, the revolutionary content of liberation theology is simultaneously released. The violent vocabulary is intentional: the responsibility of the Marxist historian, Benjamin concludes, is to prepare for a 'real state of emergency' which will precipitate the actualisation of this conjunction and forcibly change the directionality of the future.

Incidentally, Michael Löwy argues that because of his commitment to the *negation of the present order*, Benjamin's apocalyptic last writings imply a form of anarchism.[22] In a study of his early theological activism, Eric Jacobsen confirms the consistency of the anarchistic theme in Benjamin; characterising his position as 'ethical anarchism', Jacobson carefully explicates its crucial dimension of radical hope, a hope informed by the complete 'transformation of society and the individual'.[23] Redemption is synonymous with revolution in late Benjamin, where the concept of the messianic is used in a disruptive, violent and ultimately (for late capitalist teleology) destructive sense, in that it is determined to 'usher into worldly affairs a transformative age'.[24] Putting Marx's image of the locomotive of history into question, Benjamin conceives of the anarcho-messianic revolution-to-come as an emergency intervention, a desperate reaching for the communication cord.[25]

The political significance of punk in 1977 is precisely its status as a 'real state of emergency' – a moment of transformative opportunity that places all preceding criteria of meaning and value in suspension. If Punk '77 can be thematised as such a decisive moment – not a transition but an interruption of the continuum of history – as it emerges from an unrepeatable constellation of sociocultural conditions, and 'disappears just as quickly' leaving only an undeveloped 'trace'[26] behind, then everything hinges on the ontology of this trace,[27] which, impinging on the unscripted future, haunts those affected by its abortive promise: 'The past can be seized only as an image which flashes up at the instant when it can be recognised and is never seen again.'[28] In the configuration of punk suspended in the present of 1977, we recognise such a 'dialectical' image: 'the sign of a Messianic cessation of happening, or, put differently, a revolutionary chance in the fight for the oppressed past'.[29] Punk in 1976–77 constitutes an anarcho-messianic intervention in the genealogy of social history. Yet it is only by 'blasting' the epoch out of its state of suspense, as Benjamin instructs, that its latent revolutionary energies can be released, its significance as an emancipatory project be retrieved, and its political destiny be fulfilled.[30] Following Benjamin's procedure, therefore, in this chapter, a specific era – Punk '77 – is sprung from historical sequence in order to rescue a 'specific work' from its embalming effects. 'As a result of this method', Benjamin's cryptic conclusion reads, 'the lifework is subsumed and transcended [*Aufheben*] *in* the work, the era *in* the lifework, and the entire course of history *in* the era.'[31]

The future isn't what it used to be: Berardi and 1977

The rhetoric of 'recuperation' was initially inspired by the eclectic neo-Marxist critique of the Situationist International (SI), and there is little doubt about its influential role in the early elaboration of punk. Proliferating briefly throughout Continental Europe in the aftershock of the student occupations of the late 1960s, the aphoristic, neo-Dadaist semantics of the SI appealed to a post-war generation frustrated by the academic institutionalisation of the radical political tradition. Ambiguously subversive and 'street', SI-style discourse was reappropriated by the British new left intelligentsia who applied the theory-lite principle of *recuperation* to explain 'the fate of all forms of avant-gardiste revolutionary *dé-tournement* [cultural subversion], whether aesthetic or political'.[32] Due in part to the peripheral involvement of countercultural provocateurs Malcolm McLaren (who travelled to Paris during the events of May 1968), Bernard (Bernie) Rhodes[33] (later manager of The Clash) and Sex Pistols' designer Jamie Reid (who adapted *détournement* to British culture) with the anarchist clique of excommunicated UK Situationists, King Mob,[34] the *détournement*–recuperation dialectic (strategies of subversive defacement, repossessing vandalism, graffiti-activism)[35] in the context of Guy Debord's analysis of the ideological mediation specific to late consumer capitalism has had a determining influence on the theoretical canonisation of the cultural politics of punk.[36]

In the attempt to achieve retrospective comprehension, the tendency of cultural theory has been to rationalise the negative social impact of punk, yet this has the effect of deactivating its political animus.[37] Theorisation of punk (as countercultural style) is limited by an analytic focus that remains at the semiotic level. As well as ignoring certain strands within the Situationist movement itself (its critique of culture as principal facilitator of recuperation),[38] this emphasis has had a detrimental impact on the critical evaluation of the political legacy of punk.

Expressing scepticism precisely about the influence that dominant discourses exert on the process of historical transmission, Benjamin cautions that 'the attempt must be made to wrest tradition away from a conformism that is about to overpower it'.[39] Is it necessary to recall, as Keir observes, that punk critique 'was so strong it undermined all previously existing pop culture, including the position of political rock'? Subverting hegemonic codes at cultural, existential and psycho-social strata, punk's radicalism cleared a crucial space of emancipation for the formation of new kinds of subjectivity, agency and political autonomy.[40]

Recent critical directions, however, have enabled the radical impact of punk to be assessed from an alternate perspective. Functioning at a certain distance from the Situationist model, such critique circumvents the redundant *détournement*–recuperation dialectic. Mark Fisher's attempt to reassess punk and post-punk from the existential perspective of someone who admits no direct experience of it, but whose subjectivity remains metaphysically afflicted – or *haunted* – by its promissory political legacy, is a case in point.[41] Fisher speaks of a 'lost generation' born too late to participate in the cultural revolution of punk yet freighted by a melancholic longing for an epoch that has 'just eluded' them; too late for punk, our 'expectations' were nevertheless 'raised by its incendiary afterglow'.[42]

Fisher's approach is informed by Italian activist Franco Berardi, who was affiliated with the post-Marxist *Autonomia* organisation (which split from Italian Situationism following the university and factory occupations in the 1970s). Berardi, in his more recent critiques of neoliberal financial capitalism, repeatedly emphasises the specificity of the year 1977, the apex of a period of social unrest and economic crisis, when large areas of Rome and Bologna were under occupation by *operaismo* activists: 'In 1977, in places like Italy and Great Britain, this social instability was the incubator of a new cultural sensibility: political activism, social movement, and artistic experimentation melted together in the cultural movements of autonomia, punk and new wave.'[43] Identifying contemporaneous instances of creative dissent and politicised occupation by activist coalitions across Europe, Berardi links the emancipatory uprisings in Italy with the German extreme left Red Army Faction, and the 'Deutsche Herbste' street violence of 1977[44] as well with UK punk, and – paradigmatic of such convergence – urban guerrilla collectives, the so-called 'Metropolitan Indians' gathering in the terrain vague of the European capitals.[45]

Apropos these connections, the affirmative negation 'No Future' encapsulates something epochal and darkly prophetic: as the positive consciousness of tomorrow shifts, faith in progress is shaken by a general and pervasive scepticism. Capturing this shift, the eschatological refrain of 'God Save the Queen' is not simply the expression of an impulsive nihilism, but rather articulates the 'final premonition of the end of modern times, the end of industrial capitalism, and the beginning of a new age, which is an age of total violence: financial globalisation, deregulation, total competition, infinite war'.[46] 1977, Berardi concludes, is not merely a significant date for the history of emancipatory politics, but should in fact be regarded as the index of a global crisis: for in this period the entire paradigm split on its axis, and the 'history of culture, technology and philosophical thought' fundamentally changed direction.[47]

1977: punk spring

Punk '77 began with the New Year's Day gig at the Roxy club in Covent Garden. When Andrew Czezowski signed the lease and renamed the former Chaguarama club in December, the Roxy rapidly became the *locus classicus* of the London punk scene.[48] Although in existence for a mere hundred days, the venue hosted three historic concerts in the final weeks of 1976, and was preparing to inaugurate year zero with an epoch-defining gig. The Clash (with Rob Harper temping on percussion) headlined (substituting for the latest Pistols' post-'Anarchy' tour cancellation), with support bands Chelsea and Sounds.[49] 'The Roxy was started by Andrew C specifically for punk groups and its followers', Strummer recalled, 'and in a spirit of punk solidarity we agreed to kick it off on New Year's Day.'[50]

The Roxy gig ushered The Clash to the forefront of the London punk scene. When they came on stage, Kris Needs reminisced, '[t]hey charged headlong into "White Riot" with shattering energy, strutting and leaping like clockwork robots out of control'.[51] Julian Temple's handheld footage captures the lead singer with '1977' stencilled across the front of his shirt, an incongruous white Gretch in lieu of his signature Telecaster;[52] the entire ensemble projecting the 'siege mentality of a Baader-Meinhoff cell' seizing its first day.[53] On the afternoon of the gig, Mick Jones told Needs that their bespoke drip-painted and hand-stencilled fatigues constituted an essential element of the band's participatory attitude. 'We encourage the kids to paint their clothes. That way they get involved and feel part of it.'[54] With the assistance of Alex Michon, recruited as Clash fashionista by manager Bernie Rhodes, and Paul Simonon, the band cultivated a vandalised neo-Pollock-cum-Robert Rauschenberg[55] 'paramilitary' aesthetic – repurposed shirt-trouser combos daubed with house paint and car spray, covered front-and-back in the stencilled, utilitarian typography synonymous with the overall image: 'social security', '999', 'Hate and War', 'White Riot', 'Heavy Duty Discipline', 'Heavy Manners', 'Complete Control' etc.[56] (Jones wore an armband with RED GUARD appliquéd in neutralisation of Siouxsie's swastika, then the controversial synecdoche of punk in the popular media.)[57]

The 9.30 p.m. set was followed by a reputedly even better performance three hours later. Members of the Sex Pistols were among the audience who witnessed the highlight of the gig: 'I'm So Bored with the USA'. Originally a break-up epistle to an anonymous ex composed by Jones, Strummer retooled the song into a white-knuckle diatribe contra American imperialism ('You' ingeniously extended to 'U-S-A').[58] Of course, their performance of the 1 minute 40 second, post-Ramones, anti-rock'n'roll manifesto '1977' acquired apocalyptic significance that evening as Strummer thundered the final allusion to Orwell's dystopian *1984* which brings '1977's numerological coda to its sudden abrupt conclusion.[59] Here was a clear and evident sense of transvaluation, of extreme paradigm-change: 'No Elvis, Beatles or the Rolling Stones in 1977.'[60]

Placing all former criteria of meaning and value in suspension, '1977' was released as the B-side of 'White Riot' in March 1977. Intense, convulsive performances witnessed the tracks become the primal emissary proclamation of the zeitgeist. Invoking and simultaneously outdating The Stooges' '1969', the song's explicit rejection of the R'n'B paradigm and, by extension, the late 1960s psychedelic counterculture is epitomised by the audacious opening riff subversion of 'All Day and All of the Night': Jones mangles The Kinks' chord progression out of shape, twisting it around E and F where an affirmative C major is expected. The effect is sheer brutalism. Generally characteristic of British punk's ultraviolent intervention into popular culture, this cheerfully aggressive strategy of musical sabotage was perfectly enacted by the early Clash's 'telepathic' synergy. Yet, as Jones later revealed, they were actually 'struggling' with their instruments at the time.[61]

The Roxy is a significant motif in the narrative of Punk '77 for another key reason. Czezowski had already propositioned Don Letts, the African-Caribbean[62] manager and 'public image' of Steph Raynor and John Krivine's King's Road basement boutique Acme Attractions, to be resident DJ in the Roxy.[63] Letts had by that period acquired a reputation among the King's Road *flâneurs* for playing loud Jamaican dub reggae (and smoking stacks of ganja) in the store: 'I'd shaken the place with all this heavy dub', he said. 'Basically I turned it into my living room, a place to hang out and smoke and talk.'[64] Since credited with single-handedly mining a highly popular subterranean reggae space within the hard core of London punk, Letts explained: 'For the disaffected youth roaming up and down King's Road looking for something ... I had reggae and dub to ease my pain (so to speak) but my white mates weren't so lucky. So they went about creating their own soundtrack – which was punk rock.'[65]

According to Phil Strongman (a design associate of Acme), Letts was not just a retailer and DJ with a reputation for introducing dub to the London scene, he was also an important chronicler of Punk '77 through his ubiquitous super-8 camera: 'just playing records was not enough for me', Letts said, 'everyone was picking up guitars and forming bands and I wanted to pick something up and be creative'.[66] Letts's extended footage, montaged (using scissors and 'sellotape') into *Punk Rock Movie*, constitutes the quintessential 'insider documentary' of this 'long-lost world', this 'curious new age'.[67]

Arguably, however, Letts's most enduring influence was his effect on Bernie Rhodes, Joe Strummer and The Clash: 'they liked the music I was playing in the shop'.[68] Unusual mixes, pulsating syncopation, reverb effects, deep bass and, above all, the 'reportage' *verité* of reggae lyrics helped to relieve the paralysis of summer 1976, and strongly appealed to the punk search for alternative, non-mainstream sonic and socially expressive forms.[69] 'They tell me I'm responsible for the punk–reggae link', Letts admitted. 'I guess I did introduce these people ... on the fringe to a side they would not necessarily have heard.' However, as he later commented, Strummer and especially bassist Paul Simonon – as well as Rotten, Ari Up, Viv Albertine and Palmolive (The Slits) – were already interested in reggae before Letts made their acquaintance.[70] But he certainly enabled this curiosity by introducing the young rebels to hard-core protest reggae and rare Jamaican dub imports. Czezowski employed the 'Rasta brethren' to help manage the Roxy, where, according to Letts, they discovered a lucrative 'untapped hash market'.[71]

The punk/Rasta nexus facilitated by the Roxy 'was ... really crucial to the whole scene', Strummer admitted; '[i]t would've been pitiful without that, really'.[72] The political dimension of punk culture, as Letts frequently reiterates, can neither be understood nor fully explicated without reference to reggae; this applies, a fortiori, to The Clash. During this period, Simonon and (manager) Bernie Rhodes were obsessed with the militant (uniquely affirmative) iconography of contemporary reggae albums, 'especially the Jamaican ones. The ones that we really gotta lot of influence from.' Citing *Screaming Target* by Big Youth, in particular, 'Bernie was really keen to use some of that imagery ...'

Following the Roxy concert, The Clash took a break from live performance for two months. Retreating to their Camden Town rehearsal space, they concentrated on refining record-ready tracks, bringing drummer Terry Chimes back (temporarily) to replace Harper for the sessions that would lead to the 'White Riot' single release in March and the debut album the following month.

Two sevens clash

At this point The Clash, following much deliberation and debate, made the decision (which profoundly informed the direction of British popular culture) to include reggae in their repertoire. Initially reluctant, they consulted the less than enthusiastic Pistols for advice: 'we [however] could see the potential to combine it with what we were doing to make something powerful'.[73] Strummer's initial reluctance related to the white appropriation of reggae (Hammond, up-stroke chord-chops, dampened melodies, one-drop rhythms, etc.) which Rotten had cavalierly dismissed as 'cultural exploitation'.[74] Imitated without sensitivity to the political and socio-economic context, as well as to its associated visionary element, reggae is evacuated of expression and critique, rendering it caricature (so-called 'cod-reggae' – *à la* Paul Simon, Eric Clapton, Wings and, later, The Police).[75] Yet even Patti Smith's 'Redondo Beach' on the hugely influential protopunk *Horses* (1975) demonstrates that white reggae is always high-risk. '"Police and Thieves" was just ringing out all over the town', Strummer said, '[s]o we decided to cut a version of it.'[76] Attributing the astonishing effect of its hybrid form to Jones's innovative arrangement, Strummer remarked that The Clash did not try to 'assimilate' reggae.[77] 'It was punk reggae, not white reggae. We were bringing some of our roots to it, not trying to mimic someone else's.'[78]

In relation to the Anglo-American appropriation of reggae it is necessary to emphasise at least three crucial distinctions where The Clash are concerned. First, Strummer, Simonon and Jones, by their own admission, closely identified with the West Indian community (the 'Young, Bitter and Black' youth subculture) in London, which gave them an empathetic sense of their politicising socio-economic situation.[79] Jones and Simonon grew up in predominantly black areas of London; the latter, Gilbert informs us, was known to banter in Jamaican patois with his schoolmates in Ladbroke Grove.[80] In fact, Simonon suffered from a self-diagnosed 'reggae addiction', claiming that when Lee 'Scratch' Perry was headhunted to produce 'Complete Control' (1977) this was his chance to meet an 'all-time hero'.[81]

While preparing for the second album, *Give 'Em Enough Rope*, Jones and Strummer travelled to Kingston where, from the security of their hotel bolthole, 'Safe European Home' and 'Drug Stabbing Time' were composed.[82] Up until the final mixing sessions in Automat Studios in San Francisco during the 1978 'On Parole' tour, the working title for the forthcoming LP was *All the Peacemakers*, a phrase from the Junior Murvin/Lee Perry track 'Police and Thieves' covered on the debut album.

Second, as has been well documented, Strummer, Simonon and Rhodes (along with Letts) had been peripherally involved in the infamous Notting Hill carnival riots, an experience that had a profound politicising effect on Strummer and provided the inspiration for 'White Riot'. Radicalised by the public unrest and street violence witnessed on Portobello Road and under the Westway in the late summer of 1976, Strummer's song is an incitement to the indigenous British working class to revolt. Evoking the right to protest, and indicting obedience to authority, listeners are provoked by the lyrics and delivery of the song to collectivise – and, of course, *white riot* refers reflexively to the punk movement itself.[83] Caroline Coon's (slightly doctored) photograph of the band on the cover of the single referenced the sleeve of Joe Gibbs and the Professionals' 1976 album *State of Emergency*, which depicts three Rastas assuming the classic *up-against-the-wall* position being frisked by militia.[84] Indelibly identified with The Clash through photo-journalistic montages on sleeve-design and stage backdrop, the Notting Hill riots became a leitmotif in the band's iconography, a connection consolidated by the image on the back of the debut album: a Xerox of Rocco Macauley/Redondo's photo of the police baton-charging the crowd under the curved shadow of the Westway (subverted with punk supplements in Dayglo spraypaint).

Third, and most pertinent, the dimension of social protest inherent in reggae attracted British punks who identified closely with the sense of collective resistance to state authority expressed in the music (while sounding nothing like phoney Dylanesque folk-based protest songs). Through their own experience of alienation 'from the social, economic, and political forces around them',[85] the 'officially defeated'[86] in the UK – the punks, the unemployed and the increasingly radicalised squatters in London – were inexorably drawn to (dub) reggae in the summer of 1976. It must be acknowledged that, due to his instinctive comprehension of the relationship between social class and civil rights, the politics of reggae particularly appealed to Strummer,[87] ultimately making The Clash the first band to effectively negotiate the punk–reggae hybrid – the first, that is, to meaningfully inform punk's anarchistic critique of social repression, state power and 'systematic violence' with the complex messianic animus of reggae expression, reciprocally amplifying both forms without compromising either. The significance of Rastafari reggae for punk transcends the influence of musical genres, according to Letts, 'seeming to reflect what was happening right here in the UK'.[88]

Of course, this process of transformative reciprocation is most effectively expressed in the interpretation of Murvin and Perry's 'Police and Thieves' on the debut album, which under The Clash's direction is fascinatingly transfigured into a testimonial account of the Notting Hill riot witnessed the year before.[89] Consolidating punk's identification with the West Indian and black subculture in the UK, the track supplements the album with 'an almost uncanny counterpoint to "White Riot", its lyric echoing Paul and Joe's encounters with both police and thieves at the Notting Hill Riot'.[90] In an interesting observation on 'Police and Thieves', Marcus Gray remarks that the track amplifies other 'less immediately obvious reggae influences' distributed throughout the album.[91] Yet the anarcho-apocalyptic power of the track, Billy Bragg observes, paradoxically derives from the refusal to make 'concessions' to the original; transposing the time-signature to 4/4, their version achieves a new urgency: 'On an album full of powerfully polemic songs', Bragg concludes, '"Police and Thieves" stood out as the most radical cut.'[92]

Stephen King clarifies how musical form acquires the force to articulate a sociopolitical 'ethos' by examining the way reggae played an enabling role in the promotion of the Rastafarian movement in Jamaica; in the process, establishing how vernacular music helped to accomplish a strong (and politicised) ethnic identity for the disenfranchised black underclass of the shantytowns of West Kingston and government yards of Trenchtown.[93] 'Persecuted by the Jamaican authorities, especially the police, and forced to live in abject poverty, many Rastafarians perceive themselves as innocent victims of Babylon's cruelty and greed';[94] in response to the hegemonic suppression of Rastafari in the Caribbean, the countercultural protest movement was relied on to mediate its message; reggae proved to be the most effective and most popular means of spreading the word. 'By the mid-1970s', King observes, 'reggae music was experiencing unprecedented popularity in Jamaica and acclaim throughout the international community.'[95] By now reggae was widely acknowledged by European resistance movements and US anti-war student activists as a powerful, efficacious form of social protest against the oppressive apparatus of the state, imperialism and wage slavery.

Most influential in the UK during the civil unrest in the lead-up to the Jamaican elections and the state of emergency declared by Prime Minister Michael Manley in June 1976 'were the productions of Joe Gibbs, not only the "Africa Dub" instrumental series, but also the remarkable albums by Prince Far-I and Culture, which set dense rants against minimal music'.[96] Record releases from the Caribbean during the period reflected the violent conflict between PNP (People's National Party) and JLP (Jamaica Labour Party) supporters that erupted on the streets of Kingston that year: Prince Far-I's 'Heavy Manners', Gibbs's 'State of Emergency', Max Romero's 'War in Babylon' and Tapper Zukie's 'MPLA', to mention the most prominent.[97]

Black liberation and repatriation advocate Marcus Garvey became the central figure of African Zionism for early Rastafarianism.[98] Founder of the Universal Negro Improvement Association and the Red Star Line, Garvey promoted the redemption of black peoples from white supremacy and was regarded as a latter-day prophet. Inspired by the emancipation of the Israelites from Egypt, freedom from economic/diasporic slavery became the central tenet of African liberation theology. Referring to the disenfranchisement and economic disadvantage of black communities in Western societies, Garvey prophesied the divine liberation of 'all the oppressed on earth'.[99] Applied to authoritarian oligarchic control in Jamaica, 'Babylon' came to refer to the state apparatus of government, police and official Church, supported by postcolonial British and US imperialism, an extension of white hegemony *per se*, in other words, to all that sought to control, subjugate and impede the process of African emancipation.[100]

Although he died in anonymity in London in 1940, Garvey gained posthumous notoriety for his prophecy foretelling widespread pandemonium in Western civilisation on 7 July 1977 with the alignment of the sevens (7/7/77). Then, he believed, the black diaspora would be returned to African Zion.[101] In 1976, in anticipation of this apocalyptic event, the reggae artists Culture recorded an album for Joe Gibbs in Kingston: *Two Sevens Clash*. Lead singer of the trio Joseph Hill claimed (as the liner notes testify) that, on the X82 bus, he experienced a vision of Garvey and the '77 prophecy, and the lyrics of the track were revealed to him.[102]

Thus when Clash bassist and reggae-freak Paul Simonon first suggested the band-name to Strummer and Jones, Culture (and Hill's vision) were clearly the key reference points.[103] Clarifying the significance of the year for the band, their name, arguably an elision of the syntagm 'the Clash of Two Sevens', also neatly encapsulates the antagonistic political subjectivity associated with the efflorescence of Punk '77.[104] 'The 7th of the 7th '77 passed without incident in Jamaica but in an island far away a culture clash of creative chaos was in progress.'[105]

Punk stillborn: after the future

Everyone knows what happened next: manager Bernie Rhodes pressurised the band into signing a £100,000 recording contract with CBS, prompting the editor of the acclaimed fanzine *Sniffin' Glue*, Mark P(erry), hitherto impressed by the band's anti-corporate stance, to lament that punk had 'died' that day. One of the fatuous myths that have haunted The Clash since before the release of their first record, this sell-out smear has impelled fans, media supporters and music journalists ever since to adopt the refutation of this obvious falsity as a personal mission (notwithstanding Mark P's own efforts to pacify his 'one big quote').[106] However, as Perry himself is aware, his quote contains a kernel of 'ugly' truth that remains hard to digest. Something obviously untrue requires no effort to refute. As industry whistleblower Steve Albini (of US hard-core provocateurs Big Black) observes, 'the thing that everybody seems to be living in denial of is that the great majority of bands that sign to major labels not only sell fewer records than they did in their independent lives, but they make less money'.[107] He adds: 'people who get involved with major labels make less interesting music; they end up suffering personally, and as a band, aesthetically'.

Where Punk '77 is concerned, it is impossible to know with certainty if Albini's 'ugly truth' applies here as the band never had the opportunity to have an independent life; the debut album, however, intimates what might have been. While being aware of how potentially heretical this might appear in a publication devoted to the band, it is tempting to agree with Mark E. Smith's wildly unorthodox (but refreshingly critical) view that The Clash were 'very good when they started out, much better than The Pistols'. But, 'After the first album there's really nothing there.'[108] The ugly truth is that *London Calling* (1979) is (*pace* the title track) uncritically overrated; at best awkward and inflated, at worst incoherent and generically confused, the double album is symptomatic of a band in profound musical and ideological crisis.

Following the bedlam of the 'Anarchy' tour and the tabloid hysteria in the aftermath of the Bill Grundy incident, the Pistols and McLaren gradually became discredited as a musical force as their sensationalist celebrity value increased.[109] With more concert cancellations and venue closures across London, a chronic ennui and disillusionment descended on Pistols' fans, as the already moribund promise of punk became concentrated in The Clash.[110] However, Strummer, Jones and Simonon, hailed as the new agents of the Punk '77 Spring, unexpectedly delivered on the promise, and The Clash rapidly became the live turbine of the new youth revolution.

As confirmed by eyewitness testimony, their gigs were astonishing, epitomising everything the Punk Spring promised. 'Even now', Kris Needs tries to impress on the millennial generation, 'it's impossible to adequately convey the overwhelming rush of standing on the side of the stage witnessing The Clash at their dazzling peak. Nothing has ever come close' – a magnetism due in no small part to the charisma of their adrenalised lead singer. 'Everything coming off the stage you manufactured in that moment. It was really fast, really hard ... And really loud.'[111]

One of those who attended the infamous 9 May 1977 Rainbow gig[112] was protest singer Billy Bragg. 'What I witnessed that night dispelled all of my lingering doubts about punk', he recalled. The Clash 'were drawing a demarcation line between the generations and I was cheering them on as they loudly proclaimed that the Rolling Stones had no place in punk's Year Zero'.[113] In this context it is understandable that the record contract was taken as a betrayal, a hypocritical forsaking of punk's emancipatory promise that the band at this stage now singularly embodied. During this period, Needs remembers that Strummer had to negotiate (along with the pelting gob) jeering about the CBS sell-out from belligerent audiences.[114]

Be that as it may, when released on Columbia records on 8 April 1977 (six months prior to *Never Mind the Bollocks*), *The Clash* became the paradigm-defining phenomenon of Punk '77; and not because it dramatises the moment when the means of production are forcibly appropriated by the proletariat, but rather because the record, in its rough syntax, announces a new concept of cultural resistance (more relevant to Benjamin's messianic interpretation of revolution as redemption). *The Clash* enacts the sonic manifesto of an alienated and demoralised English urban prole counterculture participating in its own apocalyptic 1977 vision. Presley's death later that year seemed the fulfilment of a prophecy for the Punk Spring.[115]

Aiming towards the direct transmission of the disciplined anarchic energy of their energised and dangerous live shows,[116] the album was recorded over three breakneck weekends in the CBS Whitfield Studios in London.[117] Simon Humphrey, who supervised the production (Mickey Foote was the producer) for the record company, testifies that the band 'basically played their set and we recorded it live'.[118] Although *The Clash* is far from perfect, it is perhaps unnecessary to recall that punk was an anti-aesthetic movement valorising negative 'rough' criteria of imperfection, privation, severity. Poor production serves only to augment documentary authenticity: its chaotic, shambolic texture is, however, freakishly offset by a parameter of austerity and control. Even if Strummer sounds as though he just got up from the electric chair, his delivery is tight, economic and disciplined.[119] There is also what Gilbert identifies as its 'disguised musical sophistication'.[120] Syncopated percussion offset by bass-drum pulsation, haunting harmonica sub-frequencies on 'Garageland', overdubbed guitars on 'Police and Thieves', bass line variations in the 'White Riot' bridge. The recorded versions of the songs also take full advantage of the differential features of Strummer's gnarled adenoidal vocals and Jones's more lucidly conventional singing style to interweave aural textures ('Janie Jones', concluding choruses of 'Hate and War', call and response in 'Remote Control', falsetto vocal supplements in 'Deny' and 'Police and Thieves').

Radically discontinuous with the history of recorded music preceding it, *The Clash* transgresses every established popular convention, remaining as incommensurable with standardised culture industry product as twelve-tone composition to tonal harmony. Dirtily abrasive, visceral, turbocharged, each track on this punk disasterpiece 'scrambles the grammar' of popular music until it submits in a kind of gasp. Conventions such as the fade-out, for instance, are vetoed; with the notable exception of 'Deny' (and the cover version) every track ends at full volume with an aftershock of silence. Repealing the love and peace ethos of the Beatnik-hippie era, this hate and war record is the sonic equivalent of King Mob style urban terrorism. There is no obvious continuity with the rock tradition save the raw materials utilised by the personnel, now sounding like the lumpen instruments of the destructive character.

Reflexively embodied in the entire approach, the theme of confrontation is ubiquitous: invoking generational conflict, as well as conflict of race and class, *The Clash* has radical oppositional practice encoded in its very nomenclature – 'onomatopoeically violent',[121] the title of the album epitomises the white-riot politics of punk. And politics, as Milligan remarks in her study of the London squatting movement, should always be defined in conflictual terms: that is, as 'confrontation between opposing forces'. Conflict, she clarifies, 'constitutes a political arena as it is explicitly between those within the status quo and those without'.[122] In its combat-green sleeve, *The Clash* borrows its conflictual political syntax from underground zine and poster 'para-art'. A poor quality photocopy of Kate Simon's photo of the band taken in a Camden Town alleyway is pasted at an awkward angle and completed by the title stamped in degraded type on the bottom right-hand corner in red to maximise the colour clash with the background. Too rough to be classified as 'collage', an equally unclear photocopy of Rocco Macauley's Notting Hill riot police baton-charge photograph, sprayed sporadically in pink and orange – punk chromatics – appears on the reverse. Song titles are typed up in plastic file-tag strip, adding to its conflictual anti-aesthetic political intervention.

Seamus Nolan remarks that punk suddenly made the counterculture's promissory 'power to transform' society available to a demographic that, lacking social representation and searching for cultural identity, developed political consciousness through creative expression.[123] In this milieu, 'White Riot', as testified repeatedly in ethnographic studies, had an immensely enabling impact on the post-1960s British subculture that was experiencing the subtle forms of alienation and social exclusion that persist in Western liberal democracy. Recall the presence of early Dylan in the civil rights movement and anti-war counterculture in America; *The Clash* elicited something comparably empowering in this demographic by suggesting ways in which oppositional – anti-social – political agency is performed at the cultural (ideological) stratum.

Secret affinities

Inspired by Benjamin's rescuing-critique, I have argued that punk constitutes a rupture in the homogeneous continuum of history that places all criteria of meaning and value in question for a brief incandescent moment in 1976–77.[124] Yet even though it constitutes a decisive turning point, Punk '77 leaves only a 'trace' in history.[125] This trace was my starting point. For, no matter how compromised or frail it may be, the historical trace of the originary event constitutes the vehicle of that 'weak messianic force' that Benjamin recognised as the agency of redemption of the past and the sign of future revolutionary potential. Therefore, even if, as a 'formal gesture of rejection', the Punk Spring of 1977 may be considered to lack positive ideological content, the disruptive messianic singularity concentrated in its traces is 'more important than any positive content'.[126] Indeed, for those affected by it, the event of punk foreshadowed an entire 'new way of being', an existential fidelity that informs their entire attitude to life.[127] Examining punk as an 'experiment' in counter-hegemonic and violently creative forms of self-valorisation significantly clarifies the ambiguous political significance and radicalising effects of Punk '77: 'even in mediated form', Keir concludes, 'the message of punk was powerful enough to provoke a new wave of creativity that reached into even the smallest towns of the UK' (as well as Ireland).[128] Following Benjamin's procedure, in this chapter a specific era – Punk '77 – was identified and a 'specific work' detached from it. As a result of this method, we endeavoured to redeem the era *in* the lifework, and, in this way, sought to retrieve Punk '77 from the blastosphere and thereby prophesy the fulfilment of its political destiny.[129]

Listening to the record today, *The Clash* invokes grim silhouettes of tower blocks and brutalist high-rise estates penetrating gloomy banks of streetlights; its convulsive fragments suture a spectral montage of underpasses, traffic headlights, dark concrete, corrugated fencing, vacant car parks, 'images comparable to those which are imprinted by light on a photosensitive plate'. London in the late 1970s, a dilapidated city of strikes, riots and social unrest forever crystallised on two sides of badly scratched vinyl: 'Only the future possesses developers active enough to scan such surfaces perfectly.'[130] It remains the most articulate manifesto of the politics of punk bequeathed to a lost generation, in the hope that it may come to realise it at some undisclosed time in the future.

Notes

1 Simon Critchley, *Very Little ... Almost Nothing: Death, Philosophy and Literature* (London: Routledge, 1997), p. 99.
2 Ibid.
3 Keir, 'When Two Sevens Clash: Punk and Autonomia', *The Free Association*, September 2001, http://www.freelyassociating.org/when-two-sevens-clash-punk-and-autonomia/ (accessed 17 November 2018).
4 Slavoj Žižek, *The Universal Exception* (London: Bloomsbury, 2006), p. 18.
5 Ibid.
6 Ibid., p. 482.
7 Slavoj Žižek, *The Year of Dreaming Dangerously* (London: Verso, 2012), p. 83.

8   Žižek, *Universal Exception*, p. 482.
9   Cyrus Shahan, 'Punk Poetics and West German Literature of the Eighties', PhD thesis, University of North Carolina, 2008, p. 23.
10 Walter Benjamin, 'The Destructive Character', in *Selected Writings, Volume II: 1927–1934*, ed. Michael W. Jennings, Howard Eiland and Gary Smith (Cambridge, MA: Belknap Press of Harvard University Press, 1996), pp. 541–2.
11 Shahan, 'Punk Poetics', p. 3.
12 Žižek, *Universal Exception*, p. 482.
13 Walter Benjamin, 'Paralipomena to "On the Concept of History"', in *Selected Writings, Volume IV: 1938–1940*, ed. Michael W. Jennings, Howard Eiland and Gary Smith (Cambridge, MA: Belknap Press of Harvard University Press, 2003), p. 405.
14 Walter Benjamin, 'Theses on the Philosophy of History', in *Illuminations*, ed. Hannah Arendt (London: Fontana, 1973), p. 249.
15 Benjamin, 'Paralipomena to "On the Concept of History"', pp. 405, 407.
16 Walter Benjamin, *The Arcades Project* (Cambridge, MA: Belknap Press of Harvard University Press, 1999), p. 482.
17 Gershom Scholem and Theodor Adorno (eds), *The Correspondence of Walter Benjamin* (Chicago: University of Chicago Press, 1994), p. 300.
18 Walter Benjamin, 'Theological-Political Fragment', in *Selected Writings, Volume III: 1935–1938*, ed. Michael W. Jennings, Howard Eiland and Gary Smith (Cambridge, MA: Belknap Press of Harvard University Press, 2002), p. 305.
19 Benjamin, 'Paralipomena to "On the Concept of History"', p. 401.
20 Michael Löwy, *On Changing the World: Essays in Political Philosophy from Karl Marx to Walter Benjamin* (Atlantic Highlands, NJ: Humanities Press, 1993), p. 160.
21 Benjamin, 'Paralipomena to "On the Concept of History"', p. 402.
22 On Benjamin's anarchism, see James Martel, 'Anarchist All the Way Down: Walter Benjamin's Subversion of Authority in Text, Thought and Action', *Parrhesia* 21 (2014), pp. 3–12; Michael Löwy, 'The Young Benjamin', *Jacobin* (2016), www.jacobinmag.com/2016/01/walter-benjamin-anarchism-surrealism-marxism-theses/ (accessed 11 December 2018); and Löwy, 'Revolution against Progress: Walter Benjamin's Romantic Anarchism', in *On Changing the World*, pp. 143–63.
23 Eric Jacobson, *Metaphysics of the Profane: The Political Theology of Walter Benjamin and Gershom Scholem* (New York: Columbia University Press, 2003), pp. 212–13.
24 Ibid., p. 6.
25 Benjamin, 'Theses on the Philosophy of History', p. 252.
26 Alain Badiou, *Manifesto for Philosophy* (Albany, NY: SUNY Press, 1992), p. 20.
27 Reference to trace recalls Greil Marcus's study of punk and the European avant-garde in *Lipstick Traces* (Cambridge, MA: Belknap Press of Harvard University Press, 2009). However, the concept is used here with an emphasis on its ontological modality. For Benjamin, the traces of certain events,

expired prior to accomplishing their promise, leave latent after-effects. Materialist interventions are motivated by the impulse to *rescue* these traces. Shoshana Felman, 'Benjamin's Silence', *Critical Inquiry* 25.2 (1999), pp. 201–34.
28 Benjamin, 'Theses on the Philosophy of History', p. 247.
29 Ibid., p. 254.
30 Benjamin, 'Paralipomena to "On the Concept of History"', p. 406.
31 Benjamin, 'Theses on the Philosophy of History', p. 254 (trans. modified original emphasis).
32 Simon Critchley, *Infinitely Demanding* (London: Verso, 2007), p. 98.
33 Marcus Gray references US urban guerrillas the Weather Underground's subversive 'song book' (owned by Bernie Rhodes) which contains a song, 'White Riot', to the melody of 'White Christmas'. Marcus Gray, *The Clash: Return of the Last Gang in Town* (London: Helter Skelter, 2001), p. 158.
34 King Mob promoted tactics of active-comedic nihilism, staging subversive interventions in London throughout the late 1960s. David Wise and Stuart Wise, *King Mob: A Critical Hidden History* (London: Bread and Circuses, 2014).
35 *Détournement* is 'the reuse of pre-existing artistic elements in a new ensemble'. Debord quoted in George Robertson, 'The Situationist International: Its Penetration into British Culture', in Stewart Home (ed.), *What is Situationism? A Reader* (Edinburgh: AK Press, 1996), p. 118.
36 Jon Savage, *England's Dreaming: Sex Pistols and Punk Rock* (London: Faber and Faber, 1991); Marcus, *Lipstick Traces*; Phil Strongman, *Pretty Vacant: A History of Punk* (London: Orion, 2007); *Anarchy! McLaren Westwood Gang* (documentary, dir. Phil Strongman, 2015); Sadie Plant, *The Most Radical Gesture: The Situationist International in a Postmodern Age* (London: Routledge, 1992).
37 Hebdige's analysis of punk subculture (employing the deconstructionist concept of 'bricolage') is an instance of this trend. Dick Hebdige, *Subculture: The Meaning of Style* (London: Routledge, 1979).
38 Although SI originated as an avant-gardiste aesthetic movement, its later objective was political, aiming at the transformation of society, and it rejected *art* as 'a superior attitude'. Robertson, 'The Situationist International', p. 112.
39 Benjamin, 'Theses on the Philosophy of History', p. 247.
40 Keir, 'Two Sevens Clash', p. 12. Sabin insists that Situationism only appealed to a 'tiny cognoscenti' and had a limited influence on the ground: 'if that was punk's *secret history*', he quotes Johnny Rotten, 'then it was so secret that nobody told us'. Roger Sabin, 'Introduction', in Roger Sabin (ed.), *Punk Rock: So What? The Cultural Legacy of Punk* (London: Routledge, 1999), p. 4.
41 Haunting concerns the 'staining of place with particularly intense moments of time'. Mark Fisher, *Ghosts of My Life: Writings on Depression, Hauntology and Lost Futures* (Alresford: Zero Books, 2014), p. 191.
42 Ibid., p. 189.
43 Franco Berardi, *After the Future* (Edinburgh: AK Press, 2011), p. 46.

44 *The Baader Meinhof Complex* (dir. Uli Edel, 2008); Stefan Aust, *Baader-Meinhof: The Inside Story of the RAF* (London: Oxford University Press, 2009).
45 Franco Berardi, *The Uprising* (Los Angeles: Semiotext[e], 2012), p. 94; Keir, 'When Two Sevens Clash', p. 12. The Metropolitan Indians were communities of activist squatters in Italian cities during the occupation of universities in 1976–77. Identified with the cultural 'wing' of Italian *Autonomia*, they painted their hair and clothes. A related group, the *Stadtindianer*, were active in Germany during the 1977 German Autumn.
46 Berardi, *After the Future*, p. 94.
47 Ibid., p. 47.
48 Andrew Czezowski, 'Pogo A-Go-Go', *Mojo* 267 (February 2016), p. 85; Strongman, *Pretty Vacant*, p. 168; Gray, *Return of the Last Gang in Town*, p. 207. Strongman describes the Roxy as 'semi-derelict', a small room with an upstairs bar. See also Don Letts, *Dread Meets Punk* (2017), a montage of his own Super-8 archive footage from the period.
49 Gray, *Return of the Last Gang in Town*, pp. 208, 231.
50 Mal Peachey, *The Clash* (London: Atlantic Books, 2008), p. 108.
51 Paul Du Noyer, *The Clash* (London: Virgin, 1997), p. 28.
52 Don Letts, *Westway to the World* (Sony Music, 2001).
53 Du Noyer, *The Clash*, p. 42.
54 Kris Needs, 'The Clash', *Vive Le Rock* 42 (2017), p. 59.
55 Pat Gilbert, *Passion is a Fashion: The Real Story of The Clash* (London: Aurum Press, 2004), pp. 93–4. Simonon clarifies: 'It was a Rauschenberg thing.' Letts, *Westway to the World*.
56 Aphorisms taken primarily from Jamaican record sleeves. Needs, 'The Clash', p. 59; Peachey, *The Clash*, p. 71; Letts, *Westway to the World*.
57 Gray, *Return of the Last Gang in Town*, p. 172.
58 Letts, *Westway to the World*.
59 See footage of the performance on Letts's *Westway to the World*.
60 From the song lyrics.
61 'This just made the whole thing more alive', he adds in interview with Peachey, 'more real. Y'know.' Letts, *Westway to the World*.
62 He self-identifies as 'first generation British-born Black'. Letts, *Dread Meets Punk*.
63 Strongman, *Pretty Vacant*, pp. 87, 170.
64 Ibid., p. 170. Letts contrasts Acme with its King's Road rival – McLaren and Vivienne Westwood's SEX. Theirs 'was Eurocentric', based on Situationist 'politics'. Acme, however, was a complete 'culture clash'. 'It's like the photo of me at the riot, it represented the changing face of the city in the 1970s … When punk came along the two cultures collided.' Don Letts, 'Babylon's Burning', *Mojo* 267 (February 2016), p. 81.
65 *The History of the Clash* (TV documentary).
66 Strongman, *Pretty Vacant*, p. 171.
67 Don Letts, 'Scissors and an Attitude', *Sight and Sound* 26.8 (2016), p. 29.
68 Gilbert, *Passion is a Fashion*, p. 133.
69 Letts discussed the association of Jamaican music and punk at 'PunkLondon:

Forty Years of Subculture: A Celebration of Punk', at the BFI in 2016.
70 Peachey, *The Clash*, p. 197; Letts, 'Babylon's Burning', p. 81.
71 Letts, *Dread Meets Punk*: the 'brothers' sold ready-rolled spliffs to the Roxy's punk clientele.
72 Letts, *Westway to the World*; Peachey, *The Clash*, p. 108; Gray, *Return of the Last Gang in Town*, p. 211.
73 Gilbert, *Passion is a Fashion*, p. 134.
74 Gray, *Return of the Last Gang in Town*, pp. 225–7.
75 Gilbert, *Passion is a Fashion*, p. 134.
76 Letts, *Westway to the World*.
77 Gilbert, *Passion is a Fashion*, p. 146.
78 Du Noyer, *The Clash*, p. 45.
79 Gilbert, *Passion is a Fashion*, p. 134.
80 Ibid.
81 Ibid., p. 165; Peachey, *The Clash*, p. 132.
82 Kris Needs, 'Aces and Eights', *Vive Le Rock*, 31 (November 2015), p. 50. Simonon says he was 'really pissed off about that. Coz I really wanted to go.'
83 Strummer documents the song's provenance: 'We participated in the riot. But I was aware all the time that it was a black people's riot, i.e., they had more of an axe to grind and they had the guts to do something physical about it.'
84 Designer Sebastian Conran added '1977' to Strummer (the original slogan was 'Hate and War'): Caroline Coon, 'Behind Enemy Lines', *Mojo* 267 (February 2016), p. 77 (original photo); Gray, *Return of the Last Gang in Town*, p. 218. His trousers are stencilled 'Heavy Duty Discipline' from the Prince Far-I/Joe Gibbs produced 'Under Heavy Manners', phrases used by Jamaican Prime Minister Michael Manley during 1976's state of emergency.
85 Kevin C. Dunn, '"Know Your Rights": Punk Rock, Globalisation, and Human Rights', in Ian Peddie (ed.), *Popular Music and Human Rights Volume I: British and American Music* (Farnham: Ashgate, 2011), p. 29.
86 Fisher, *Ghosts of My Life*, p. 184.
87 Dunn, 'Know Your Rights', p. 30.
88 Letts, *Dread Meets Punk*.
89 By the end of 1976 the band acknowledged reggae as the 'most vital contemporary musical genre'. Gray comments: 'the entire band's interest increased dramatically once the Riot gave a local context to its wrathful denunciation of Babylon'. *Return of the Last Gang in Town*, pp. 156–7.
90 Ibid., p. 228.
91 Ibid.
92 Billy Bragg, *The Progressive Patriot* (London: Black Swan, 2007), p. 238.
93 Stephen King, 'Protest Music as Ego-enhancement', in Ian Peddie (ed.), *The Resisting Muse: Popular Music and Social Protest* (Aldershot: Ashgate, 2006), p. 110.
94 Ibid., p. 113.
95 Ibid., p. 111.
96 Savage, *England's Dreaming*, p. 237.
97 Gilbert, *Passion is a Fashion*, p. 135.
98 Ibid.; King, 'Protest Music', p. 110; Savage, *England's Dreaming*, p. 237.

99 Brown in King, 'Protest Music', p. 110. For black liberation theology, Jahweh 'is involved in the history of a struggling people: the deliverance of the children of Israel from bondage in Egypt is also the story of deliverance of an African people enslaved in America'. Marc Ellis, *Toward a Jewish Theology of Liberation* (London: SCM Press, 1988), pp. 67–8.
100 King, 'Protest Music', p. 112.
101 Gilbert, *Passion is a Fashion*, p. 135; Strongman, *Pretty Vacant*, p. 166; Savage, *England's Dreaming*, p. 237.
102 Letts discusses Garvey's influence on UK punk (via Culture) in *Dread Meets Punk*.
103 Although he claims that it was the frequency of the word 'Clash' in the *Evening Standard*. Letts reveals that Culture was a particular favourite of the band; the LP was constantly on the turntable (*Dread Meets Punk*).
104 Other contenders included the title of a Big Youth song. Gray, *Return of the Last Gang in Town*, p. 156.
105 Letts, *Dread Meets Punk*.
106 Perry, in mollifying response to Jones's threat to dump him in the Thames, significantly moderated his earlier judgement in his review of *The Clash* in *Sniffin' Glue* (June 1977). Randal Doane, *Stealing all Transmissions: A Secret History of The Clash* (Oakland, CA: PM Press, 2014), p. 42.
107 Kevin Dunn, 'Never Mind the Bollocks: Punk Rock and Global Communication', *Review of International Studies* 34.1 (2008), p. 204.
108 Mark E. Smith, *Renegade* (London: Viking, 2008), pp. 43–4.
109 When the Sex Pistols were drafted in to fill a vacant slot on Thames TV's early evening chatshow *Today* on 1 December 1976, due to a last-minute cancellation by EMI's supergroup Queen, host Bill Grundy incited his interviewees into using obscene language live on air. 'Go on', he scoffed, 'say something outrageous', to which Pistol Steve Jones replied, 'You dirty bastard! ... you dirty *fucker*.' A hilarious nationwide moral panic ensued, provoking the *Daily Mirror*'s infamously resonant headline: 'The Filth and the Fury'; Strongman, *Pretty Vacant*, pp. 150–4. See also *The Filth and the Fury* (dir. Julien Temple, 2000). The footage of the Pistols and the Bromley Contingent drunk dancing and larking about on the set behind the rolling credits is behaving-badly gold dust.
110 Bragg, *Progressive Patriot*, p. 235; Gray, *Return of the Last Gang in Town*, p. 201.
111 Letts, *Westway to the World*.
112 The Clash's White Riot concert at the Rainbow Theatre in Finsbury Park on 9 May 1977 gained notoriety for the disorderly behaviour of the audience, who left destroyed seating in a pile at the front of the stage. Gray, *Return of the Last Gang in Town*, p. 246.
113 Bragg, *Progressive Patriot*, pp. 236, 237.
114 Needs, 'The Clash', p. 59.
115 Strummer was photographed wearing a subverted Elvis T-shirt during this period. He designed the 'Chuck Berry is Dead' T-shirt for Rhodes.
116 Humphrey in Gilbert, *Passion is a Fashion*, p. 143.
117 Neil Spenser, 'The Clash', *The Ultimate Music Guide: The Complete Story*

       of the Clash, Uncut, August 2017, p. 20.
118 Gilbert, *Passion is a Fashion*, p. 145.
119 Regarded as too damaged, Strummer's guitar was omitted from the mix; he insisted on playing his Telecaster nevertheless. 'I'm in there chundering away with the bass-drum and the snare.' Spenser, 'The Clash', p. 20.
120 Gibson, *Passion is a Fashion*, p. 148.
121 Danny Kelly in Du Noyer, *The Clash*, p. 41.
122 Rowan Tallis Milligan, 'The Politics of the Crowbar: Squatting in London, 1968–1977', *Anarchist Studies* 24.2 (2016), p. 16. 'The first Clash rehearsal was in a squat in Davis Road … in Shepherd's Bush.' Mick Jones, 'Introduction', in *The Complete Story of the Clash, Uncut*, August 2017, p. 3.
123 Seamus Nolan, *Subvert all Power* (Dublin: Upstate Theatre Project and the Arts Council, 2016), p. 2.
124 Simon Reynolds's study of post-punk music culture, *Rip it Up and Start Again: Postpunk 1978–1984* (London: Faber and Faber, 2005), proposes the counter-hypothesis that the evolution of alternative music after 1977 was more influenced by David Bowie and the Bowie-produced releases of 1977 (*Low*, *Heroes*, and Iggy Pop's *The Idiot* and *Lust For Life*) than any of the first-generation punk recordings.
125 Badiou, *Manifesto for Philosophy*, p. 20.
126 Žižek, *Year of Dreaming Dangerously*, p. 83.
127 Alain Badiou, *Ethics: An Essay on the Understanding of Evil* (London: Verso, 2002), p. 41.
128 Keir, 'When Two Sevens Clash', p. 13.
129 Benjamin, 'Theses on the Philosophy of History', p. 254.
130 Benjamin, *The Arcades Project*, p. 482.

6
What if Keith Levene had never left The Clash? Punk and the politics of novelty

Pete Dale

The purpose of this chapter is partly to query the 'year zero' mythology of 1977 era punk, partly to question the idea that a discrete 'post-punk' music can be understood separately from 'original' punk, and partly to explore more general questions around music, novelty and tradition. The latter concern is something I have been exploring in theoretical work for some time now. The Clash are used here largely as a case study with which to explore some of the theoretical ideas I have been developing. In the conclusion, I focus closely on the question that has been at the heart of my work for many years: will radical innovation produce radical politics or can radical/leftist politics be better served by artistic products that are more 'traditional' (i.e. less ostentatiously novel) in character?

Punk is a long tradition within which 'the first wave' represents only one episode. Indeed, 1970s UK punk was not even the first music to be described as 'punk rock': Dave Marsh used these words in 1971 in the US magazine *Creem* to describe the American 'garage' group? and the Mysterians.[1] It is well known that the word 'punk' was circulating in a range of music-related contexts prior to its use in the UK from 1976 onwards, such as the magazine/fanzine *Punk* published by Legs McNeil and John Holmstrom between 1975 and 1979. The UK punk rock scene of 1976–78 is not even necessarily the most influential era within the overall punk tradition. The relatively recent flowering of punk in the Eastern hemisphere, for example, arguably relates more strongly to the various strands of 1980s-derived US punk: Minor Threat, Black Flag, Nirvana, Green Day and so forth.

Consider, on this point, Kevin Dunn's revelation in his detailed monograph *Global Punk* that Indonesia currently has 'the largest punk community in all of Asia, if not the world'.[2] Emma Baulch, meanwhile, has demonstrated that Bali in particular 'was awash with Green Day' from at least 1996 onwards.[3] Baulch suggests that the influence of Green Day may have been overstated by the Indonesian bands themselves, interestingly enough, but she is clear nevertheless that Green Day and Nirvana cover versions, rather than Sex Pistols or Clash cover versions, were being performed by Indonesian bands as the punk scene emerged in that country.[4] She also states that 'Green Day's music echoed throughout the province' of Bali in the mid-1990s.[5] That said, by 1998 UK punk bands such as The Exploited were beginning to influence a separate set of more 'underground' bands.[6] However, The Exploited were not a first-wave UK punk band and, in any case, Baulch's account suggests that US groups such as NOFX, Bad Religion and Green Day provided the initial impetus for the Indonesian punk scene which would eventually become, if Dunn is to be believed, the biggest in the world.

Of course, one can argue that without the likes of The Clash and Stiff Little Fingers one would not get a group such as Green Day. One can equally say, however, that you could not have had The Clash and Stiff Little Fingers without, say, The Kinks and The Who. After all, popular music scenes do not come from nowhere and the lineage that produced most of the UK's first-wave punk in 1976–78 is transparently obvious: the average listener would not struggle to recognise the similarity between, say, the opening bars of the Sex Pistols' 'God Save the Queen' and the trademark openings of numerous Eddie Cochran hits. Where certain bands did suggest a less obvious debt to the rock tradition (Alternative TV, for example), a debt to the past is nevertheless readily identifiable (ATV's more avant-garde work came after the first wave of punk, for one thing, while their early material is quite musically conventional).[7] Nothing comes from a vacuum, after all, despite the 'year zero' pretensions of the UK punk rock movement around 1977.[8]

Nevertheless, first-wave UK punk retains a certain fascination: it *was* a shockingly novel movement and did excite many people. As everyone knows, the Sex Pistols were of pivotal importance in this regard, but The Clash, as I have shown elsewhere, were also highly influential upon individuals as significant as Steve Ignorant (Crass) and Billy Bragg.[9] I have also argued, in my work on the traditions of punk, that the facile idea of a chain of influence with some 'original' agent deserving priority over all that follows (the Pistols begat The Clash who begat Crass who begat countless 'anarcho-punk' groups, and so forth) is highly problematic in political and philosophical terms.[10] However, punk has repeatedly provided tinder for left-leaning sentiments and socially progressive ideals, and hence is certainly worth talking about from a left perspective. First-wave UK punk should (and, indeed, does) remain of interest for both academic and non-scholarly discourse, then; but we should resist the temptation to grant it some unique and rather magical power. The Sex Pistols and The Clash were far from the 'be-all-and-end-all' of punk; but they certainly combine with other first-wave punk bands to form an interesting case within UK popular music history as well as British sociocultural history more broadly.

However, it is the music-specific aspect of The Clash that I wish to focus on here. More particularly, I want to look in detail at the harmonic character of The Clash's eponymous first album, wherein they restrict themselves, in the main, to predictable diatonic progressions. The strongest exception to this harmonic conservatism is 'What's My Name', which was co-composed with Keith Levene – an outstanding guitarist among the punk generation who was originally a member of The Clash (before they made any recordings) and who would go on play a crucial role in John Lydon's post-Pistols group Public Image Limited (PiL).

What is the 'political' significance of The Clash's musical conservatism? Does music require novelty in order to kindle political engagement or, conversely, do the innumerable 'epiphanies' experienced by young people at Clash gigs outweigh any aesthetic reservations one might hold? By the end of the chapter, I hope to offer some tentative answers to these two questions. I begin, however, with some discussion of the musical content of the album *The Clash* in general, followed by some detailed discussion of the harmonic character of 'What's My Name'. I then enquire, in the third section of the chapter, whether the elements of harmonic interest unearthed in 'What's My Name' suggest that Levene's relatively 'advanced' musical instincts mean that, in some alternative reality, The Clash could have been a more avant-garde group. Is the common assumption of greater musical complexity in 'post-punk' (relative to the 'original' punk) necessarily well founded? And even if post-punk is more complex – even if Keith Levene had not left The Clash, allowing the group to retain a greater level of musical interest – why assume that a greater complexity would be more valuable as, say, propaganda for the left? This, in short, is the core question of the chapter.

The eponymous debut album

The Clash by The Clash was not the most musically groundbreaking album of its era by any means. Take the opening track, 'Janie Jones': a drum kit beats out crotchets and quavers without syncopation, a guitar strikes a straight E major bar chord and a voice descends the 'do-re-mi' of the first three steps of the major scale (the opening notes of 'Three Blind Mice', that is). We eventually move up to the dominant chord, B major, thus following the most standardised element within European music – the core harmonic detail, for example, of pretty much every hymn that lead vocalist John 'Joe Strummer' Mellor would have sung at the private schools he attended. As we move back to the tonic chord (E), bassist Paul Simonon offers a D natural as he descends through E–D–C#–B. This D natural does not belong to E major (where we would find D#) but does belong to A major: the bass line, in other words, has prepared our ears for a modulation to A major by flattening the seventh degree of the E chord which the guitarist is playing. The move, which is typical of the kind of rock'n'roll 'boogie' bass one finds in countless 1950 hits, is highly clichéd as harmonic patterning (preparation for modulation to the sub-dominant position being created through addition of the dominant seventh note to the tonic chord, that is).

It is no coincidence, furthermore, that the lyrics focus upon being 'in love with rock'n'roll', 'getting stoned' and sex (Janie Jones, born Marion Mitchell, was notorious in the 1970s as a host of sex parties): this is supposed to be a good, upbeat rock'n'roll song. Or is it? The question hinges, I would suggest, partly upon a decision as to whether The Clash intend some irony or sarcasm with the lyrical turns just mentioned. If one listens a little further in to 'Janie Jones', it turns out that there is good reason to suspect that The Clash are rather sceptical about the adequacy of the escapism undertaken by the office worker about whom they are singing. Consider, for example, the mention of 'payola': our office worker should 'send for the government, man!' given that he lacks this monetary benefit. The clear implication is that the system is corrupt at the top, while the office worker receives little or no benefit from that corruption; indeed, 'the boss at the firm always thinks he shirks' and, therefore, we might not be surprised that the worker seeks solace in rock'n'roll, drugs and sex. Is such escapism an adequate solution to the problems that the character in the song faces? The song isn't exactly a sociological diagnosis or Marxist analysis of the difficulties facing the working man, but it would be hard to deny that we are encouraged at least to view the described situation critically. Indeed, there is good reason to perceive 'Janie Jones' as a critique not only of drugs and sex (which, of course, the hippies had tended to prioritise as central facets of their 'freedom') but also of rock'n'roll itself.

Musically, however, this *is* a fairly straightforward rock'n'roll song: as mentioned above, it 'rocks' steadily (i.e. without syncopation), uses the familiar components of the 'three-chord trick' and offers guitar work and a vocal melody that are simple and entirely congruous to the patterns established since the 1950s. Postponing for now the question as to how problematic this mismatch is, we can note that the bulk of the remainder of *The Clash* conforms to similarly established musical patterns – and, like 'Janie Jones', combines them with socially conscious lyrics. The album's second track 'Remote Control', for example, begins with an emphatically conventional I–V–IV–I sequence in C major. There is some interest (unusualness, that is) in the I–iii–IV–VI–II verse sequence, to the extent that the major form of the submediant chord is employed (VI, which is A major in this key) followed by the major supertonic chord (D major, chord II in C major). The step down from II to I as the verse is repeated is not a dominant to tonic set-up but, that said, it is not so extraordinary even within the context of rock/pop's typically restricted harmonic palette. The development section where the vocalist sings 'Don't make no noise...' (not really a chorus, in the sense that there is less of a hook here than one finds in the verse) uses a fairly predictable IV–V repeated switch with the VI–II closure from the verse being employed again. The breakdown section at 1.40 is a rather unimpressive reiteration of a mixolydian trick frequently used by The Who, while the ensuing guitar solo, though reasonably pleasing for a rock fan such as this author, is far from being unusual – indeed, the opening 'trick', which extends through two-thirds of the twelve-bar break, is taken directly from Chuck Berry. The last four bars of this guitar break are rather well played and are in advance of the capabilities of, for example, Steve Jones of the Sex Pistols, it is fair to say; but the guitar break and the musicality of the song overall are not surprising and are not unusual in a rock or pop context.

Again, though, the lyrics are politically provocative and sociologically interesting. 'Who needs the parliament?', the singer asks; after all, 'they're all fat and old [and] queueing for the House of Lords'. In the end 'repression', which we hear chanted four times, is what we are experiencing: parliament and 'big business', the song seems to say, provide 'remote control' of our options and, in the last analysis, 'you gotta work' whether you want to or not. Not quite a full-blown exposition of Gramsci's theory of hegemony, the lyric nevertheless pushes in the same general direction – but it does so without offering many, if any, musical surprises.

This general pattern proceeds almost all the way through the album. Track three, 'I'm So Bored with the USA', follows the hymnal I–IV harmonic structure throughout with the sole exception of a modal bVI chord (C major, that is, given the E major context of the rest of the song) in the choruses; but the lyric implies a critique of the cultural imperialism of US foreign policy. 'White Riot', which follows 'I'm So Bored...', has provoked great discussion for its lyrical focus upon racial tension, but musically it is fairly predictable, again following the hymnal I–IV switch for the bulk of the song.[11] Actually, 'White Riot' does surprise a little by modulating down a whole tone from A to G for the verses, while the use of a C major to A major change in the pre-chorus ('Everybody's doing just what they're told to...') is also reasonably inventive; but, like 'I'm So Bored...', this modality is kept to very minimal levels. 'Hate and War' is a lyrically provocative song which focuses on two of punk's favourite themes; but the harmony is based entirely around the three-chord trick, that most conservative of harmonic configurations.

At this point on *The Clash* (or, at least, on the UK version of the album)[12] we encounter 'What's My Name'. The song stands out, for reasons which I explain below. 'What's My Name' is followed by 'Deny' and the latter apes a little of the harmonic interest from the former; for example, the use of the C chord in the verse (a bIII chord, given the clear set-up of A major as 'home'). We can also note a decorative and arpeggiated high guitar figure at one point that adds a rich ninth to a B minor chord and a jazzy major seventh to the G major. Despite these elements of intrigue, 'What's My Name' is significantly less harmonically stable than 'Deny', as we will see. In lyrical terms, that said, the attack on a 'liar' in 'Deny' suggests a classic punk call for simple truths and, therefore, we can see at least a little political impetus of some stripe here.

'London's Burning', the last song on the first side of *The Clash*, begins with a V–I fall: vocalist Joe Strummer cries the song's title on a D natural (V) and then the band 'reply', as it were, with G major (I). This 'perfect fifth' is the heart of musical tradition in Europe and, although one can reasonably claim that it remains perfectly satisfying as a musical effect, it is about the most conventional musical element a rock or pop band could possibly prioritise in a song. Having given us this musical germ (the interval that introduces 'Baa Baa Black Sheep' and 'Twinkle Twinkle Little Star', among other nursery rhymes), the group settle into a I–bVII–IV–V sequence that they stick with for the rest of the song. (Perhaps aware that they risk listener boredom through repetition, the sequence is moved up from G to A for the last part of the song, but this 'truck-driver' modulation is, as Dai Griffiths has shown, one of the oldest tricks in the book.)[13] One can actually sing the titular melody of 'London Bridge is Falling Down…' quite consonantly over this chord sequence and, in more than one respect, it is fair to say that the song is somewhat childlike in its simplicity as music. The lyrics, however, provoke the listener by suggesting that 'watching television' is 'the new religion' and hinting at the squatter mentality (the singer is 'looking for a home' among 'the empty blocks').

The second side of *The Clash* follows the same kind of harmonic and lyrical patterns that had been offered on the A-side: primarily major key and/or three-chord-trick-based harmonic sequences with occasional modal usages of bVII and/or bIII chords. Modulations can be found in songs such as 'Cheat' (moves from A major to C major and then, eventually, E major), 'Protex Blue' (opens with a D-rooted modal sequence then modulates to an unusual C-rooted modal harmony) and '48 Thrills' (vacillates between E major and G major). However, once the modulation has taken place, the new key is always fairly stable. Lyrics about work ('Career Opportunities'), drugs ('Cheat', '48 Thrills') and contraception ('Protex Blue') are on offer while 'Garageland' seems to sum up something of a Clash ideology in just three verses (and using a three-chord trick in the verses with a IV–iii–ii–I rundown in the pre-chorus and chorus). 'Police and Thieves' is anomalous both stylistically and by virtue of not involving the 'Strummer/Jones' writing team (the song is a cover of a Junior Murvin/Lee Perry number).

As an album, then, *The Clash* consistently blends fairly (and quite often very) harmonically conservative music with fairly politically minded lyrics. The combination proved to be very popular, it is fair to say, with a significantly sized audience: there can be little argument that they were second only to the Sex Pistols within the first-wave UK punk milieu, in terms of popularity. However, there is good reason to wonder what might have happened if the group had adopted a less musically conservative approach. Could they have been more popular still? Alternatively, might a more musically radical sound have better complemented the group's lyrical tendency towards sociopolitical critique? I begin to approach these questions by considering the more musically challenging character of 'What's My Name', relative to the rest of *The Clash*.

'What's My Name'

According to Levene, 'What's My Name' was something 'I totally wrote on my own'.[14] The record sleeve of *The Clash*, however, claims that the song was jointly composed with Strummer and Jones, attributing only one third of the composition to (erroneously and, given the song title, rather ironically) 'K. Levine'. To some extent we can leave such forensic arguments to the lawyers but, for the record, my analyses would suggest that Levene's claim that 'I wrote on all the tunes, not just one-third of one tune' may have some legitimacy.[15] Some of the best-remembered songs on *The Clash* – 'Garageland', 'Career Opportunities', 'Janie Jones', 'White Riot' and 'London's Burning' – fit well, harmonically speaking, with the songwriting style of subsequent Clash albums and are thus more credible as outright Strummer/Jones compositions. Other songs discussed above, however, such as 'Deny', 'Cheat', 'Protex Blue' and '48 Hours' in particular (and, more narrowly, the first chord of each chorus in 'I'm So Bored with the USA' with which, one could argue, American culture is symbolically rejected through dissonant harmony) might well be claimed to have Keith Levene's 'fingerprints' upon them, as it were.

What those just-mentioned songs have in common with 'What's My Name' is a certain tonal/harmonic ambiguity. For example, as noted above, 'Protex Blue' uses two modal (and thus non-standard) structures, the second of which is more especially unusual by virtue of a surprising (given the C-rooted context) B chord followed by F major. Which of the song's two modal roots (D and C) has overall priority in terms of key? It is not quite clear and as a result the decision to end on C feels somewhat arbitrary, particularly given the opening guitar riff on F major which audibly offers Bb (and thus implies F as 'home' as well as rendering the D, which arrives at the outset of the first verse, as quite a surprise).

'What's My Name' is more ambiguous still. Take the opening bars: the rhythm guitar strums on B but the lead guitar starts out on E natural, thus creating a Bsus4 harmony; the rhythm guitar then seems to move up to E and down to A. The latter two chords are odd given that, as the drums enter, the bassist plays the more obvious F# down to D. The obviousness of these notes derives from the fact that the backing vocalists sing 'woah-oh' across the same interval. Interestingly, lead vocalist Joe Strummer does not really follow this pattern: he drones on the B root for his first line ('What the hell is wrong with me?') and then rises to C# and D for his second ('I'm not who I'm s'posed to be...'). We can also note that live clips of the band performing 'What's My Name' currently available on YouTube (such as the Manchester Belle Vue performance filmed by Granada TV for the *So It Goes* programme in November 1977) show Strummer offering only vocals, as opposed to playing rhythm guitar as he more typically would on stage and on recordings.[16] Additionally, we can observe that the studio rendition of 'What's My Name' seems to have the rhythm guitar buried in the mix after the opening bars, with a decorative lead guitar dropping in intermittently, but the overall mix sounds rather 'empty' relative to the rest of the album.

Was Strummer confused by the ambiguity of the B–F#–D sequence and struggling to work around it as both vocalist and guitarist? Perhaps; we can note that he reduces the vocal melody to a rap on B natural in the Belle Vue footage and other live performances, even handing over vocal duties to bassist Paul Simonon at a 1985 Roskilde Festival performance. (The YouTube footage of the latter performance is also interesting because the lead guitarist – a replacement for Mick Jones, who had left in 1983 – accidentally plays the major third of the opening B chord at the outset of the song. The guitarist corrects himself by playing the minor third the second time he performs the phrase, but his evident confusion supports my argument that the tonality of the song is highly ambiguous.)[17] The reason B–F#–D is confusing is that the B feels like home (by virtue of its positioning in the sequence and the prioritisation of B by the vocalist). Meanwhile the D chord implies B minor, and yet (as the onstage error by the guitarist in the 1985 Roskilde performance just mentioned indicates) the thrust of the first chord brings B major to mind. (It is hard to tell, but my ear suggests that Strummer is playing a B major chord on the rhythm guitar in the version on *The Clash*; we can note that he is reduced to standing in the background playing root notes on the bass in the Roskilde performance.) In short, I would argue that we hear the D chord as a surprising harmonic twist.

This harmonic uncertainty is only compounded when the chords rise across E–F#–G–A for the song's chorus, all in major chord position. The D# within the F# major chord would indicate B major as the key, which would then mean that the E and F# chords at the outset of this sequence were IV and V of the tonic key. This would mean that the D major chord in the verses is bIII of the tonic key, and such modality is certainly at play in 'What's My Name'. The crucial question for present purposes, however, is whether B major really is our tonic key. The G and A major chords suggest otherwise: they imply, to at least some extent, D major as the home key (thus G and A would be IV and V of the D major while the E and F# would simply be the major form of the ii and iii chords one should expect in D major).

The middle eight ('Dad got pissed so I got clocked...') somewhat adds to the impression of D major as possible tonic: the harmony switches from D to A in what feels like a possible I–V movement. However, if A major were the tonic key, the full sequence of the middle eight (D–A–D–E) would be a classic subdominant-orientated bridge consisting of IV–I–IV–V. We need also to observe that the band resolves on to E major at the close of the song, and this *does* 'work' as a resolution (by which I mean that few listeners would perceive this as a markedly interrupted cadence and most, indeed, will hear it as reasonably good 'sense').

So far, then, I have proposed that B major, B minor, D major, A major and E major can all be 'felt' as the tonic key in this particular song. This is not a puzzle that we can simply unlock with some 'correct' answer: indeed, some of these ambiguities (such as the question as to whether we are in D major or A major during the middle eight, or whether we are in B major or E major during the chorus) occur fairly simultaneously rather than, as it were, sectionally. Tonal ambiguity, then, is knitted into the song and, I would say, is highlighted by the decorative lead guitar which falls across F# and F natural (both major and minor third of D major, that is) on its descent to D natural during the verses. This is done as the rhythm guitar and the bass guitar play D and the effect, for me, somewhat recalls the ragtime of Scott Joplin. 'What's My Name', in short, is harmonically richer and more peculiar than anything else on *The Clash*. It seems fairly certain that Keith Levene's harmonic skills brought this richness into play. What, then, if The Clash had retained Levene as their guitarist instead of ejecting him in 1976?

The contrast between Mick and Keith

It is reasonable, I would argue, to characterise Mick Jones and Keith Levene as polar opposites in musical terms. Perhaps this is to overstate the case, but the overstatement might allow us to broadly illuminate two differing poles of musicality – even, I think, if the characterisation is a little caricatured. For some insight into the musical instincts of the former, an interview in Daniel Rachel's *Isle of Noises* is probably as good a source as any.[18] Regarding songwriting, Jones asserts to Rachel that 'there's a natural law to it somehow ... the natural tune is already there telling you what the natural tune is'.[19] Tautological though this statement clearly is, it shows us that Jones is happy to operate within a given musical system: 'I'm just trying to receive ... get in touch with all the stuff that's going on out there in some way, or let it come to me so that other people can enjoy.'[20] Jones is no avant-gardist; rather, he wants to engage listeners with broadly familiar musicality: 'You've got to have a tune otherwise you're going to bore everybody.'[21] He is aware, it seems, that the early Clash (probably, I believe, due to a combination of neophyte experimentation and the influence of Levene) were more modal, harmonically unconventional and (subtly) dissonant. This element was dropped by the time they were writing *London Calling* (circa 1979), Jones hints: 'in the music it was a bit more chunky before and I made it smooth'.[22]

The 'chunky' element, I would suggest, is the modal tendency and/or the tendency to modulate without preparation that one can sometimes find on *The Clash*. By *London Calling*, chunks (as it were) of harmony were not so awkwardly juxtaposed, it is fair to say. Jones had/has some awareness of harmonic principles and practices: 'It's like a puzzle ... the E chord is the same up here after twelve frets. Plus in the A position [the bar-chord that apes the open A, as opposed to the bar-chord that apes open E, he seems to mean] it's here on the eight fret or something.'[23] Although Jones actually means the seventh fret, it is clear that he has thought about harmonic relations: 'On the same fret you can do the A again in the D position. So it's like a graph.'[24] The graph he has just described, however, provides options for E, A and D chords: a rather restricted palette which is expanded on some songs on *The Clash* but more heavily relied upon by the time of *London Calling*. The latter album has significant stylistic diversity, of course, and it should be noted that harmonic experimentation is only one form of potential adventure in music. Nonetheless, it is certainly the case that *The Clash* offers more harmonic surprises than *London Calling*.

Levene, judged by the music of PiL (of which he was a founding and musically crucial member), also has a working knowledge of traditional harmony. We can note on 'Poptones', for example, that he creates a nimble pattern around A major that descends delicately through the major seventh and sixth on its way down to the fifth degree of the scale. This is one sign of a working facility with conventional harmony, but there are many others in the PiL repertoire. Levene once commented that 'people thought I was classically trained', with good reason, I would suggest, even if he really only 'knew the E chord, and ventured into E minor'.[25]

Levene, however, chose to 'play outside of the chord', as jazz musicians will put it: to expand his harmonic palette with extra-triadic notes that are dissonant to some ears but are heard as a consonance (of sorts; an interesting sound, at least) by enthusiasts. Examples of such pleasing (to some ears, at least) dissonance in the PiL repertoire are innumerable: 'Albatross' (the opening track from *Metal Box*), to select a song almost at random, is full of harsh 'off' notes although the initial E minor-based guitar figure is consonant enough. The question, moreover, is *why*? If you are capable of making music that is easy to listen to, then why make it difficult? Why go 'out there' when you can stay inside the conventions and, many will presume, thus have a wider appeal?

Part of the answer to these questions could be commercial: as I have noted elsewhere, 'noise' can have a special appeal, and if the audience for avant-garde music is often a smaller one, it is nonetheless the case that dissonant music can draw a crowd.[26] In some cases – PiL perhaps being a case in point, given the commercial need (or arguable need) for Lydon to mark out a difference from the Sex Pistols – noisy music can be more commercially successful than something that, at face, seems more consonant. (Clearly the words consonant and dissonant are to some extent in the eye/ear of the beholder – some people will complain that be-bop jazz, for example, sounds 'out of tune' – but this is a problem that I shall leave to one side for present purposes.)

Some enthusiasts of dissonant and noise-based music appear to believe that such music can somehow escape both the logic of the market and the (perceived to be contrary to true artistry) desire to engage audiences. We can note, for example, Jacques Attali's prioritisation in his celebrated *Noise: The Political Economy of Music* of 'the production, by the consumer himself, of the final object, the movie made from virgin film'. According to Attali, this Barthesian consumer 'will thus become a producer and will derive at least as much of his satisfaction from the manufacturing process itself as from the object he produces'; indeed, he 'will institute the spectacle of himself as the supreme usage'.[27] Such self-facing production-consumption leads nowhere, we might reasonably object; the productive-consumer's supreme spectacle of himself has no exterior value, and the movie made from virgin film can be seen by no one else, one fears. Paul Hegarty, in a more recent and (for this author at least) more nuanced consideration of the noise/music relation, has acknowledged that the idea of noise as an easy escape from capitalism should be challenged by a Marxist.[28]

I am inclined to hesitate, given this, before declaring that Keith Levene's more musically 'adventurous' (if this is the right word, and I am inclined to think it may not be, given its pejorative implications) playing is more 'progressive' or 'radical' than that of Mick Jones. The two musicians were clearly pushing in differing directions. Brian Cogan has reported that 'Levene was forced out' of The Clash.[29] Levene himself claims that he jumped rather than being pushed: because The Clash 'weren't complicated enough [musically] ... I thought "they're going to do it whether I'm there or not" so I'm gonna go off and do something else.'[30] Either way, the fit between the ambitions of The Clash, on the one hand, and Keith Levene's musical instincts, on the other, seems to have been a poor one. We have seen something of Jones's populist instincts in the quotations offered above. For Levene, by contrast, '[w]hat happened to me was once I got good enough to know the rules, I didn't want to be like any other guitarist'. He clarifies that he 'didn't go out of my way to be different' but 'just had an ear for what was wrong. So if I did something that was wrong, i.e. made a mistake or did something that wasn't in key, I was open-minded enough to listen to it again.'[31]

The difference between the two approaches should be clear by now.

The question that provides the title to this chapter remains to be answered, however. I attempt a provisional answer in conclusion, with a special focus on the political implications of the choice between musical experimentation and musical traditionalism/conservatism.

Conclusion

What if Keith Levene had remained a member of The Clash? Perhaps they might have been more musically unusual (more 'interesting') and yet perhaps for this reason they might have grabbed the interest of fewer listeners. Perhaps, however, their 'legend' could have loomed larger still, in the annals of popular music history, than it actually does. To speculate in this way is, arguably, a waste of time. Levene left, and thus we had two separate bands that are somewhat emblematic of two distinct trajectories: The Clash, who seem to embody much of the 'old school punk' tendency, on the one hand, and PiL, who are certainly one of the main 'post-punk' bands, on the other.

I would be reluctant to insist upon these emblematic trajectories as a stark choice between 'punk' and 'post-punk', in the way that Simon Reynolds has tended to do.[32] As I have emphasised above, a group like the (early) Clash actually had a not-inconsiderable level of musical experimentation within their sound, at least at the harmonic level (partly courtesy of Keith Levene, granted, but similar harmonic instability can also be noted in, to give just one example, 'New Rose' by The Damned).[33] Not all post-punk bands were especially avant-garde, furthermore: for example, the song 'Rip It Up and Start Again' by Orange Juice (which gave Reynolds's book on post-punk its title) is a fairly lightweight piece of funky pop, musically speaking. Post-punk, in any case, should not be limited to 1984, the year that Reynolds takes as his end point. As David Wilkinson has recently shown, the question of novelty, politics and avant-gardism remains an important one about which we still need to think carefully in the twenty-first century.[34] In a sense, indeed, we are still very much in a post-punk moment.

That being the case, the emblematic choice between avant-gardism and traditionalism remains an important one. If a musician, today, aspires to promote the cause(s) of the Left, should she follow the example of the (post-debut) Clash or of Keith Levene's band PiL? Should she, in other words, seek to use experimental musical aesthetics as a component of her radicalism (as PiL and many other groups like them did) or, alternatively, should she seek to engage her listeners with familiar-sounding music (as The Clash and other 'old school' punk bands tended to do)? In the latter mode, after all, she could promote the values of the Left through lyrical content (as The Clash quite often did) or through the methods of production (the DIY methods that The Clash did not adopt but that innumerable punk and post-punk bands, of course, did). In the former mode, perhaps the most important element of Left-radicalism – what you *say* and, more important still, what you *do* – can get confused with aesthetic considerations to the point where, arguably, the 'message' gets lost. How many people say they were inspired to take an interest (or an active involvement) in politics because of PiL? Fewer, I am sure, than were inspired by The Clash in the manner which, as noted above, the likes of Steve Ignorant, Billy Bragg and countless others were.

I am not calling, that said, for the kind of 'socialist realism' that was prioritised by Lukács at the expense of the actually highly valuable aesthetic experimentation of, for example, Brecht.[35] It would be a huge mistake for the Left to return to such fundamentalism if it were once again to consider the tension between aesthetics and politics that so preoccupied key leftist theorists of the 1920s and 1930s. Heaven forbid that the work of PiL, or of comparable musical experimenters of the current era, should be criticised for the 'formalism' that key modernists were once tarred with by (typically) Soviet-based critics. I think, nevertheless, that the disambiguation of aesthetic judgement from political action is important if we would seek to reinvigorate the Left such that, in the distant or immediate future, it could revive its fortunes and perhaps even supersede its greatest successes. We should not assume that such an effort would be 'pie in the sky': what has been achieved before can be achieved again. More importantly still, we must learn not only from the successes but also from the failures of the past.

A crucial element within this is the aesthetic decision involved in the effort to engage or challenge audiences. Facile aesthetic engagement can risk the appearance of revolution but without the kind of critical 'electricity', if I can put it like that, that a truly revolutionary moment requires. How many Clash fans were up for much more than a good night out by, say, 1981? Doubtless the populist instincts that guided Mick Jones in his aesthetic decision making risked building a fanbase at the expense of building a movement. On the other hand, however, the 'oblique techniques' that Simon Reynolds associates with post-punk bands such as PiL surely risk being so oblique as to inspire almost nobody and ultimately say little or nothing.[36] After all, even Reynolds (surely one of the greatest advocates of the experimentalism of the immediate aftermath of first-wave punk) acknowledges that so-called post-punk music became 'dry' after a few years, demanding a return to a 'loose' and 'intuitive' musicianship which I take to be emblematic terms for the musical traditionalism of the likes of Mick Jones.[37]

Perhaps if Keith Levene had never left The Clash their music would have been a lot more interesting and their message a lot more politically effective, but there is no point in wishing for a different past. There is every reason, however, to assume that we – we, in the broadest possible sense – can control our future. As we move forwards, questions around innovation and tradition will be worth considering carefully for those of us who still believe that art – again, taking the term in its broadest possible sense – can contribute valuably to social change.

Notes

1. Paul Gorman, *In Their Own Write: Adventures in the Music Press* (London: MPG, 2001), p. 66.
2. Kevin Dunn, *Global Punk: Resistance and Rebellion in Everyday Life* (London: Bloomsbury, 2016), p. 25.
3. Emma Baulch, *Making Scenes: Reggae, Punk, and Death Metal in 1990s Bali* (Durham, NC: Duke University Press, 2007), p. 92.
4. Ibid., p. 95.
5. Ibid., p. 27.
6. Ibid., p. 126.
7. The avant-gardism of the later ATV owes a clear debt to the likes of Art Ensemble of Chicago and Sun Ra in any case, as Perry has himself admitted. See Simon Reynolds, *Rip it Up and Start Again: Postpunk 1978–1984* (London: Faber and Faber, 2005), p. 79.
8. As Simon Reynolds puts it (to give just one example), 'punk declared 1976 to be Year Zero', *Rip it Up*, p. xx.
9. Pete Dale, *Popular Music and the Politics of Novelty* (London: Bloomsbury, 2016), p. 64.
10. Pete Dale, *Anyone Can Do It: Empowerment, Tradition and the Punk Underground* (Aldershot: Ashgate, 2012).
11. For discussion of race and punk, with a significant focus upon The Clash and the particular song in question (which gave the book its title), see Stephen Duncombe and Maxwell Tremblay, *White Riot: Punk Rock and the Politics of Race* (London: Verso, 2011).
12. *The Clash* was issued in the US, belatedly in 1979, with a radically different running order and some songs omitted as well as others added.
13. Dai Griffiths, 'Elevating Form and Elevating Modulation', *Popular Music* 34.1 (2015), pp. 22–44: for Griffiths, the 'truck driver shift' involves, essentially, a basic modulatory upwards shift of melodic and harmonic material, typically by a semi-tone or whole tone.
14. Jason Gross, 'Keith Levene Interview', *Perfect Sound Forever*, February 2001, http://www.furious.com/perfect/keithlevene.html (accessed 12 September 2016).
15. Ibid.
16. https://www.youtube.com/watch?v=iNE8Ebklesc (accessed 18 November 2018).
17. https://www.youtube.com/watch?v=f0tbrXp4IxM (accessed 18 November 2018).
18. Daniel Rachel, *Isle of Noises: Conversations with Great British Songwriters* (London: Picador, 2014).
19. Ibid., p. 158.
20. Ibid., p. 159.

21 Ibid.
22 Ibid.
23 Ibid., p. 154.
24 Ibid.
25 Interview by Dave Simpson, 'How We Made: Jah Wobble and Keith Levene on Public Image Ltd's *Metal Box*', *The Guardian*, 13 February 2012, https://www.theguardian.com/culture/2012/feb/13/jah-wobble-keith-levene-metal-box (accessed 13 September 2016). I would suggest that Levene is a little disingenuous here, given the evidence of his playing and his claim to have spent eight hours practising on guitar each day during his teens; Gross, 'Keith Levene Interview'.
26 Dale, *Anyone Can Do It*, p. 28.
27 Jacques Attali, *Noise: The Political Economy of Music* (Minneapolis, MN: University of Minnesota Press, 1985), p. 144.
28 Paul Hegarty, *Noise/Music: A History* (London: Continuum, 2007), pp. 51–2.
29 Brian Cogan, *Encyclopedia of Punk Music and Culture* (London: Greenwood Press), p. 38.
30 Ivor Levene, 'The Clash, PIL Founder Keith Levene Sets The Record Straight', *California Rocker*, 2016, http://www.californiarocker.com/2016/06/09/exclusive-interview-clash-founder-keith-levene-sets-record-straight/ (accessed 13 September 2016).
31 Gross, 'Keith Levene Interview'.
32 For example, Reynolds argues that 'Punk's approach to politics – raw rage or agitprop protest – seemed too blunt or preachy to the post-punk vanguard'; *Rip it Up*, p. xxii. While Reynolds is entitled to claim this view for himself, it does not tally well with my innumerable conversations with music fans who were collecting records during the era Reynolds focuses upon (1978–84), as well as many musicians of that era. One could listen to Crass, The Clash, the Fire Engines and Scritti Politti without feeling misaligned, in fact; and many musicians to whom Reynolds ascribes the status of 'post-punk' actually viewed themselves as punks. I would dispute the idea of a hard distinction between punk and post-punk, therefore.
33 For discussion of the harmonic interest in 'New Rose', see Dale, *Popular Music and the Politics of Novelty*, pp. 80–2. Oddly, Allan F. Moore argues that there is limited harmonic interest in 'New Rose': *Rock: The Primary Text – Developing a Musicology of Rock*, 2nd edn (Abingdon: Routledge, 2016), p. 131. My analysis shows that this conclusion was hasty on Moore's part.
34 David Wilkinson, *Post-Punk, Politics and Pleasure in Britain* (London: Palgrave, 2016), esp. ch. 7.
35 Theodor Adorno et al., *Aesthetics and Politics* (London: Verso, 2007).
36 Reynolds, *Rip it Up*, p. xxii.
37 Ibid., p. 520.

7
'The beautiful people are ugly too': The Clash as my 'true fiction'

Martin James

When, in late 1999, The Clash released their post-split live album *From Here to Eternity* and previewed Don Letts's documentary film devoted to them, *Westway to the World*, the media were invited to a launch party at a private members' club in West London[1] where music critics and record label personnel rubbed shoulders with celebrities, musicians and supermodels. The event offered a clear indication of the huge gulf that existed between the band's romantic mythology as the embodiment of punk authenticity and their status as revered leaders of a *cool London* aristocracy. This chasm was brought into sharp focus when the band made a brief appearance at the party and pressed flesh with the capital city's self-proclaimed 'beautiful people'. Rumours quickly circulated that rather than spend too much time with the 'fake' celebrity friends, they'd spent most of their evening together in the fish and chip shop next door – authenticity performed and intact.

This scenario was nothing new, however. The tensions between the public perception of punk authenticity and the private reality of the privilege of stardom had long been linked to The Clash. From *Sniffin' Glue* editor Mark P.'s proclamation that the band had 'sold out' when they signed to CBS[2] to this launch party where they had chosen to sit in a chippie rather than talk to the likes of Kate Moss, the history of The Clash presents a litany of contradictions, each as complex as punk itself. Indeed, The Clash did embody UK punk's dilemmas of authenticity in so many unexpected ways. For fans of the band, that may even have been a part of their appeal.

Prior to that launch party, members of the audience at a special cinema screening of the band's *Westway to the World* documentary would inadvertently reveal just how strong that dichotomous relationship between mythology and reality remained in the hearts, minds and memories of their fans. Halfway through the film, as Joe Strummer delivered one of his renowned sermons on 'the truths of punk and The Clash', *Sniffin' Glue* and *NME* writers Danny Baker and Danny Kelly stood up and stormed out, proclaiming loudly that this was 'nothing to do with punk'; that the documentary bore no resemblance to their experience of either band or subculture.

It struck me at the time how important it seemed for both of these journalists to remain in the position of gatekeepers to the public notion of 'authentic' punk. I was also struck by the arrogance of this outburst, that they believed theirs were the definitive memories of what punk was, memories that they believed held more importance than those of the other hangers-on and media friends. More importantly, however, I recall thinking 'How the hell would they know what The Clash were really like? While the fans sweated it out at the front at the gigs, those self-styled punk-journalists stood side-stage, or at the bar, hanging out with the in-crowd and looking down on the band's following. How would they know what it was like to be a fan of The Clash?' *My* memories are more authentic, you see.

It was an admittedly naïve reaction to their equally naïve outburst. But, taken with the experiences of the launch party, it raises a few questions about perceptions of the band's authenticity, the extent to which this was managed and mediated by external forces for whom notions of authenticity were brand values for their industries, and how rarely the authenticating and often oppositional voices of the fans were heard.

The silence of the fans...

The silence of the fans is in large part due to the ways in which popular music histories are constructed. Sarah Thornton notes that four criteria are generally used to assign historical importance to particular music-makers and genres.[3] These are sales figures, biographical interest, critical acclaim and media coverage. Each of these criteria has inherent problems, however. Sales figures form the basis of lists that claim to cover popular music's past but are based solely on recorded and released artefacts, thus excluding fan recordings or un-registered DIY products. Furthermore, they reduce the fan simply to the level of passive consumer or bystander. Biographical interest has the effect of personalising and simplifying complex historical processes. In this instance, punk is reduced to a narrative that prioritises the individual members of The Clash within the London punk scene. Critical acclaim tends to produce 'canons' of the 'best' music which are constructed through a range of biases that have little to do with fans. Finally, media coverage often presents as 'windows on the past' rather than texts that construct events and values. Media reports are partial interpretations of events, rather than factual accounts. The fans' voice is all too often omitted in favour of the voice of the music journalist as 'enlightened fan' or the musician as biographical subject.[4]

All four approaches to the construction of histories produce an emphasis on simple timelines of events with a selection of key moments and personalities deemed to drive change. In other words, they tend to lead to totalising histories. The inclusion of the fans' voice can create a rupture in this simple timeline in which participants problematise facts as myth, or mythologise events as personal 'true fiction'.[5]

All the young punks (new boots and contracts)

Few popular music scenes or genres have experienced the high levels of investigation that UK punk has attracted since late 1975. Where such rock sub-genres as prog, glam or pub rock had been given space to grow towards a sense of maturity, from its emergence punk quickly came under the critical microscope of both the music media and the newly emergent popular music studies. This interest can be viewed through authenticity discourses that had come to the fore in the rock music press from the late 1960s. The dominant ideologies of popular music criticism emerged in the specialist magazines of the US and the alternative underground press in the UK in the 1960s. Magazines such as *Crawdaddy* and *Rolling Stone* in the USA emerged through the need to locate the power of popular music as cultural signifier. Such critics took American history as the starting point and employed the tropes of 'individualism and independence'; the frontier spirit and revolution produced an 'objective' account of rock as the music of 'great men' of a 'great nation'.[6] This process prioritised rock music's masculine, authentic potential over pop's feminine, trivial disposability and was key to authenticating rock music in opposition to all other popular music forms. This was not an uncommon trope in the late 1960s and early 1970s when rock bands performing their own material live were presented as being more authentic than pop bands who performed other people's songs and existed largely as a music industry concept.

In this era, rock critics were mainly unpaid amateurs who in most cases were aware of the role they had in forging new ideas. Simon Frith has noted that 'the ideology of rock – the arguments about what records mean, what rock is for – has always been articulated more clearly by fans than by musicians (or businessmen)'.[7] As non-professionals, these writers structured their craft through the interests and language of themselves as fans. By employing the ideology of the fan, these writers 'valorized authenticity and originality, and developed a mythologized account of rock musicians that considered their work as art'.[8] This aspect of the fan's immersion in the romantic notion of the artist as originating genius is key to understanding the underlying ideology of the popular music critic whose key tools for understanding music texts were the dual themes of authenticity and originality. Musicians were thus mediated through the discourses of the music press 'both as authentic spokespeople for their generation and as Romantic artists'.[9]

With the emergence of the professionalised rock critic, ideologies of authenticity became a central focus for the new rock press. Thus rock became authenticated through the authentic and authenticating voices of the music critic as cultural intermediary. Little surprise then that when punk first emerged, much of its oppositional stance was focused on a rock press that was deemed to be out of touch. It no longer represented the youth. It was *inauthentic*. Or rather, it was still clinging to the performed rock-era authenticities of musicianship and spectacle.

Punk's authenticities may have given primacy to the 45rpm single over the long-playing album, the self-taught non-musician over the educated 'muso', and the immediacy of the scene participant over the apparent distance between rock star and fan, but it also revolved around many similar concerns as those presented by rock: the primacy of live performance over the rhetorically live, the foregrounding of a perceived marginalised underground over a self-serving mainstream and the high focus on musical and extra-musical activities as subcultural expression. Perhaps unsurprisingly then, punk authenticity focused heavily on subcultural display.

Research on subcultural authenticity has focused primarily on style, which in turn fetishises material culture and its consumption as both inevitable and unavoidable dimensions of youth subculture. Perhaps the best-known work in this area is Dick Hebdige's *Subculture: The Meaning of Style*, which presents punk primarily as a culture of display and in so doing reduces the subculture to its material qualities, thus emphasising its inevitable descent into mass consumer culture.[10] For Hebdige, punk's moment of authenticity can only be located in those initial phases of subcultural formation prior to it becoming subsumed by consumer culture.

There are two problems with this position. First, this overemphasis on the materiality of style flies in the face of the original ethos of punk, which emphasised individual choice over collective uniform. Secondly, the inevitability of the commercial market place subsuming subcultures denies the lasting activities and impacts of DIY cultures associated with punk. In terms of collective subcultural style, a brief look at the photos of the earliest UK punks reveals a range of 'looks' that encompassed the subverted city gent, the sadomasochist, the fetishist, the Ramones clone and the leather-clad, spikey-haired punk cliché. Indeed, first-wave punks also deployed hair of varying length, colour and style. The earliest UK bands were equally versed in expressing the individual over the collective, with no two presenting the same uniform style – The Damned, the Sex Pistols, The Adverts etc. were distinctive from each other both as bands and as individuals within those bands. The Clash's adoption early on of uniformly stencilled clothing offered recognition of the power of the collective image that could be argued to be a deliberate attempt to codify a collective punk style. It was through this that they were able to present the image of 'the last gang in town', a key narrative in their collective biography. However, these stylistic concerns were often presented through the illusion of, and allusions to, punk's DIY activities. The Clash's Alex Michon-styled stencilled clothes were contrived to look as much a part of their DIY self-expression as their highly controlled earliest 'showcase' performances in their *Rehearsal Rehearsals* studios.

Fanzine editor Tony Moon's renowned illustration 'here's a chord, here's another, here's a third, now form a band'[11] gave rise to the notion that the auto-didactic performer was itself evidence of DIY ideologies among the earliest punk bands. The reality, however, was that these first bands were less interested in DIY record production and distribution, or even gig promotion, than in building an illusion of creative control through the portrayal of a rejection of mainstream, or parent, cultures. Hebdige and his colleagues at the Centre for Contemporary Cultural Studies may have theorised subculture through an emphasis on class and resistance as homologous positions, thus noting 'rejection' as located in the dismissal of an idealised mainstream society. However, they failed to note the dimensions of subcultural activity that punk's DIY ethic offered beyond rejection: namely reflexivity and self-actualisation. Reflexivity represents the ways in which the individual lives a life that is true to their own ideals, which sit in opposition to that rejected idealised mainstream. Self-actualisation can be viewed as 'being' as opposed to 'doing'. In order to remain true to personal ideals, 'being' the subcultural participant through style alone is not enough. In order to gain subcultural authenticity, it is important to actually take part in the processes of subcultural production. Most notably this can be achieved through DIY activities.[12]

This position creates an important step in the understanding of subcultural authenticity, in that it de-emphasises the mass and focuses on the individual. In the process, it gives voice to subcultural participants, including fans, in the construction of punk authenticity. The emphasis on individual over collective creates space for a greater value on autobiographical experience as authentic voice. DIY becomes located in the 'doing' of an activity and the 'being' of personal expression of the experience of that activity. The very existence of autobiography is a DIY process.

By applying this lens to the construction of history, emphasis is removed from the fetishisation of the collective defining the scene and instead relocated to the individual, active, authenticating participant. In recent years, this approach has seen an increase through the proliferation of punk autobiographies and oral histories. The former has lately seen a marked increase in numbers, with artists as disparate as John Lydon, Viv Albertine and Chrissie Hynde producing confessional memoirs as colour to their versions of 'absolute truth'. Oral histories have provided space for previously overlooked individual participants to offer their hitherto undocumented, subjective, personal perspectives on punk's key historical events.[13] These have brought to light numerous contradictory stories of many of punk's early actors who had previously fallen outside the canon, with the suggested lack of authorial gatekeeping supplying the text with an added sense of authenticity. The same is also true of The Clash's eponymously titled official book, produced after Strummer's death, which places the band in a position of both authority and authenticity, 'telling it like it was, in their own words...' without the overt interjection or opinion from a journalist.[14]

Books on The Clash have positioned the band as the focal point of the punk subculture. Like other biographies on punk's key figures, they are sensationalist texts either written from a fan's perspective but with fandom rarely foregrounded, or from a privileged 'insider' view that is defined against the fan masses.[15] In general, punk autobiographies have the egotistical drive of the need for immortality, while 'official' histories are given eye-witness extensions that place the storyteller and their version of events at the centre. Oral histories find the critical focus squarely located in the words of key participants within the scene and its associated industries. They attempt to fill the gaps left by the selective retelling of 'official histories' but, despite occasional dissenting voices, rarely question the grand narratives of punk. This is largely due to the silent voice of the compiling and editing author who is likely to adhere to a legitimised narrative for storytelling simplicity.

These types of texts raise interesting questions as to the critical value of the colloquial and sensationalistic representations of personal experiences when compared to a 'scholarly' article. Are we able to learn more about the punk subculture through auto/biographical retellings of the story of The Clash by music critics or participating musicians? Can we learn more about the punk scene by analysing through a fan's observations and memories? Do my personal recollections of The Clash have any critical value? According to their own rhetoric, The Clash would consider themselves and their fans to hold the only truly authentic stories.[16]

Helen Reddington argues that giving voice to the first-hand accounts of fans has the potential to question the grand narratives of punk and relocate the hidden, or forgotten, histories and write them into being.[17] The details omitted from official histories offer a rich source for investigation and are invariably to be found in the memories of those people who were involved at the time. But does this suggest that the 'lost' voices of The Clash fans are in any way more 'authentic' than those of the legitimised cultural intermediaries of the time?

'The beautiful people are ugly too': my 'true fiction'[18]

I was 14 when I first 'left home' to follow The Clash. It was early 1977 and the impact of punk rock was just beginning to be felt in the nation's classrooms. Like so many kids of my generation, the cocktail of punk's apparent unbridled anger and my own hormones proved too potent to contain. In the course of what seemed like only a few weeks my voice broke, I gave my mum cheek, cut my hair short, converted my flared jeans to drainpipes, acquired baseball boots and a ripped T-shirt, and got beaten up. This was for being 'a punk', thus setting a pattern that was to define the next few years of my life.

My first Clash gig was at the Harlesden Coliseum in 1977. I told my parents I was staying at a friend's house. My friend did the same and we duly 'left home'. For two kids from the middle-class town of Marlow-on-Thames, it seemed like the punk-rock thing to do.

Harlesden Coliseum was decrepit. The fake alabaster decor was in an advanced state of decomposition, the flecked wallpaper peeling off in strips to reveal disintegrating walls. The carpet was sticky underfoot, the air dense with the smell of damp, stale cigarettes and body odour. It constituted the perfect setting for my first encounter with the London punk scene. It also seemed the perfect venue for The Clash, who took the stage to taunts about their newly signed deal with CBS Records. The band's reaction was to deliver a set of all-consuming ferocity.

The picture is still clear in my head: Joe Strummer screwing his face up to snarl at – rather than into – the microphone, his leg pumping uncontrollably like a piston; Mick Jones attacking his guitar and his amp as if he hated them (they kept packing up, as if they hated him); peroxide-blond bassist Paul Simonon swinging his instrument low like a weapon, a slow-burning cigarette hung constantly from his bottom lip in defiance of the laws of physics. It doesn't go away, that kind of imagery, not when you encounter it for the first time.

After the gig, I worked up the courage to approach Joe Strummer. He was holding court at a makeshift bar, enjoying a couple of beers and praise for the show. I waited until the crowd thinned, wandered over to him and said hello. He seemed to me to be the epitome of cool in his Clash uniform of heavily stencilled combat gear. But it was his teeth that really compelled my attention. They appeared to be decaying in front of my eyes, ravaged, presumably, by a combination of negligence, bad dentistry and cheap speed. As he spoke, a continuous stream of spittle flew from his mouth.

I attempted to make intelligent conversation. I asked him why he sang a song called 'White Riot' while the DJ played reggae all night – did it, I wondered, annoy him at all? The spittle turned to froth. Did I not understand that 'White Riot' was all about his respect for black people and their stand against oppression? Had I not listened to the lyrics, in which he sang that he wished white people would take the same positive position?

Well, no actually. First of all, The Clash hadn't actually released the record at this point so there was no way I could have analysed his lyrics. Secondly, I hadn't grown up in multiracial Notting Hill Gate. And despite going to gigs in the multiracial town of High Wycombe, I had never previously been forced to face up to my own implicit racism. It was an attitude that had been born from the simple fact that there were no black people in Marlow. I was ten when I met my first black kid. Some nice, white, middle-class family had adopted him. I can still remember being told in the playground that if the black kid touched me his colour would rub off on me. Even as a 14-year-old, race riots – or indeed the very concept of 'racism' – meant little to me.

So Strummer forced my eyes open. And to confirm my new-found awareness I started drinking Red Stripe in High Wycombe's Rasta pub, The Red Cross Knight, and, when The Clash hit the road again in May 1977, I skanked enthusiastically to the band's version of Junior Murvin's roots-rocking classic 'Police and Thieves'. I became a vocal supporter of the Rock Against Racism movement. And when, in April 1978, The Clash played the RAR Carnival at Victoria Park in Hackney, there I was handing out badges, unquestioningly.

Back in Harlesden, however, the tongue-lashing that Strummer meted out went on and on and left me reeling. This was not what one expected of narcissistic rock stars. He did stop eventually, at which point he put his arm round my shoulders and told me to 'piss off 'ome'. I stumbled into the Harlesden streets feeling as if I'd just been pulled up by a teacher. It was while I reflected sombrely on this that I was knocked out cold by another punk and robbed of the £1.20 I had to get home. It wouldn't have happened, of course, if my attacker had realised that I was now a close friend of Joe Strummer.

So how exactly did a middle-class kid from a middle-class town come to follow The Clash around? Well, as a young teenager it certainly wasn't their political stance that excited me. At that time the dole meant nothing to me and, as I've already mentioned, I was completely ignorant of any concept of race politics. In retrospect, I think I was drawn to the macho air that surrounded the band. It may not appeal much now, but as a teenage boy their tough-guy, outlaw image was something to aspire to. The Clash, far more than the Sex Pistols or The Damned, were a gang. And, more to the point, they made us – their hormonally challenged disciples – feel like we were also part of the same gang. They were, they argued, the same as us and everything about them portrayed an us-against-them attitude.

That gang vibe was a key component of the punk 'stance'. Kids like me were never hard enough to be skinheads. In fact, like most punks, I was happier to write poetry than fight. But like it or not, aggro attended punk wherever it went. The media waged a daily war on us; complete strangers adopted the blood sport of 'punk hunting'. We just took it on the chin, or wherever else the blows landed, because we had a cause. We were martyrs, the beatings a rite of passage. We would show our wounds to younger, aspiring punks. The cuts and bruises were much, much more meaningful than button badges. And we got great stories out of it: I remember bragging about being jumped on by a gang of Teds, when in reality a single Elvis impersonator had punched me for spitting at him. We were only reducing ourselves to type. I was a punk: spitting is what we did. He was a Teddy Boy: hitting punks is what they did. He probably told his friends that he'd taken on a gang of us. The fact that we sat next to each other in double English on a Tuesday afternoon would certainly have been left out of the narrative.

Punk offered the chance of reinvention. We were all keenly downwardly mobile, throwing away what we saw as the entrapments of middle-class life in favour of what we perceived to be working-class attributes. This meant swearing a lot, chewing imaginary gum and sneering at 'the straights'. The mad rush to punk self-reinvention was especially notable in the generation about to head off for university. Virtually every 18-year-old went off as a hippie, only to return at Christmas quoting the first Ramones album, hair shortened (side bits still over ears though), styled by Oxfam.

My own three-strong gang comprised Nutty (the son of a toilet-roll salesman), Gerard (who later became briefly famous for finding an original painting by John Lennon in a skip) and myself. But by the summer of 1977 our number had swelled considerably. Among the future DJs, movers and shakers of the late twentieth century, Roald Dahl's grandson used to hang out with us. Can't remember his name. He was at Eton at the time. And one of the girls started to bring along her boyfriend. His name was Steve Redgrave, a huge, quiet fellow. He wore a torn school shirt with the names of his favourite punk bands written in ballpoint all over it. But that was as far as he went. He had other interests. He amiably put up with us giving him stick for not being punk enough and puffing up and down the Thames in a rowing boat when he could be going to gigs and changing society.

At the time, the most uncool thing you could be was a 'weekend punk'. It's what the London cognoscenti called us Thames Valley youngsters (despite the fact that many of this same self-styled in-crowd were Thames Valley locals who would commute to the gigs). But 'weekend punks' is exactly what we were. Correspondingly, in time-honoured anthropological fashion, we would sneer 'weekend punk' at anyone who didn't measure up to our exacting standards: wearing the right clothes, buying the right records or being seen at the right gigs. Steve Redgrave was a full day short of qualifying as a weekend punk.

In May 1977 I 'left home' on a number of occasions to follow The Clash's 'White Riot' tour around the country. These adventures were funded by savings from odd jobs and, of course, Christmas, birthday and pocket money. I even started dealing in second-hand records at school and later, in a particularly enterprising move, selling such bootleg classics as the Sex Pistols' *Spunk*. We got to the gigs on a mix of naivety and bravado. We often hitched and relied heavily on punks in other places for food. We sometimes even managed to grab a sandwich from the band and their entourage. Obviously, there was also a degree of subterfuge involved. In fact, you could say that The Clash taught me to lie convincingly to my parents and, on occasion, to my friends. My entire family was oblivious to what I was up to. I was never gone long enough for them to become suspicious. I was, however, now spending enough time in the band's orbit to be on nodding terms with them.

Joe I'd come to see less as a pedagogical figure and more as a cool older brother. Paul was always the one I most wanted to be like – he seemed street-tough but indefatigably concerned with the welfare of other people. Mick I was less sure of. His sneer was always unsettling. He had no inhibitions about showing his dislike for us juvenile 'weekend punks'. Topper seemed mildly uninterested in either us or the attention he received for being the newest addition to the band. A year later in June 1978 he and a few friends would attend Marlow Fair. It was a few days after the release of '(White Man) In Hammersmith Palais' and he received more than a little attention both from the by then swollen ranks of the Johnny-come-lately 'weekend punks' and the local Teddy Boys. Among the latter was Lurch, the supersized Ted who had made our lives hell for the previous twelve months. When he tried to take on Topper and crew he found his match and was quickly sent away, quiff somewhat bedraggled and crepes muddied. Topper immediately became a hero to Marlow's young punks.

Back in 1977 though, I was having the time of my life. I'd been to Eric's club in Liverpool and the Electric Circus in Manchester. I'd joined in with my fellows and ripped up chairs at the Rainbow in London (an act that we repeated a year later for Siouxsie and the Banshees) and talked my way backstage on numerous occasions to chat with Clash iconographer, filmmaker and Roxy club DJ Don Letts. I even blagged my way, blind drunk, into sleeping on the hotel-room floor of one of the band in Leicester. To this day I've no idea whose room.

In the year that followed I took in a few one-off dates around the country, each time 'leaving home' only to return early the next morning. It was in June, on the 1978 'Clash On Parole' tour, that I decided to bite the bullet and actually run away to follow the band on a permanent basis. The first date was at Aylesbury Friars. I was suitably adorned in The Clash's uniform, wearing white jeans, red military jacket (both embellished with home-sewn zips) and ripped Clash T-shirt. After the gig, one of the hangers-on (who I now realise was Ray Gange who starred in the Clash film *Rude Boy* – although I was studiously indifferent to the ever-present cameras at the time) handed me a button badge giving me backstage access. The dressing room was a whitewashed breezeblock box with mirrors on every wall. The floor was a rubble of beer cans, empty amphetamine wraps and comatose punks. I went straight up to Joe and told him I was coming on the road with the band. He told me to 'piss off 'ome' again. Undaunted,

I turned up the following night at Queen's Hall in Leeds. This time Joe told me I was an idiot. So I spent the night on the floor of Mick's room, along with a horde of stranded fans eking out their own space among the cans, wraps and guitar cases.

This wasn't the greatest fun in the world and the following day I decided to go home. Paul rather sweetly offered his floor for future dates if I decided to continue with the tour. However, by now I'd made the discovery that the romance was better than the reality. My bed at home in Marlow was preferable to Mick Jones's hotel-room floor in Leeds and the illusion of being a part of The Clash's extended family had somehow just dissolved. It had never figured in my fantasy that I would actually have to share the experience with other fans. I was an individual you see. Other people's love affair with The Clash meant nothing to me. The band was the only gang I wanted to be a part of.

The last gang in town

The trustworthiness of these recollections can easily be challenged by questions around accuracy. Furthermore, it could be suggested that, as this 'oral history' was originally written for the *Independent on Sunday* in 2004, some of the events I recall were further shaped for the newspaper's readership. However, the same could be said of all published or broadcast works that draw on autobiographical materials. Certainly the official oral history account, *The Clash*, is as carefully mediated as any of the biographies of the band, whether written by professional fans or former roadies.

Perhaps the most revealing aspect of my account is the evidence of The Clash's habit of offering their hotel-room floors to fans. It is an act that has been alluded to over the years, but it has yet to be explored from the perspective of those fans who actually engaged with the band in this way.[19] To accept the band's generosity as an aspect of their punk credentials would at this time have required the mediation of *the last gang in town* ideology to extend beyond the band to include the fans too. Although this would have authenticated the fan experience through punk's oft-claimed rejection of hierarchy, it would have created a rupture in the punk narrative presented by a media that needed stars to sell papers. The fan experience was less interesting than the object of fandom. As a fan, however, the very rejection of the star system was a huge part of the appeal of *the last gang in town*. To me, The Clash weren't stars but figureheads who represented an egalitarian movement. It was a naïve ideal that would almost inevitably be challenged over time.

My own account suggests an atmosphere of intimidating machismo, with gangs of primarily young men performing punk's anti-social collective identity – not violent, but certainly aggressive and abrasive. Indeed, the fans as a collective seemed to represent the antithesis of my own personal romantic concept of punk. Despite punk's supposed embrace of the outsider, within this gang I felt like the wrong type of outsider. Despite being attracted to what I perceived as punk's egalitarianism, I was acutely aware of my own position in punk's social hierarchies. I was a middle-class kid from a middle-class town who possessed none of the social capital that I read about in the music press each week. Like many of my contemporaries, I was first-generation middle class. My parents, from fiercely working-class North-East England stock, had moved south in an effort to better themselves and provide a brighter future for their family. I found myself caught between the ideologies associated with my family history and the new middle-class views of my own personal experience. In retrospect, The Clash captured this class collision. They embodied the dilemma that existed between the authentic 'real' and the authenticated myth.

In the *Independent* piece I discussed the notion of 'weekend punks', through which participants assessed each other's claims to authenticity through the concept of subcultural commitment. As I have noted, the commitment was judged through a range of means including style, class and, perhaps more significantly, geography. The whole story of punk has been told through bands associated with key industrial cities such as London, Manchester and Newcastle. With the exception of Bromley, the suburbs were omitted from the narrative. Becoming close to The Clash and their fans seemed to accentuate this in my own mind and I became very aware of my Home Counties origins. By not being a London punk I felt I could only be part-time in the eyes of other members of the fan entourage and within the broader narrative of punk, no matter how deep my dedication to The Clash. Ironically, I now realise that most of these seemingly 'authentic' fans who followed the band or posed for the cameras at London's Roxy were also suburban commuter-punks. It was in the suburbs that DIY ideologies were truly able to flourish. Indeed, with the obvious and short-lived exception of Buzzcocks' *Spiral Scratch* EP and their self-promoted Manchester Lesser Free Trade Hall gigs, there is little evidence of that first wave of UK punk performers being particularly averse to the offer of 'new boots and contracts'.[20] As with Buzzcocks, punk's DIY activities would emerge through those punks who were denied the privileges of living in or near London being forced to put on their own gigs in village halls, press up their own records or sell cassettes of their demos.

The acceptance of early punk's suburban life creates a rupture in the accepted capital city, year zero narrative. My home town of Marlow is a satellite of High Wycombe, a place that is steeped in historical significance for punk and post-punk. It was here that Buzzcocks' Howard Devoto and Pete Shelley first saw the Sex Pistols supporting Screaming Lord Sutch at the High Wycombe College of Higher Education union bar on 20 February 1976, and booked them to play the Lesser Free Trade Hall dates in Manchester later that year. Also present at the gig was promoter Ron Watts who booked the band to play his venue, the Nag's Head in High Wycombe, and London's 100 Club, site of the legendary *Punk Festival* held on 20 and 21 September 1976.

High Wycombe's place in the popular narrative of UK punk's formative period is well documented through the impact that the Sex Pistols' gig had on the band's career. What is less well represented is the impact on the crowd. Popularly presented as being a room full of hippies, the audience also featured 'a whole load of David Bowie freaks and Roxy Music freaks'.[21] Watts notes: 'High Wycombe ... had an element of youth that were into the new scene much earlier than elsewhere outside London...'[22] Significantly, most of the Bromley Contingent had yet to see the Sex Pistols live at this stage.

On Thursday 18 November 1976, an unsigned Clash, complete with Joe Strummer sporting newly bleached hair, played a low-key gig at a half-full Nag's Head. Strummer had already played the venue with his previous band, The 101ers, earlier that year. Furthermore, a pre-Strummer Clash had been taken to the Nag's Head by original vocalist Billy Watts, a High Wycombe local. Along with the A&R personnel who made up half of the crowd were *ZigZag* magazine editor Kris Needs (reviewing the gig for *Sounds*); future *GQ* magazine editor Dylan Jones; Folk Devils guitarist Kris Jozajtis, who at this time fronted a band called Death Wish that counted Dylan Jones as their roadie; soon-to-be Killing Joke drummer Paul Furgerson and art student Stephen Jones, who would become a renowned milliner, who both played in art-punk band The Pink Parts at this time; Howard Jones's brothers Roy and Martin, who would later form Red Beat and sign to Killing Joke's label Malicious Damage; and Mark Reilly, singer with 80s group Matt Bianco, who at this time played in a band called The Xtraverts with occasional SEX employee Nigel Martin.[23] A number of these same people had been present at the Sex Pistols' 1976 gig.

Like much of the early punk activity in the suburbs, High Wycombe's contribution became secondary to the totalising narratives of McLaren and Westwood's SEX boutique and the Bromley Contingent. It could be argued, however, that High Wycombe's importance to the suburban punk scene is pivotal. Indeed, by the time I'd decided to follow The Clash, High Wycombe was a renowned site for punk activity. A site that, like much of punk's suburban life, has now been largely written from history.[24]

Time is tight:
a postscript to my adventures with The Clash

In August 2004, after interviewing Paul Simonon and Mick Jones in a private members' bar on Portobello Road in West London, I stayed on with Paul to enjoy a few pints until I had to leave to catch the last train home. I made my excuses and a quick exit. As I reached the door, Paul came running after me with his phone number. 'If you've missed it, give me a call and you can kip at ours.' I felt like I was 14 again – but I went home anyway.

Notes

1. A special screening of the documentary film *The Clash: Westway to the World* took place at the Coronet cinema in Notting Hill, London on 21 September 1999. This was followed by a party for the launch of both the film and the live album *From Here to Eternity* at London's exclusive Cobden Club, also in Notting Hill.
2. It has often been claimed that Mark P.'s statement that 'punk died the day The Clash signed to CBS' can be sourced to *Sniffin' Glue*. In fact, this is an example of punk mythology. According to his quote in John Robb's *Punk Rock: An Oral History* (London: Ebury Press, 2006), he actually said this 'on a TV show' (p. 328). However, it is not entirely clear which TV show this was and no recordings of the interview are known to be in existence.
3. Sarah Thornton, 'Strategies for Reconstructing the Popular Past', *Popular Music* 9.1 (1990), pp. 87–95.
4. Ulf Lindberg, Gestur Gudmundsson, Morten Michelsen and Hans Weisethaunet, *Rock Criticism from the Beginning: Amusers, Bruisers, and Cool-Headed Cruisers* (New York: Peter Lang, 2005).
5. In their book *Writing Culture: The Poetics and Politics of Ethnography* (Oakland, CA: University of California Press, 1986), James Clifford and George E. Marcus explored the boundaries between ethnography and fiction, advocating a self-reflexive approach to writing that acknowledged its role in the creation of 'true fictions' (p. 7). The term 'true fictions' takes into account the fabricated nature of ethnography and acknowledges that the cultures being written about are subject to invention through a narrative that privileges published over unpublished accounts of an event. 'True fictions' allow previously silenced participants with 'new angles of vision and depths of understanding' (p. 9) to write themselves and their experiences into the narrative.
6. Chris Atton, 'Writing about Listening: Alternative Discourses in Rock Journalism', *Popular Music* 28.1 (2009), pp. 53–67.
7. Simon Frith, *Sound Effects: Youth, Leisure, and the Politics of Rock 'n' Roll* (New York: Pantheon, 1981).
8. Atton, 'Writing about Listening'.
9. Ibid.
10. Dick Hebdige, *Subculture: The Meaning of Style* (London: Routledge, 1979).
11. Tony Moon's illustration 'here's a chord, here's another, here's a third, now form a band' was first published in his fanzine *Sideburns* in 1976, and not in *Sniffin' Glue* as is often wrongly stated.
12. This development of DIY is explored in depth in Alistair Gordon's doctoral thesis, 'The Authentic Punk: An Ethnography of DIY Music Ethics', Loughborough University, 2005.

13 Perhaps the most notable punk oral histories are Robb's *Punk Rock*, and Legs McNeil and Gillian McCain, *Please Kill Me: An Oral History of Punk* (London: Little, Brown, 1997).
14 The Clash, *The Clash* (London: Atlantic Books, 2008), back cover matter.
15 Notable biographies of The Clash include Marcus Gray, *The Clash: Return of the Last Gang in Town* (London: Helter Skelter, 2001) and Pat Gilbert, *Passion is a Fashion: The Real Story of The Clash* (London: Aurum Press, 2004). Keith Topping's *The Complete Clash* (Richmond: Reynolds and Hearn, 2003) offers a biography through an analysis of the band's song catalogue, while *A Riot of Our Own: Night and Day with The Clash – and After* (London: Orion, 2003), by former road crew member Johnny Green and long-time fan Garry Barker, presents a privileged insider's view of the band.
16 The Clash, *The Clash*, p. 98.
17 Helen Reddington, *The Lost Women of Rock Music: Female Musicians of the Punk Era* (Aldershot: Ashgate, 2007).
18 'The Beautiful People are Ugly Too' is an outtake from the band's *Combat Rock* sessions and was only available on the bootleg album *Rat Patrol from Fort Bragg*, until it received an official release on the 2013 box-set *Sound System* (Columbia, 2013). A version of this section of this chapter originally ran in the *Independent on Sunday*, 26 September 2004, as part of an interview with Paul Simonon and Mick Jones in support of the 25th anniversary reissue of *London Calling*.
19 Caroline Coon's *1988: The New Wave Punk Rock Explosion* (London: Omnibus Press, 1982) is one of the very few publications to refer to the travelling fans.
20 The Sex Pistols' first Lesser Free Trade Hall gig in Manchester has been the subject of much debate in both the popular music press and academia. Sean Albiez notably challenges the myths of the gig, which is seen as one of Manchester punk's foundational events, becoming a cornerstone of the city's own narrative. As such the authenticity of legend is called into question. See Sean Albiez, 'Print the Truth, Not the Legend. The Sex Pistols: Lesser Free Trade Hall, Manchester, June 4, 1976', in I. Inglis (ed.), *Performance and Popular Music: History, Place and Time* (Abingdon: Ashgate, 2006), pp. 92–106.
21 Author's interview with milliner Stephen Jones who was present.
22 Ron Watts, *Hundred Watts – A Life in Music* (Birmingham: Heroes Publishing, 2006), p. 151.
23 As there is no detailed documentary evidence of the people who actually attended this gig, I have created this list by collating personal interviews with High Wycombe's earliest punks and via a brief interview with the Nag's Head promoter Ron Watts, who sadly passed away in 2016. He suggested that the audience was 50 per cent made up of A&R men, but did concede that the rest were local punks, many of whom, he claimed, had also been part of London's 100 Club scene until punk had been banned from the venue.
24 For further detail on High Wycombe's contribution to the UK punk story see M. James, 'No I don't like where you come from, it's just a satellite of London: High Wycombe, the Sex Pistols and Punk Transformation'. *Punk and Post Punk*, 7.3 (2018), pp. 341–62.

PART III
'It could be anywhere, Most likely could be any frontier, Any hemisphere': The Clash around the world

8
'Up and down the Westway' or 'live by the river'? Britishness, Englishness, London and The Clash

Conrad Brunström

'We weren't little Englanders.'
'War is just around the corner. Johnny hasn't got far to march. That's why he is coming by bus or underground.'

Joe Strummer[1]

The idea of a revolution that needs to be accessible by public transport underpins much of the 'sense of place' revealed by the music of The Clash. Johnny's marching distance is defined by bus routes and relevant tube lines. The ambiguity, both of The Clash's music and Strummer's own commentary on The Clash's music, makes it unclear whether Johnny's march home from the nearest bus stop marks the end or the beginning of violent confrontation. This chapter will consider the ways and means by which a particular version of being a Londoner contributed to The Clash's eclectic global engagements. It will argue that it was their peculiar sensitivity to a very specific sense of place that facilitated their sense of the world at large. In so doing, they stand as the most elegant and relevant challengers to current British Prime Minister Theresa May's notorious claim that 'if you believe you're a citizen of the world, you're a citizen of nowhere'.[2]

Urban life reconfigures time and space in obvious ways. In a major metropolis, physical distance, imagined as the crow flies, becomes irrelevant and people become networked on the basis of lines of communication over which they have little or no control. Even without a coherent transport network, a metropolitan environment creates spaces where people socialise based on shared preferences rather than physical neighbourhoods. This process precedes the Industrial Revolution. A feature of sociability in London, arguably ever since the rebuilding of the city after 1666, has been the proliferation of club culture at the expense of parochial identity, elective rather than geographical identification. This process was captured at its earliest phase by pioneering journalist Ned Ward, whose description of London clubs demonstrates an early and excited recognition of a newly rebuilt and expanding city that is strange to all of its inhabitants, a city in which nobody feels completely at home and in which, by necessary implication, nobody need feel entirely unwelcome.[3] Elective socialisation does not render specific London districts irrelevant or characterless. Far from it. But the specifics of London locality only make sense insofar as unusual lines of communication converge on or radiate from them.

Although The Clash's core (and extended) membership hailed from a variety of places, the specific locality most associated with The Clash is an area of Ladbroke Grove/Notting Hill, close to the Westway, and it is fitting that the most famous graffito associated with the band was daubed on one of its supporting concrete pylons.[4] The Westway marks the eastern extremity of a highway intended to carry cars as far as Oxford and Birmingham, and to invite motorists from far-flung regions to drop in to the inner-city neighbourhood of Marylebone with dramatic abruptness. This chapter will argue that the experiential reality of this environment informs the achievement of The Clash not just thematically or sociopolitically but rhythmically. Dropping in facilitates dropping out.

Notting Hill is not a place inhabited by people who were 'born and bred' there. Ever since the Second World War it has been populated overwhelmingly by incomers.[5] Joe Strummer himself arrived in the area only after the most strange and rootless childhood and adolescence imaginable, becoming part of an elaborate culture of collective squatters' rights and responsibilities. To 'drop out' into a squatter's lifestyle is not to evade responsibility but rather to engage a fresh set of reciprocities based on a structured attempt to make equality of access sustainable. The 101ers, created from this environment, were an eclectic squatters' band, whose experience demonstrated an intense and urgent sense of place.

Up and down the Westway

It is fitting, if confusing, that the Westway, which towers over Ladbroke Grove, is referenced prominently in 'London's Burning', one of the band's earliest signature songs. Strummer's description of it as 'a great traffic system' can only be described as lazily ironic from the perspective of either its users or those who live in its shadow. Strummer's sneering vocals emphasise the obvious untruth that the Westway is an aesthetically exciting highway that accommodates high-speed driving. 'Speeding' on the Westway is not a viable proposition in daylight, and anyone who can think of no better way of spending the night than driving on this stretch of road needs their head (and, perhaps, other parts of their anatomy) examined.

It is only at night that the fantasy of high-speed driving on the Westway could hypothetically be fulfilled. Only if you have no home to go to or no work to come from can you drive at speed on it, and the only thing to do once you have reached the Hanger Lane gyratory system is to turn around and drive back again ('up and down'). The distance between the beginning of the Westway and the first plausible 'turnaround' is a mere seven miles, so assuming that 'speeding' implies driving at least at the speed limit, at most seven minutes of excitement at a time are available. There are also traffic lights on parts of Western Avenue which would have to remain friendly. However, any experiential argument regarding the merits of this form of recreation remains moot so long as neither The Clash, nor their core fanbase, have access to cars.

The song's chorus refers to the tedium of this ludicrous motorised paradise more explicitly, repeating the number 'nine' five times. The addition of two more nines to an emergency phone number offers the suggestion that even the emergency services may be too lethargic these days to pick up. The idea of 'burning with boredom' resonates through a larger corpus of late seventies punk. The quest to make boredom excitement, or rather to celebrate nervous potential energy derived from a frank acknowledgement of boredom, achieves choric authority in 'Bored Teenagers' by The Adverts, as well as Buzzcocks' early single 'Boredom'. The Clash themselves, of course, referenced boredom with titular centrality in 'I'm So Bored with the USA', a song that belatedly and paradoxically functions as a proleptic riposte to Bruce Springsteen's most famous song of the 1980s. The most significant and repeated fact about Janie Jones's would-be lover is that he finds his job boring. To be bored with the United States has more obvious political consequences, however, in the context of global cultural and economic imperialism. The agitprop crudity of the song's verses denouncing Yankee imperialism are redeemed by the frank complicity of the chorus, with the very word 'bored' dragged painfully over three syllables, each initial of USA given a staccato loneliness, and the final admission of incompetence serving to demonstrate that this song is not so much about the USA as the media saturation of American culture and the sense of marginalisation and passivity that this saturation breeds among consumers. (The spacing of the initials may be a felicitous by-product of the fact that the song was originally intended as a more straightforward anti-love song called 'I'm So Bored with YOU').

The Westway is an apt symbol of politicised boredom. Nuzzled under the Westway, an unusable arterial road (certainly for a young, unemployed demographic), The Clash declare that the freedom of the open road – a frankly American cultural import – is both inescapable and impossible at the same time. An American vision of personal liberty is patently ludicrous and overwhelmingly proximate, and The Clash function, quite literally, in its shadow, bored by the USA yet fixated by the Westway. The delicious irony of referencing 'boredom' in the chorus of a song, literally 'climaxing with boredom', represents a defiant rejection of pre-programmed desire, a determination to avoid the tramlines of whatever it is that urban consumer desire is meant to follow. Perhaps the supreme celebration of boredom and consumerism performed in the 1970s is 'Repetition' by The Fall (1979), which takes repetitive chord sequences to the very brink of endurability (and, many would say, beyond). Few emotions are as sincere as 'boredom', and from the point of view of enraging an older generation, few are as effective. To be comprehensively bored is to evade channelling and redirection. From a generational point of view, a posture of consistent boredom represents a statement of defiance against the parental voice offering constructive ways of spending your time. To be bored, in London, meanwhile, following the logic of the Johnsonian maxim, is to assert boredom with life as we know it.

Jon Savage describes North Kensington's desolation thus:

> Notting Hill's radical pretensions and realities both highlighted and masked the real hardship that existed at its outer fringes. In 1975, the areas around Chippenham Road and Elgin Avenue, Freston Road and Lancaster Road were a scrapyard vista. Where there wasn't rubble, there were remnants of Victorian housing stock. Just like parts of Camden Town, most of Docklands, and pre-media Soho, these empty spaces seemed then to embody an emotional truth: this is what England is *really* like.[6]

The 'reality' effect of these neighbourhoods is generated from their deflationary sense of failure. They are 'real' only insofar as more desirable neighbourhoods are 'unreal' – unreal insofar as all advertising is 'unreal'. The inner suburbs, not just of London but of cities around the world, took on an authenticity that developed in direct proportion to official political narratives that insisted that those that the economy really cares about are meant to live elsewhere. (Following the gentrification of inner London in the decades since The Clash's rise and fall, advertising has adjusted itself accordingly, and 'authentic' London is even harder to locate or celebrate.) In the 1970s reality was accessible only by selecting that which best resisted profitable fantasy.

Don Letts's documentary on The Clash, *Westway to the World*, would be equally descriptively titled if the direction of travel were reversed. Letts's film consists of a mixture of original film and the band members themselves talking in a leisurely fashion. Although Letts himself is well aware of the Westway's social significance, no further commentary is made on it in the course of the film. It is understandable that the single most iconic 'Clash' graffito is engraved on this structure. If the Westway verse in 'London's Burning' is intended ironically, the subsequent verse, which describes the kind of environment where Mick Jones grew up with his grandmother, is not. It describes feeling lost in a 'subway', unsure which confusingly similar exit leads to which confusingly similar tower block. This subway refers not (as in American English) to the underground rail network, but rather to an underpass under a road not unlike the A40. Underpasses, piss-stained excuses for pedestrian access, serve to alienate and confuse those forced to use them. Underpasses feature prominently in *A Clockwork Orange* as sites of threatened and actual violence. Morrissey invites and then forecloses a redemptive underpass (where a chance might come at last) in one of his most famous lyrics. In this environment, even the wind (howling because loudly focused between high-rise developments) is without a home. The Westway not only sanctifies the motor car, it stigmatises the pedestrian and, by means of the degradation of the subway, attempts to obliterate the carless from the view of the only people deemed to 'matter' by policy makers.

Thanks in no small part to The Clash, the Westway has achieved iconic status in any discussion of social realism in a popular musical idiom. The Jam posed beneath the Westway for the cover of their second album *This is the Modern World* (1977). Decades later, it was predictable that Blur (those studious magpies) would decide that it was strategically evocative to reference the Westway in no fewer than three of their songs, despite none of them enjoying any biographical connection whatsoever with the A40.[7] Blur sang about the Westway because they understood that referencing it confers a sense of instant social relevance, that it had achieved a kind of iconic resonance within a version of recent London social history.

It is interesting, meanwhile, that punk film-maker Julian Temple has recently made a film about another city, Detroit, with a road scheme that has hollowed out its own inner periphery, while offering a startling glimpse of new forms of life that are improvised in spaces that seem so inhumane that the natural world has already started to reclaim them.[8] Likewise, Edward Platt's *Leadville: A Biography of the A40* (2000) has much to say about those lives that are carved up and confused by a highway that offers a version of the American dream that has not worked especially well even in America.[9] The fascination of the book is the discovery of life where life should not be possible. Just as biologists are compelled by the possibility of life at the bottom of Lake Vostok in Antarctica, so the possibility of life clinging to the A40 between White City and Hanger Lane hardens the conviction of Platt's readers that we cannot possibly be alone in the universe. In the 1970s (or more accurately, in the decade following the partial but fatal collapse of Canning Town's Ronan Point residential tower block in 1968), Le Corbusier ceased to be Imaginer-in-Chief of the vertical, motorised city and was replaced by J. G. Ballard. The effect of these great arterial roads (the very term 'arterial' anticipates the medical metaphor of congestion that such roads seem inevitably to provoke) is to divide and separate and reconfigure time and space in new ways. Any etymological connection between Ballard's 1973 novel *Crash* and a band formed three years later called The Clash, geographically indebted to a dystopian road project, cannot, alas, be proved.

The A40 purports to join London to Oxford, but it meanwhile separates East Acton from West Acton. The Westway and Western Avenue create wastelands that are still, inexplicably, habitats. Platt's book describes how house-proud pensioners, surprisingly conservative squatters, the angry, the acquiescent and the bewildered all live cheek by jowl. *Leadville* covers a period in the mid-1990s when 'The Avenue' (itself a peculiarly suburban and arboreal term for a concrete gridlock) was to be destroyed so as to extend the Westway's broad disengagement from pedestrian life. With a change of government in 1997, this project (and road-widening in general) was abandoned, leaving the author with a sense of anxiety over the inability of officialdom to acknowledge any sense of monumental (or human) waste associated with this project.

The narrator of the book is virtually carless. His car withers and dies as his exploration of the road progresses. Many of the residents of Western Avenue are carless too, but like many Londoners they are defined by traffic that they have no personal stake in. A sense of oppressive and polluted heat pervades this book, which treats the paradoxes of utopian suburbanism:

> Who could carve a lonely enclave out of a foreign world – and contrive within it a self-contained landscape – if so uncompromising a reminder of the outer world's foreignness as an arterial highway tore noisily through the midst of it?[10]

The elevated section, the 'Westway' itself, was constructed between 1964 and 1970, exactly contemporary with the Labour government and its buoyant technocratic agenda, and it represented the greatest single investment of concrete ever committed to a UK construction project up to that time. Its impact on nearby neighbourhoods has been incalculable, changing forever not merely a section of London, but how London regarded itself in terms of a wider world. The Westway leads, indirectly, not merely to the outer suburbs, but to Heathrow Airport and the possibility of transcending the London/England/Britain tension of overlapping identities altogether. For Londoners, the gestural inflection of any kind of escape is always westward, a function of any city in which the prevailing winds blow from west to east, making the west side more desirable as its air is relatively uninfected by urban fumes.

The Sex Pistols, who converged on the King's Road from North London and Shepherd's Bush, did not experience the same brutal imposition of a traffic scheme upon their neighbourhoods. A large part of the success of the Pistols consisted of the collaboration of intellectual pretension with working-class menace, and its two indispensable ingredients, John Lydon and Steve Jones, embodied this necessary alliance. The shop at 430 King's Road owned by Malcolm McLaren and Vivienne Westwood where they converged was a stone's throw from the World's End pub, itself a chauvinist joke about the Johnsonian notion that the last house in London is the last house in a world worth knowing about. While the World's End has not marked the western edge of London for centuries, it continues to mark the western extremity of a version of inner London, and has been, for some years, the name of the shop previously called, *inter alia*, Let it Rock, SEX and Seditionaries.

The home turf of their biggest rivals was also the setting for the supermarket in which The Clash would feel ill at ease. The song expresses a yearning for a home that was not a home. The narrator was not so much born as 'fell out' and 'falling/dropping' is a rhythmic as well as a sociopolitical leitmotif for The Clash. The narrator has no point of origin other than a falling motion that has never stopped. The supermarket seems to represent the commodification of identity, as well as a bewildering environment in which it is easy to get lost. No longer a happy shopper, the supermarket only further confuses any idea of belonging. The Clash, unlike the Pistols, were never tied to any particular shop. The suburbs 'back home' which offered, in the 1970s, the dominant official narrative of homeliness suggest a suffocating version of the *heimlich* in which cosiness becomes claustrophobia and privacy becomes a prison. 'Home' is not back in the suburbs, but the suburbs still claim a monopoly of representation when it comes to 'homeliness' – a quality that England likes to claim but that inner London repudiates.

'Something about England': London, England and Britain.

London is a city that mediates ideas of England and Britain. Although, since 2016, Britain has been a nation *sous rature*, awaiting its own ignominious dissolution while failing (or refusing) to make any positive case for any community of constituent nations, for many in London in the 1970s (and subsequently), 'Britain' and 'British' seemed preferable adjectives to 'England' and 'English' – terms that are too ethnically exclusive to embrace. 'Britain' appeared at least to affirm a civic identity, and as a consequence immigrant communities in London traditionally championed their right to be regarded as British rather than English.[11] The choice to use 'England' rather than 'Britain' is instructive, even (or perhaps especially) when it seems most careless. The practice of using 'England' and 'Britain' interchangeably remains prevalent, yet this interchangeability cannot efface the differences of emphasis that such choices reveal.

Billy Bragg, who has long championed a form of inclusive English nationalism, hails, revealingly, from further afield, the *locus classicus* of Barking, which usually defines itself as Essex rather than London. For people growing up in an inner London suburb, 'England' can feel like an alien country. If there 'ain't no black in the Union Jack', then the St George's cross feels like a standard of albino whiteness. The image of the St George's cross with a white transit van parked nearby proved a critical and prescient signifier of supposedly alienated 'whiteness' during the Rochester by-election campaign of 2014 and throughout the subsequent UK general election campaign of the following year. It is notable, however, that The Clash reference 'England' and 'English' far more often and more prominently than they do 'Britain' and 'British'. This preference does not, however, imply secure ethnic affiliation (certainly not from Strummer, born in Ankara to a Scottish mother), since the 'Englands' referred to are generally distant, estranged and/or unattainable. Indeed, The Clash's London rejects both 'Britain' and 'England' as stable identities.

Although a very multi-ethnic community huddles beneath it, the Westway is the ultimate symbol of an attempt to make London accessible to a stereotypical version of Little Englishness. Those who have to work in London but wish to live in homogeneously white, affluent and spacious housing developments were to imagine themselves speeding down the A40 and dropping in on the city centre without the enforced heterogeneity that public transport enforces. It offers a London for people who hate London.

It is notable that a song such as 'Something about England' emerged on the conspicuously internationalist triple album *Sandinista!* (1980), in which England appears not as home turf so much as one failed state among many. It is a title that suggests a scornful afterthought, a recognition of a point of origin that now seems arbitrary. The production exposes Strummer's vocals awkwardly against a piano accompaniment, while guitars are kept far in the distance, as though recorded in a different country and phoned in to the studio barely amplified. This is a recording that is all about an idea of distance and estrangement.

The song offers a reminder that one of the chief influences on the design of modern London was Hermann Goering, and that uneven post-war redevelopment betrays its debt to a world war even when (especially when) it seeks to efface it. As The Clash explored history as well as geography, time as well as space, it was clear to them that the effort of post-war rebuilding involved leaving certain people behind. The song evokes a war veteran who grew up in the shadow of the First World War and songs such as 'It's a Long Way to Tipperary', which references Piccadilly and Leicester Square. The inhuman architects of the post-war world have hollowed out familiar urban spaces in order to privilege a profitably bourgeois and expansionist suburbia. The two wars fuse together in the muddled and traumatised imagination of a person born between the wars, one of which destroyed a generation and the other of which destroyed a city.

Geography is not, of course, destiny. Political attitudes are not predetermined by postcodes. However, social commentary is never more powerful than when it is *detailed* social commentary, and the more localised the observation, the more potent the detail. It was the genius of The Clash, and Joe Strummer in particular, to examine how a particular kind of paradoxical urban deracination can command a peculiar and authentic lyrical and rhythmic authority. The white man in Hammersmith Palais is, and is not, at home – just as every thoughtful Londoner is intoxicated and appalled by the cityscape that they only half-willingly inhabit. All Londoners are dislocated yet curious – 'looking for fun'. 'Fun' itself, defined as a state of relaxed exhilaration, is a thoroughly politicised commodity and access to it is strictly controlled in most urban environments. Nowhere is the fearful quest for fun more dramatically and politically staged than in the context of carnival.

'Looking for fun...': The Clash and reggae

The relationship between The Clash and reggae, and with London reggae's appropriation of Notting Hill on an annual basis (reinforced by Strummer and Simonon's participation in the Notting Hill riots of 1976), is illustrative of how the instrumental technique of 'dropping out' showcases empty spaces, places where individual instruments and voices are left stranded, with particular words and phrases framed by pockets of reverberative silence. The 101ers, and thereby Joe Strummer, and thereby The Clash, therefore grew up out of the experience of 'dropping out' of conventional employment and residency into a squatting culture that just happened to be dominated by the eastern end of a great road that drops down into London, a neighbourhood that is, absolutely not coincidentally, saturated with reggae music. As Don Letts remarked, in a *vox pop* in Julian Temple's film *Joe Strummer: The Future is Unwritten*, all white bands draw inspiration from black artists, but 'Strummer and Jones were inspired by people who live next door'.

In an eloquent rhapsody on dub published in 2003 by Greg Burk in *LA Weekly*, the point is made that there is an alternate African-Caribbean understanding of postmodernity in which reconfigurations of space and time are accomplished at a rhythmic level. Dub, more than any other musical movement, was concerned with the technological possibilities of loneliness and deracination:

> Jamaican dub is more subversive than Burroughs or Derrida because it's more populist: The huge bass – designed for irresistible dance action via monster sound systems – goes straight for the body. No PhD required [...] In dub, the bass (the base, the foundation) is you, the only permanence that matters. Drums, guitars, horns and keyboards may rise and fall or drop out of the mix suddenly and completely in a starburst of against-the-beat echo, but the bass almost always keeps playing its riff, just as you try to do in a world of uncertainty.[12]

The moment of loneliness when everything except the bass line has been stripped away, the sense of being reduced to a chilling core identity (consider the constant referencing of 'bones' in the world of dub), is central to the vulnerable yearnings of the Strummer persona throughout '(White Man) In Hammersmith Palais'. Equally lonely is 'Complete Control', a song as mythologised as anything The Clash ever produced. The first guitar solo, coming after 'even over this song', is meant to sound as though it has been imposed as an obligatory feature of an established rock'n'roll song, and succeeds both on its own terms and as an ironic commentary on the song, with Strummer mockingly applauding Mick Jones as a 'guitar hero' in what may be the first recorded usage of this term. The second solo, following 'lemme see your other hand!', exhibits far more of Lee Perry's fingerprints, its resonant echoes allowing a glimpse of proximate void.

When Joe Strummer announces himself in the song as 'Joe Public', a very public crisis of identity is being broadcast. 'Joe Public' is not some embodiment of the General Will that bubbles up spontaneously from the streets. 'Joe Public' is an abstraction that is invoked in lazy journalese, usually in the context of what 'Joe Public' will and will not put up with. It's a label that implies predetermination. The inherent challenge facing any performers who gain global recognition involves the fact that they are cut off from their original constituency. The ability to sing to the world at large seems at odds with having anything specific and relevant to sing about. As Paul Simonon recalls in Don Letts's film, with disarming honesty, talking to Joe Strummer after their CBS signing: 'We can't sing about career opportunities any more 'cos ... we've now got some cash y'know.' Unwilling either to retreat into apolitical mysticism or fake a street-level existence they could never again 'enjoy', the medium and the message of a politicised rock band had never been more estranged.

What saved The Clash from political oblivion was the fact that their radicalism had *always* been tangential and slightly second hand, in part because they had inhabited a very real urban territory in which a degree of deracination was the norm rather than the exception. Despite its apparent simplicity, 'White Riot' is work of self-aware cultural cringe, in which the defiant community spirit evidenced by Rastas at the 1976 Notting Hill riots is co-opted in an attempt to provide a basis of emulation, given some hypothetical and uncertain reaffiliation. The Clash were never the voice of a specific, definable community, ready to fight their own battles. At their most successful, they were about a confusion of communities and a constituency of disaffected urban youths uncertain as to which proximate battle was most urgent and authentic.

The persistence of reggae cadences in The Clash's work would prove instrumental in the sacking of Topper Headon, which occurred as a result of Joe Strummer determining that a 'rocksteady' beat was essential to whatever definition of The Clash was worth preserving. As Strummer himself observed: 'maybe you can play the saxophone when you're on heroin, but not the drums'. The Clash's reggae-cadenced preoccupations, critical to the identity of the band from its inception, could not be sustained by a drummer who floated free of the disciplines that reggae demands.

The notion of intersectional solidarity expressed musically is, of course, highly contested. In a somewhat gloomy article published in *Social and Economic Studies* entitled 'Babylon Makes the Rules', Mike Alleyne declares: 'As reggae artists continually cross borders between organic eclecticism and overt commercialisation, critical consideration must be given to the extent to which textual integrity and cultural specificity are compromised or lost in alternative relation to the economic and creative gains of interfacing with wider audiences.'[13] Alleyne threatens at times to out-Adorno Adorno in his insistence that moving into a mainstream inevitably involves sacrificing integrity. Adorno proclaims that:

> The assent to hit songs and debased cultural goods belongs to the same complex of symptoms as do those faces of which one no longer knows whether the film has alienated them from reality or reality has alienated them from the film, as they wrench open a great formless mouth with shining teeth in a voracious smile, which the tired eyes are wretched and lost above. Together with sport and film, mass music and the new listening help to make escape from the whole infantile milieu impossible.[14]

According to Alleyne's analysis, for any music to be heard in a wider world controlled by global capitalism, compromises amounting to dilution must be made, and for 'otherwise marginal music' to be true to itself, it must (presumably) remain marginal. Alleyne's conclusion is as despondent as his introduction: 'Much evidence points to a critical imbalance in the negotiation process, whereby the overriding factor of capital generation operates disjunctively with artistic creativity, imposing pressures on the text which must in some way accommodate these transformative forces to gain access to discourse with an audience.'[15] What Alleyne's thesis requires in order to fully enclose its pessimism in detailed empirical terms is a discussion of how precisely the original strength of reggae's truth claims are compromised by commodification, the qualitative and formal changes that are imposed, and precisely why these impositions are deemed commercially necessary.[16]

Alleyne's pessimistic analysis makes considerable sense when applied to his specific example of Chris Blackwell's reproduction of Bob Marley, but is less relevant, perhaps, to the mainstreaming of reggae cadences as a result of the global success of The Clash. It is possible to retain a sense of place ('cultural specificity') and interface with wider audiences if you can exploit the fact that cultural specificity can include a global vision that is implicit in the dynamics of local geography. The Clash did not have to escape West London in order to conquer the world – they merely had to unlock the global politics that were already concentrated in West London. The Clash were able to reject the notion of having to choose between local authenticity and global fame, insisting that to express the truth of a locality necessitates an understanding of the global forces that determine the lived conditions of bounded and intimate human conditions.

'I come from a long way away': The Clash far from home

The Clash's ability to comment on such varied international struggles was no chameleon quality and did not evidence either the wish or the ability to dissolve into any given situation. James Peacock has recently described the narrator of 'Red Angel Dragnet' thus:

> From his privileged dialectical position – a long way away yet critically engaged in affairs – the protagonist can credit himself with a certain perspicacity; to paraphrase, he knows a fine thing when he sees it. This perspicacity is enabled partly by the geographical distance of the cosmopolitan and partly by the ironic distance surely evident in 'fine thing', which puts one in mind of the exasperated phrase 'chance would be a fine thing' and implies that the subject matter of the song must be treated with ambivalence.[17]

Peacock is able to reference Julia Kristeva in support of the value of 'the stranger' in terms of social structuration (and he might well have referenced also the much earlier work of Georg Simmel).[18] The ambivalent gaze of the stranger has the effect of legitimating a version of critical authority for The Clash, and a further *verfremdungseffekt*[19] is achieved by showcasing the unfamiliar vocals of Paul Simonon on this track, which offers a commentary on the 'Guardian Angels', volunteers who offered protection to passengers on the New York subway network. I would expand Peacock's already complex reading of this song by suggesting that its perspective derives from a faraway city which is itself embedded with strangeness and distance, exemplified above all by the northern edge of Notting Hill, where homes (squats?) are improvised and nobody feels 'naturally' at home. This is not merely a commentary on one city from another, but a commentary on urban strangeness in a transatlantic context. The stranger lives among us, but sooner or later the stranger is all of us, even when we think we're on home turf.

This strangeness is reinforced by 'First Night Back in London' (1982), issued as a B-side to 'Know Your Rights'. Seventeen months after *Sandinista!*, with its wide-ranging canvas of overlapping international concerns, this record offers a homecoming that is no homecoming – a recognition that the persecutions that the band have charted across the world are waiting for them back 'home'. London defines but does not delimit The Clash, and within hours of a traumatic taxi ride, Strummer is phoning Heathrow Airport to inquire about stand-by tickets to Borneo.

The Clash were a globalist band but rooted in a particular time and space, a time and space which, in turn, staged a version of rootlessness symbolised by the shadow of the Westway, itself not so much an authentic biographical point of origin as a convenient marker, a marker which not coincidentally divides communities more than it defines them. The political intelligence of the band consisted not merely of social realist lyrics, but in a commitment to rhythmic unorthodoxies that made 'dropping out' something more than a lifestyle choice and instead a larger reflection on lives lived without choice. It is notable that the most famous single image associated with The Clash – the *London Calling* cover photograph of Paul Simonon smashing his bass guitar – was taken by Pennie Smith not in London but in New York. London calling to New York is also New York calling to London. Between 1999 and 2002 Strummer would introduce personal playlists on the BBC World Service using the same phrase: 'London Calling'. The song and album title itself evokes, of course, the wartime broadcasts from Berlin by William Joyce (better known as Lord Haw Haw) that were introduced with the repeated phrase 'Germany Calling ... Germany Calling'. Joyce's broadcasts were delivered in an almost absurdly deliberate and exaggeratedly aristocratic English accent, an irony further complicated by the fact that Joyce was an Irishman born in New York, an Irishman who left Ireland during the War of Independence as a teenager when his vocal support for the Black and Tans had made him the likely target of IRA retribution. A street-fighting fascist thug (a sort of Lilliputian Ernst Röhm to Oswald Mosley's Lilliputian Hitler), the legality of Joyce's subsequent trial and execution for 'treason' hung on the dubious circumstance of his having applied for a British passport. William Joyce is a figure who represents a kind of super-inflation of identity politics based (paradoxically but not atypically) on fractured identity. As Mary Kenny has noted, Joyce's 'Englishness' was a very careful and deliberate effort of self-fashioning.[20] He also stands as a reminder that Nazism cannot be safely 'othered' as a Germanic aberration, but can stand as the grimly logical destination of a version of willed and excessive Englishness. The fact that Strummer's elder brother embraced fascism shortly before committing suicide gives this 'Joycean' allusion a particularly personal resonance.

If 'Germany Calling' is from Berlin but *for* Britain, it makes sense that 'London Calling' is from London but *for* the rest of the world, albeit delivering an anti-fascist worldview. Just three years separate 'London's Burning' from London's drowning. The detumescence of the song, with its anti-clarion call of 'don't look to us', is epimethean in its declaration of 'the fire last time'. Beatlemania is evoked and dismissed as a moribund fake, and the only 'swinging' going on in any attempt to rebrand 'Swinging London' is that of a police truncheon. London calls to faraway towns, but calls in a state of bedraggled pain and impotence, in a way that evokes William Joyce's final drunken *Götterdämmerung* of a Berlin broadcast.

In a detailed discussion of the musical sophistication of the *London Calling* album, which treats it in its totality as a coherent 'concept album' (to use a despised term), Matthew Gelbart describes the detailed effects that the title track provokes:

> The music begins with an aggressive beat that is completely even (no stressed back beats): a clear march topos. But given the larger ambivalence it is entirely unclear who is marching in this dystopia. It may be the zombies, or it may be the police with their 'truncheon thing'. On the other hand, it may be the band's own personae and their followers reacting against the bleak situation. The mood continues as the song ends in a state of tension as well. Not only does Strummer cut off ambiguously mid-sentence (it is unclear what he is even saying, perhaps 'I never felt so much like…'), but the song also ends with a bleeping Fit that resembles a Morse code S-O-S, calling out in ominous dissonance over the tonic E minor chord (extending an earlier gesture: a ringing dissonant high F# on the guitar at the end of the second chorus, 1:52–4). The modification of this guitar sound to resemble a radio signal in the final seconds of the song ties into the song title's BBC World Service radio call reference; but more importantly it leaves a profoundly uneasy feeling: the song is all problem and no solution.[21]

This bleak assertion of impotence has not prevented the appropriation of the song by mainstream entertainment media to denote any film or television programme set in London, always to evoke a sense that London is somehow 'cool' or 'exciting'. The urgency of guitar chords communicates faster than Joe Strummer's lyrics.[22] Just as Jamie Reid's designs for 'God Save the Queen' have become tamed over time to the point of becoming a variant flag instead of a vandalised flag, so a song about London's creative as well as physical destruction has merely added to the soundtrack of the commodification of London's cultural capital.

A central orthodoxy, not merely of The Clash's story but of the story of punk rock, and perhaps the story of rock'n'roll at its most urgent, is the notion that annihilation is preferable to commodification. The end of the 1970s was marked by a prevalent panic about London flooding, contemporary with the building of the flood barrier downstream. Schools within the flood zone held emergency drills and maps were distributed indicating the areas of London likely to be suddenly inundated in the event of the wrong kind of high tide.[23] Estimates were circulated of the potential fatalities and the economic cost of a great London flood. It is not an exaggeration to say that imminent flooding came second only to full-scale nuclear apocalypse in the list of sudden forms of annihilation that haunted Londoners between 1974 and 1984, the decade of the Thames barrier's construction, as well as the decade that approximates to the creative existence of The Clash. To 'live by the river' without fear is, logically, to embrace a swift demise in preference to a long-drawn-out struggle for survival, in the same way that in the event of a full-scale nuclear war, London would be a useful place to embrace vaporisation rather than have to undergo months or years of agonising existence in an irradiated wasteland.

Afterword: you can't live in a home that should not have been built

Mick Jones sings lead vocals on 'Up in Heaven (Not Only Here)'. Jones's own experience of high-rise living informs the band's sense of empathy for those whose prescribed housing forms part of a grand plan over which they have no control. Since the first draft of this essay was completed, a further shadow has fallen across the Westway. The blackened shell of Grenfell Tower dominates the landscape that gave birth to The 101ers and the poet activist we know as 'Joe Strummer'. Its unique and haunting profile is visible across a great swathe of inner West London. A decisive and irrefutable marker of the tragic price of social exclusion, it commemorates people who were incinerated in part because of government cutbacks to the legal aid budget, depriving them of the ability to force Westminster Council to act on tenants' fire safety concerns. The view from the Westway now is an incandescent reminder of The Clash's clarion call to ensure that ordinary people 'know their rights'.

Notes

1 Quotations from *Westway to the World* (dir. Don Letts, 2000).
2 *The Telegraph*, 5 October 2016, http://www.telegraph.co.uk/news/2016/10/05/theresa-mays-conference-speech-in-full/ (accessed 12 August 2017).
3 Ned Ward, *The Secret History of Clubs* (London, 1709). For a discussion of the sociological significance of Ward, see Tanya Cassidy '"People, Place, and Performance": Theoretically Revisiting Mother Clap's Molly House', in Christopher Mounsey and Caroline Gonda (eds), *Queer People: Negotiations and Expressions of Homosexuality 1700–1800* (Lewisburg, PA: Bucknell University Press, 2007), pp. 99–113.

4 Listed as one of the ten most memorable examples of London graffiti by Tom Bolton in *The Londonist*, 7 January 2015, https://londonist.com/2015/01/10-london-graffiti-slogans-from-the-last-50-years (accessed 14 August 2017).
5 For a discussion of the threatening fascination of Notting Hill, focusing on the notorious Rillington Place murders, see Frank Mort, 'Scandalous Events: Metropolitan Culture and Moral Change in Post-Second World War London', *Representations* 93.1 (2006), pp. 106–37.
6 Jon Savage, *England's Dreaming: Sex Pistols and Punk Rock* (London: Faber and Faber, 1991), p. 112.
7 'For Tomorrow' (1993), 'Fool's Day' (2010) and the rather more obvious 'Under the Westway' (2012).
8 Julian Temple (dir), *Requiem for Detroit* (Films of Record, 2010).
9 Edward Platt, *Leadville: A Biography of the A40* (London: Picador, 2000).
10 The architectural critic J. M. Richards, quoted in ibid., p. 176.
11 A 2013 survey by the University of Manchester confirms the persistence of this tendency for non-white correspondents in England to identify as 'British' rather than 'English', https://www.ethnicity.ac.uk/medialibrary/briefingsupdated/who-feels-british.pdf (accessed 12 July 2017).
12 Greg Burk, 'Dub', *LA Weekly*, 30 October 2003.
13 Mike Alleyne, '"Babylon Makes the Rules": The Politics of Reggae Crossover', *Social and Economic Studies* 47.1 (1998), p. 66.
14 Theodor Adorno, 'On the Fetish-Character in Music and the Regression of Listening', in Andrew Arato and Eike Gephardt (eds), *The Essential Frankfurt School Reader* (New York: Continuum, 1985), pp. 286–7.
15 Alleyne, 'Babylon Makes the Rules', p. 77.
16 In a footnote to an article on Adorno's refusal to elevate any form of jazz to the status of serious music, Theodore Graycyk remarks: 'Ironically, Adorno's charges have found their way into the lyrics of rock music, including such hit songs as The Byrds' "So You Want to be a Rock 'n' Roll Star" (1967), and punk/new wave songs of The Sex Pistols, "EMI" (1977), The Clash, "White Man in Hammersmith Palais" (1978), and Elvis Costello (Declan McManus), "Radio Radio" (1978).' Theodore A. Grayck, 'Adorno, Jazz, and the Aesthetics of Popular Music', *The Musical Quarterly* 76.4 (1992), p. 541.
17 James Peacock, 'From a Long Way Away: New York and London in The Clash's "Red Angel Dragnet"', in Samuel Cohen and James Peacock (eds), *The Clash Takes on the World: Transnational Perspectives on the Only Band that Matters* (London: Bloomsbury, 2017), p. 193.
18 Julia Kristeva, *Strangers to Ourselves* (New York: Columbia University Press, 1991); Georg Simmel, 'The Stranger', in *On Individuality and Social Forms*, ed. Donald Levine (Chicago: University of Chicago Press, 1971).
19 The Brechtian distancing effect.
20 Mary Kenny, 'Lord Haw Haw', *History Ireland* 18.2 (2010), pp. 8–9.
21 Matthew Gelbart, 'A Cohesive Shambles: The Clash's "London Calling" and the Normalization of Punk', *Music & Letters* 92.2 (2011), p. 253.
22 Note, for example, the hit television series *Friends* ('The One with Ross's Wedding', 1998). This appropriation occurred during the early years of the Tony Blair premiership, the honeymoon period of so-called 'Cool Britannia'.

23 'An important characteristic of British floods is that potential warning time is very short, compared, say, with continental Europe or most of the USA and Australia.' Edward C. Penning-Rowsell and John W. Handmer, 'Flood Hazard Management in Britain: A Changing Scene', *The Geographical Journal* 154.2 (1988), p. 215.

9

'Cashing in the bill of rights'? The Clash in New York, in myth and reality

Harry Browne

This essay begins not with a song or a concert but with a book – and not just any book, but *Route 19 Revisited*, Marcus Gray's doorstopping study of the production of *London Calling*, a classic for completists, aptly described by another writer as 'exhaustive/exhausting'.[1] The book's title is, it seems to me, an irresistibly and quite wonderfully clever take on studying the album's intersecting relationships with London and the United States of Americana. Route 19 is, you see, the bus route that is evoked in the opening 'pre-lyric' of 'Rudie Can't Fail', the cross-London journey along which, Gray argues, much of the (nineteen-track!) *London Calling* was conceived and produced. But the number 19 is also (wait for it) an inversion of the number 61, as in the title of perhaps the greatest and most deep-down American Bob Dylan album of them all, *Highway 61 Revisited* – itself a reflection upon, and radical revision of, the whole idea of roots music, named for the road that runs for 1,400 miles near the Mississippi River from Minnesota to New Orleans. In his album's title song, Dylan casts Highway 61 in the role of, as it were, the route of all evil.

As is well known, the cover art of *London Calling* is itself a revisionist take on another roots-ripping American classic, Elvis Presley's eponymous debut album, with the pink and green cutout-style lettering running down the left and across the bottom of the sleeve. The British edition of Gray's book, published in 2009, beautifully apes the album's cover on its own dust-jacket. (Sadly the 2010 US edition opts only for a grim evocation of 1970s London on its cover.) Not only is the British edition's title in those familiar cutout capital letters – 'Route 19' in pink down the left, 'Revisited' in green across the bottom – but there's a stunning monochrome image of the band in onstage action bleeding out to blackness at the cover's edges. This time, unlike on the record sleeve, there's no Paul Simonon, bass-smashing or otherwise, to be seen in the photo – just Mick Jones in soft-focus and mid-air, about to thrash a chord, his back to the camera, and Joe Strummer deep in shut-eyed singing, clutching his microphone stand, his back to the audience. Photographed, the flap tells us, by Chris Walter, this is a perfect, near-abstract image of the two men, Mick all in white, possessed by guitar heroics; Joe in shades of grey, possessed by words. The audience is dark, but close, and you can make out some faces, young, absorbed, with no consensus about where precisely they should be looking at The Clash in full flight. Just beside Joe's right hand in the foreshortened perspective, one long-haired guy is looking out of the frame, presumably at Paul or Topper Headon; beside him a taller guy, his face bisected in the shot by the mic-stand, seems to be sizing up Joe. Caught in one of the greatest pictures ever taken of one of the greatest bands ever to play, these guys – and the following fact, for me, transcends the thousands of other facts contained in the book – are two of my closest high-school friends, Mark Malfa and Eugene Sobczak, of Paterson, New Jersey.

The book doesn't indicate a venue or date for the photograph. My first guess was Bond's in New York's Times Square in the summer of 1981, but Gray's book concerns *London Calling*, so perhaps 1981 wouldn't be right; and sure enough the photographer's website captions the photo as simply 'The Clash 1980'.[2] That meant that the photo, in order to include my pals, could only have been taken at our musical home-from-home, the Capitol Theater in Passaic, New Jersey. Incredibly, there is a nearly full video available online of the 8 March 1980 gig at the Capitol.[3] The visual quality is not especially good, but there is no doubt: these are the outfits and the stage set-up, this is the show from the photo. To quote Strummer and Jones: *Yes, I was there too* (we'll get to how much of what they said is true in due course). Somewhere there in the darkness behind Joe, it was my first Clash gig, though far from my first time at the Capitol – my friends and I, all age 16, were expert at securing good tickets at the 3,000-seat (barely) converted cinema, which was about four miles from my home, about three miles from where New Jersey's own (yes) Route 19 meets the Garden State Parkway. All along these highways and another ten miles or so into New York City, we were in fact good at securing tickets everywhere, including, armed with our fake IDs, drinking New York venues such as Bond's; our trailing gang of less plausibly grown-up kid brothers were treated by The Clash to alcohol-free matinees during that legendary 1981 stand at Bond's, and ended up dancing on the stage.

Still, if we – white ethnic, mostly working-class, male adolescents from unhip fringes of the New York and New Jersey area – were there, in Passaic, Times Square, Asbury Park, Pier 84, Shea Stadium, where was *there*, precisely, in our story and the story of The Clash? While we were watching, how was the rather generic, albeit brilliant, Americana of 'I Fought the Law' and *London Calling* transformed over the course of 1980 and 1981 into the very specifically urban, New York-focused concerns and musical influences of *Sandinista!* and *Combat Rock*? And how did The Clash's relationship with the US, and particularly with the likes of us in the audience, intersect with the (increasingly racialised) politics of authenticity, on both sides of the Atlantic – a politics that had been crucial to the identity of punk and of The Clash in particular?

American dreams

The story of the Americanising of The Clash has been told before, of course. There is an English punk version of the story that finds it quite reprehensible, whereby The Clash signing to CBS is a greater transgression of the punk ethos than the Sex Pistols on EMI, because the former involved national as well as cultural treachery. For the most part, though, the band's expansionary westward development up to and including *London Calling* meets with approval from British writers and critics, at least in retrospect, with allowances made for the sonic wrong-turn of *Give 'Em Enough Rope*. There is no such consensus about what happened thereafter, with a critique of The Clash's 'selling-out' to US concerns and values looming large in many contemporary and historical accounts from Britain; anglocentric and punko-centric accounts regard America as the place The Clash went to fade into irrelevance or worse, with perhaps a nod (or headshake) to the legendary chaos of that two-week 1981 stint at Bond's. Like the pre-Pepper Beatles and the Pistols before them, The Clash, in this account, died on the American stage – with Shea Stadium perhaps the historically freighted sepulchre. Meanwhile, the US-based literature on the subject tends to continue to indulge in familiar wide-eyed wonder that The Clash, and Joe Strummer especially, deigned to grace the United States with their divine presence – with the only regret being that we could not, at that dawn of Reagan time, supply these gods of rock radicalism with a more cool, diverse and politically engaged audience at their concerts.

'British music lovers don't like abandonment', writes Sean Egan.[4] In his perceptive and comprehensive book on The Clash's recorded output, that author, a rock journalist of particularly long standing and distinction, both wryly dissects and unintentionally embodies the disdain of British audiences and critics for the changes wrought on the band by US influences. Having noted that from early in their career the London 'music papers adopted the pious role of Jiminy Cricket to The Clash's supposedly wayward Pinocchio',[5] Egan proceeds to heap both piety and retrospective condescension on The Clash's inability to withstand the temptations of American lush-life. 'I Fought the Law', for example, partook of a mere 'stylized rock 'n' roll bad boy aura' – didn't Jiminy warn Pinocchio about those bad boys? – and was 'a crossover with the Americana supposedly anathema to them ... the perfect example of a process which, though perhaps inevitable, unavoidably had the smack of compromise'.[6] Egan even criticises the band's decision to lead off the *Cost of Living* EP with the track. Contrast that with American writer and musician P. Merriam Clark's take on the recording: it's the 'one Clash song that captures the punk energy of 1977–78 while fitting into the "eclectic Americana" category of 1979–80'. He adds: '"I Fought The Law", with its rockabilly feel, rebellious lyric, and infectious melody, may be the quintessential Clash song.'[7] For many US listeners of my generation it was the first Clash song we heard, exploding from our radios early in 1979, and retains that quintessential status.

But how, in any case, had Joe Strummer, previously nicknamed 'Woody' and the leader of an R&B pub-rock band, The 101ers, ended up fronting an ensemble whose core fans regarded 'American' as dirty, anathema or at least 'compromised'? Clearly The Clash had laid down a marker with 'I'm So Bored with the USA', and among the English punks of 1976–78 there was rarely much discussion of the recent origins of their musical scene in New York's East Village. The punks eschewed the devotion to obviously American sounds that had characterised the likes of The 101ers. (Caribbean sounds soon became, of course, a different story.) The US was seen as embodying the slick, the soft, the packaged, the fake, qualities that the punks rejected. When The Clash managed to put together their first tour of the States early in 1979, they provocatively – and with typical punky devotion to transgressive echoes of the Second World War – called the tour 'Pearl Harbour'. Suggesting that they had come not to bring peace but rather Japanese attack aircraft, this was scarcely a warm affirmation of the Special Relationship. At the very least, it might be regarded as passive-aggressive.

They were not entirely new to the US on that tour. Joe and Mick had gone to the States to finish *Give 'Em Enough Rope*, with producer Sandy Pearlman putting that much-despised US-friendly sheen on their English sound. (Pearlman himself had been one of the founding writers on *Crawdaddy* in the late 1960s, and could be fairly regarded as one of the fathers of a certain canonical 'rockism' that the punks had supposedly set out to destroy.) While they were there, in mid-1978, the pair discovered Texas's own 'I Fought the Law' on a San Francisco jukebox, and on both coasts they were sufficiently moved by their encounter with the rock'n'roll homeland to pen a sort of anti-'Bored' anthem, 'Gates of the West' – a song that ironically never appeared on a US release in the band's lifetime. A mixum-gatherum of urban and musical imagery bridging New York and London, the song (released in May 1979 on that British *Cost of Living* EP) is lent a sweet plaintiveness by the delicate irresolution of its harmonics and of Mick's vocal. And its climactic promise that 'there's a move into the future ... for the USA!' might be regarded as prophetic.

On their 1979 jaunts The Clash toured the USA, travelling for absurdly long times and distances, with a steady diet of classic country-and-western tunes on the bus stereo, as Johnny Green's road-managing memoir tells us.[8] You can almost hear that country-music mix-tape, and the sound of the open road, on *London Calling*. In the review of that album in *Melody Maker* James Truman could hear it, writing: 'The Clash have discovered America, and by the same process, themselves.'[9] By the time I saw them a few months later, The Clash were taking to the stage, everywhere, to the sound of Tennessee Ernie Ford's 'Sixteen Tons', and had featured a string of R&B legends as opening acts, including Bo Diddley and Lee Dorsey.

This was all well and good, but their decision to tour extensively and to record in the US through much of 1980, climaxed by a US-oriented single, 'The Call Up', resulted in 'commercial freefall and reputational decline among ordinary punters in their home country', writes Egan, adding that said punters had 'a grievance with real legitimacy'. Conceding that 'working a lot in the United States despite their anti-U.S. cultural imperialism beliefs was arguably just an irony of life' for The Clash, Egan concludes nonetheless that the band 'were now losing touch, a potentially fatal fact for artists whose entire image revolved around them knowing the score'.[10] Gavin Martin notes that as The Clash toured the US and continental Europe, but not Britain, in 1980–81, 'the riots raged in Liverpool, London, Manchester and Bradford ... The Clash were derided as failed rebels, irreverent [*sic*] poseurs, deserters even.' Most cruelly of all, Martin writes, 'The Clash were about to be dismissed as brutally as the punks had dismissed the hippies five years before.'[11] By the time faint word came in from New York in May 1981 about the Bond's near-riots in Times Square, the view back home had hardened: The Clash were paying for their neglect of those ordinary British punters, together with 'the increasing risibility of their clothing, and the declining power of their music ... not just in worsening chart positions but in a crescendo of contempt'.[12] When it became known in the winter of 1981–82 that their next album would be called *Rat Patrol from Fort Bragg*, 'the groans of contempt at the military-esque Yankophilia could be heard all over the band's homeland', writes Egan, who, sharply averse to hip hop culture himself, heaps some of his own contempt on the band's work with New York rappers and graffiti artists in this period: 'The Clash by this point were comically susceptible to anyone with a semblance of an outlaw aura.'[13] Presumably there had been no signs of such susceptibility back in London in the 1970s, or at least it hadn't been comical then.

Gaining touch

I am not generally one who succumbs to technological determinism, but it is hard to imagine such a view of The Clash's irrelevance and loss of principle surviving in the age of the internet and social media. Indeed, from the US perspective, in 1980–81 The Clash might be said to have been 'gaining touch' rather than losing it. The transatlantic divergence of opinion remains striking. While my own geographic and 'Clashographic' origins certainly put me in broad alliance with the US perspective, it must be said that its utter lack of cynicism is in some respects more wearying and disheartening than the hyper-critical vigilance of the British consensus. The very titles of American twenty-first-century edited volumes such as *Let Fury Have the Hour* and *Punk Rock Warlord* (about Joe Strummer) say something about the hagiographic adoption of Joe in particular by US fans and historians.[14] (The latter book does contain some criticisms of Strummer – virtually all of them from English writers.) Of course, the literally iconic wall-painting of Joe Strummer has stood for years on a wall in Tompkins Square in the gentrified East Village, and indeed is arguably a marker of the neighbourhood's gentrification. In the American telling, there is no doubt that The Clash were martyrs to their own principles, fighting the Man at every conceivable turn but let down both by CBS and, more importantly, their inadequate American fans – not to be confused with 'ordinary punters' back in Blighty. US writers also don't seem as concerned about the maintenance of punk purity – as one puts it: 'Strummer's eclectic influences helped change punk into a more inclusive, diverse and much more interesting genre than it should have been'.[15] The ceaseless earnestness of The Clash as they emerge in most of the American tellings, and the equal earnestness of those writing about them, reminds us that they were replaced as favourite transatlantic band in the hearts of US fans by the Irish bastion of sincerity known as U2. As the American editors of *Punk Rock Warlord* write: 'Placing a huge burden of responsibility on himself to deliver on the promise of changing the world, Strummer seemed to make the same demands on his ideal audience.'[16] Oh, if only we could have been *ideal*.

In truth, the critique of the music industry and of the fans in much of the American literature is fundamentally identical: neither suits nor audiences, the lament goes, really understood that punk and The Clash were *like totally* different from what existed before and around them. One piece quotes a record label 'telling its marketing people to package punk/new wave just like mainstream rock … "The idea is to have strong graphics, and then the format doesn't matter that much."'[17] A survey of the Atlanta audience at the first US Sex Pistols gig in 1978 found that they were 'not that different from standard rock audiences, namely middle-class, white, and in attendance more out of curiosity than commitment'.[18] It goes almost without saying that, in the eyes of the writers, this marketing and this audience is terrible, but it gets said anyway. One enormously well-meaning American studies scholar, having ticked off the tragic markers of early eighties US conservatism, from sitcoms to Stallone, allows his prose to reach extraordinary heights of bleeding-heart meaninglessness, worthy of extended quotation:

> Within a society they believed to be rapidly declining, The Clash were convinced that hope could only be restored through the direct

intervention of humans. As musicians, they felt empowered to facilitate this transition, but found that much of their American audience either missed the point or did not want to think about it.[19]

Perhaps the members of the dumbass American Clash audience were prepared to wait for the direct intervention of robots to do any required hope-restoration work.

For all the ludicrous generalisations about both The Clash and their audience contained in literal nonsense like this, it is a matter of historical record that American audiences, including ones that I stood in, were indeed dumbass disappointments to Joe at the very least. In New York in 1981 and 1982 Strummer 'castigated the crowd' for abusing black opening acts, 'and he and other Clash members continued the tongue lashing of their fans in print during interviews' – trying to 'shift the political and musical mindsets of their mostly white punk audiences'.[20] Indeed, as noted above, it is doubtful to what extent these audiences can be described as 'punk' at all, being largely, and at the front of the crowd in particular (for reasons I will explain further below), white suburban teenagers and young men who didn't necessarily identify strongly with any musical subculture more specific than 'rock', or perhaps heavy metal. As Alex Ogg writes, The Clash found 'an audience for whom punk was harsh, alien and largely incomprehensible'.[21] Being English, Ogg seems to regard this development negatively.

Will Straw's wider analysis of the American rock audience in this period is highly pertinent: he argues that it defined itself, by virtue of geography, outside the urban culture of disco (black, Latino, gay) and the avant-garde artistic subcultures with which punk/new wave in New York, in particular, was associated. He writes:

> [T]hose living elsewhere would have little or no opportunity to experience or become involved in either of these cultures. Suburban life is incompatible for a number of reasons with regular attendance at clubs where one may hear records or live performers; its main sources of music are radio, retail chain record stores (usually in shopping centres), and occasional large concerts (most frequently in the nearest municipal stadium). These institutions ... in conjunction with suburban lifestyles ... defined a form of involvement in rock culture, discouraging subcultural activity of the degree associated with disco or punk, for example.[22]

Straw's characterisation of the rock fan with little connection to any genre other than metal continues: 'there was nothing to indicate that heavy metal listeners were interested in tracing the roots of any musical traits back to periods preceding the emergence of heavy metal'. And he concludes: 'Any "rebel" or non-conformist imagery in heavy metal may be seen as a function of its masculine, "hard" stances, rather than as a conscious participation in rock's growing self-reflexivity.'[23]

Who are you?

So was that us, in those New Jersey and New York audiences? Suburban, part of the 'disco sucks' generation, drawn to The Clash by their hardness, unconcerned by their place in rock history, and ultimately too musically and politically conservative to connect with their deeper evolving concerns – especially when those concerns took them into African-American places? The answer, inevitably, is both Yes and No – but mostly No. In places like Passaic and Paterson where we came from, more 'urb' than 'sub', our conservatism and our segregation were, you might say, hard-fought and incomplete. Living cheek-by-jowl with various subcultures, in reach of the cool clubs but unlikely to get in, we were not as dumb and insular as we looked. In my Paterson high-school class, split with uncanny precision into black, white and Latino thirds, Mark, Eugene and I, and most of the other white boys, loved metal but revered the Rolling Stones, The Who and The Kinks, and vaguely appreciated their antecedents. We fell in love with girls who preferred to go dancing with the Latino boys. Some evenings we went to school gatherings to which our African-American classmate Mike Cameron brought his unfeasibly large and expensive sound system and got straight down to the business of helping to invent rap. But rock was our thing, and when we went out together it was generally with rock in mind: reared on the rockist prejudices of the 1970s, we embraced punk only when it was absolutely clear to us that it was a sub-genre of rock, and the dressing-up side of punk was left largely to the females who hung around with us. I am eternally grateful to the black friends who taught me to dance to the sound of 'Disco Inferno', but I rarely put the steps to work until I went away to college; for our music, we just bounced. We were lucky enough to have the Capitol right down the road, where the tickets were usually sold direct from the box office; for other venues we knew all the best Ticketron locations; if school needed skipping to queue for tickets, that slightly risky duty could be circulated among us. Some of us worked part-time, but most of our parents were still riding the wage highs of the post-war *trente glorieuses* and could afford to slip us ten or twenty bucks at a time.

Such largesse was not universal in impoverished Paterson. My best friend, Vernon Jackman from Barbados, couldn't afford concert-going. He was preoccupied with the question of whether Bob Marley had sold his soul for success; he loved The Clash's cover of 'Police and Thieves', but he wasn't coming with us to the Capitol. Nonetheless, somewhat to our surprise, and reflecting the reggae audience's interest in how The Clash had adopted and adapted rude-boy sounds, that March 1980 audience in

Passaic was remarkably integrated – which is to say, a little bit integrated, remarkable by the standards of a segregated entertainment scene. I remember distinctly that a day or two later my favourite radio DJ, New Jersey's own Vin Scelsa on New York rock station WNEW-FM, noted during his programme that he had never seen a concert audience like it: hippies mixed with punks mixed with Rastafarians. Combined with the noise and message of The Clash, he said, it made for a heavy and even slightly uncomfortable atmosphere, with no one quite sure what on earth they were seeing and with whom they were seeing it.

Two points are important to make here. One is that while there was certainly a scattering of West Indians who came out to see the reggae Clash on that tour, there was not any notable number of African-Americans – that is, black people from the United States – to be seen: evidently, The Clash's borrowings from the likes of Bo Diddley were not enough to engage contemporary black audiences, nor did Joe's 'Oh mi corazón' bring out any Latinos. The opening act on that tour was a cheerful R&B oldies act, Lee Dorsey, who had scored a minor US and UK hit in the ancient year of 1966 with 'Working in the Coal Mine', but who again clearly was not a draw for black 'ordinary punters' in 1980 – had such punters enjoyed a significant cultural practice of attending white concerts, which indeed they did not. The second point is that the hippies and Rastafarians, whom I remember and whom Vin Scelsa remarked upon, are nowhere to be seen in Chris Walters' stunning photograph from this concert. Of perhaps thirty visible faces in that photo, just one is black, with relatively short, undreadlocked hair, and from the same age bracket as every other audience member in the picture, in which The Clash themselves are the senior citizens. No one looks all that punky either. The Capitol Theater, in the heart of the black and Latino downtown of a heavily black and Latino little city, was a place where white teenagers always managed to get the best tickets. On the odd occasion when we did so for profit rather than for fun, we sold them to 'scalpers' (touts) who generally seemed to sell them on to ... white teenagers.

We white teenagers were, it should be said, unfailingly polite – well, by the standards of a rock audience faced with an opening act – to Lee Dorsey, who was as old and as musically irrelevant as our fathers. We could no more imagine displaying any sort of racist reaction in his direction than we would have done at the African-American sax player blowing King Curtis-style riffs in New Jersey's own E Street Band. Nor did reggae worry us: we loved the enormous spliffs on show in *The Harder They Come*, and having no significant reggae scene that we knew about in our schools, didn't regard the music as any territorial threat. The Clash's fantastic reggae and the solidarity it represented with West Indian communities was just another part of the wonderfully exotic London-ness of the band.

Crossing over

But 1980 and 1981 saw our rock heroes from abroad wander off in the direction of the dance music and rap against which we had defined our tastes locally. The Rolling Stones' 'Emotional Rescue' hit like a blow to the gut in the summer of 1980 and divided opinion sharply. But that song was pedestrian and antiquated, a regular Lee Dorsey number, compared to what The Clash gave us the next winter, something straight off Mike Cameron's turntables: 'The Magnificent Seven'. It was (nearly) impossible to deny the song's ... well ... magnificence. But at least when The Clash took to the stage with it, they played their instruments – not like those rappers who were, as Sean Egan notes with bemused disgust, not even musicians.[24] That, at least, would have comprised some part of the rationalisation for the disgraceful and undoubtedly, in effect, racist behaviour that befell Clash opening acts such as Grandmaster Flash and Kurtis Blow in 1981 and 1982. It's my recollection that as opening acts go, the Jamaican dub MC Mikey Dread got off a little bit easier than the New York area rappers Flash and Blow, but this may have been down to confusion rather than lessened hostility. It didn't help matters that, in 1981, the way Bond's resolved its fire-marshall problem, its over-selling of the venue, was to honour Ticketron tickets in week one, and then the tickets bought at its own box office in Manhattan in the newly minted week two: this meant that the audience for the first week of New York shows was comprised of virtually uncut suburbia, with all the unhip animus that entailed. I recall, nonetheless, as we ran into the venue after a long day queuing under the eyes of suspicious cops, that Joe Strummer hung around the lobby trying to chat to people about their views. With shame, I recall that I opted instead to go on into the hall so I could get right next to the stage. I never, ever booed any Clash opening act, but I was perfectly positioned to watch the spit and objects fly. (The persistence of such attitudes even in a changing music scene was extraordinary: several years later I accompanied my little sister to see white rappers the Beastie Boys back in the Capitol, and their opening act, some black guys who called themselves Public Enemy, got stick from the overwhelmingly white audience.)

Despite our hostility to their rapping friends, what The Clash were doing with new black American music was unprecedented – except perhaps for their own precedent with reggae in London in 1977, but this time playing their own songs rather than Junior Murvin's. As early as December 1977 the American critic Lester Bangs, writing in *NME*, had spotted their special talent: they were 'the closest thing yet to the lost chord, the missing link between black music and white noise, rock capable of making a bow to black forms without smearing on the black face'; most perceptively, he added: 'they actually play better and certainly more interestingly when they slow down and get, well, funky'.[25] The only other great white group of the classic rock era to adopt contemporary rather than dated black styles were, arguably, The Beatles with their early Motown and girl-group songs: but these were respectful covers of radio-friendly crossover hits, not the re/creation of cutting-edge black sounds. Famously, The Clash settled into Electric Ladyland studio in downtown Manhattan, and on days off Mick would shop in Brooklyn for rap records. What is often neglected in stories about the Americanism of *Sandinista!* and *Combat Rock*, about 'the increasingly US-obsessed Strummer',[26] is that the lyrics were, for the most part, still unmistakably Joe and unmissably English. For example, 'The Call Up', based on American protests about the reintroduction of registration for the military draft, uses a phrase as its title that an American would never use, and its Marines chant in very English accents. Sometimes the transatlantic voyage in a song is jokey, as in 'The Sound of Sinners', a near-parody of African-American-style gospel that ends with the voice of an English vicar bidding his congregation good-bye. And the occasional presence of Mikey Dread's extraordinary dub production completes a sort of Atlantic-Caribbean triangle.

Joe Strummer was extraordinarily proud that The Clash had not only produced a great hip hop song in their own idiom, but also that they made it big in the black community: 'It was a huge hit in New York that summer on WBLS. I want to point out that because we always get passed over in these hip-hop histories.' And though he didn't take credit for the influence that The Clash undoubtedly had on subsequent political rappers, he noted rightly that 'in respect to addressing the ills of capitalism and providing a smart class analysis, underground hip-hop, not the pop-culture stuff, picked up where punk left off and ran full steam ahead'.[27] It's a far cry from Sean Egan's utterly bizarre conclusion that 'the fresh, vibrant aura hanging over rap music in 1980 soon turned into something more sinister, even despicable ... [H]istory shows that rap music ultimately consumed both The Clash and rock itself.'[28] Such negativity, however, should not divert us from the not-wholly-answerable question of how The Clash went down, and were remembered, in black American musical circles. Neither the language nor the moral urgency of the accusation of 'cultural appropriation' was as prevalent then as later, but certainly many white acts imitating black sounds could expect some mockery at least: I recall Sting and the Police, for example, being hit with some brickbats for their reggae-lite. The Clash, however, were simply too obviously respectful of their black influences to find themselves on the receiving end of critical attacks. And the degree to which hip hop legend Chuck D would subsequently cite The Clash as an influence means that later revisionism has also been hard to come by.[29] It should be noted, however, that, as Joe suggests, it isn't their rather good hip hop tracks – not only 'Magnificent Seven' and 'Lightning Strikes' but the between-albums single 'This Is Radio Clash' – that makes them forebears to

Public Enemy but rather their political stance. In hip hop history, the genre's racial crossover is generally seen as coming years after The Clash, who are indeed neglected pioneers.

Clash trash

How deep was the band's immersion in urban America? By his own admission, during the heady 1980 Electric Ladyland days, Strummer 'never went out in New York! I can't believe it. Maybe once, to get a beer.' He continued:

> But it was the most beautiful time ever. To be at 8th street on New York, in Jimi Hendrix's studio, everything on a roll. You know what New York was like then? You'd get up at 10 in the morning and you'd get a cab to go to the studio. Rocketing downtown, the driver would stick his hand back with a grass joint. Cool as fuck! I was thinking, 'This is New York.'[30]

The Clash were generally exceptionally sharp and self-aware cultural tourists – as 'Safe European Home' and '(White Man) In Hammersmith Palais' testify. There is arguably a case to be made, nonetheless, that the extraordinary run at Bond's in the spring/summer of 1981, the pride of their hip hop hit, the rappers and graffiti artists on their stage, their confrontations with the suburbanites in their audience, all combined to inflate their own sense that they had very quickly gone native in New York. One often-overlooked aspect of that inflation was their relationship that summer with New York's archetypal cinematic artist, Martin Scorsese. The director cast them and their friends in *The King of Comedy* in a small scene, one that shrank away ultimately to almost nothing, in which they mock Sandra Bernhardt on a midtown street and she calls them 'street trash'. Even the hopeful, plaintive Mick Jones of 'Gates of the West' could scarcely have imagined that before long they would be official Scorsesian New York trash. Photos from the shoot indicate that The Clash were dressed neither like traditional punks nor like their audience, but rather like Village hipsters, justifying Justin Wadlow's observation that in New York The Clash were often less working-class heroes than 'elegant dandies'.[31] The Scorsese connection would emerge, too, on *Combat Rock*'s 'Red Angel Dragnet', which appropriates the famous 'rain' speech from Scorsese's *Taxi Driver*, and is at least as politically problematic as that film, without its sheer brilliance. There is a whole series of New Jersey connections here too: Robert De Niro's character in *The King of Comedy* is from Clifton, the small town between Paterson and Passaic; Allen Ginsberg, who joins in on the rather more successful 'Ghetto Defendant', was from Paterson; and the incident described in 'Red Angel Dragnet' took place in Newark – which, as Amiri

Baraka points out, has a strong claim to be the real historic black musical capital of the New York area.[32]

In any event, that brief account of just a couple of songs from *Combat Rock* begins to belie that album's image as the ultimate Clash sell-out as they careened towards their inevitable end. This album was The Clash *all'Americana*, to be sure, but beyond the hits 'Rock the Casbah' and 'Should I Stay or Should I Go', they were traversing the USA's haunted backstreets rather than the main drag, immersed in what Stanley Cohen persuasively calls a 'Vietnamization' of their artistic vision.[33] Perhaps nothing captures their ultimately terminal American dilemma in this period better than the double-A-side single of 'Should I Stay...' and 'Straight to Hell' – the former a conventional rocker, a piece of Mick's American dream come to life; and the latter an extraordinary, dark, world-spinning vision of Joe's American nightmare, experienced in 'any frontier, any hemisphere', complete with 'Amerasian blues' in Vietnam.

Terminal popularity

Nonetheless, by the time The Clash were back on stage in New York in the summer of 1982, in the wake of that album's release, they weren't especially hip at all: they were, rather, near the top of the popular music charts. The effect of the expansion of their US audience was its further whitening, young white males being, as noted, most suited to the costly acts of work- and school-avoiding endurance required to secure prized concert tickets, this time for a series of outdoor shows on Pier 84, which reached out from Manhattan into the Hudson River towards New Jersey. That year, when Joe confronted audiences who had flung objects at Kurtis Blow, he did so with a positively menacing Travis Bickle-style mohawk haircut. On 'Red Angel Dragnet', Kosmo Vinyl had read the *Taxi Driver* lines and Paul Simonon had sung the rest of the song, but here now was Joe embodying Bickle. 'Why don't you throw bottles at me if you're so tough?', I recall him saying, pointing to his shaven head. The punkiness of the mohawk as a fashion statement has generally been exaggerated, and on Joe Strummer that summer it seemed much more to signify 'hard'. All that exposed scalp also made him look scarily pale, and in combination with the cinematic allusion to a white vigilante rampage, it was the complete opposite of any of the racial cross-dressing (to use Eric Lott's famous phrase)[34] that you might expect from someone whose music had become so deeply influenced by black culture.

They were still welcoming rappers to open for them, and The Clash continued to resist subcultural specificity in appearance and sound. But for all their sophistication, their hits undeniably signalled something mainstream and white American about their work, not least in the way 'Rock the Casbah' was happy to play along with, rather than angrily skewer, dominant anti-Muslim political prejudices. For The Clash to come to this point, surely the end was nigh. As Greil Marcus writes:

> In a certain sense, Strummer was never a real rock 'n' roller, because he trusted neither fun nor money; thus the chart success of The Clash had to mean nothing to him. You could draw two different conclusions from the failure of punk to change the world and its sometime success on the charts: you could conclude that the punk critique of everyday oppression and spectacular entertainment was wrong – or you could conclude that it was correct, and the enemy more invisible, than even the most conscious punks had dared to think.[35]

The suggestion is that The Clash had found themselves sucked across on to the wrong side of the hegemonic line, and therefore Strummer, an adherent of Marcus's second conclusion, had to purge the band of its own invisible enemy (Mick Jones, to put it bluntly), and in the process destroy it. It's impossible to say, in the aftermath of that destruction, if The Clash ultimately left us transformed or merely entertained. (Some nights on Pier 84 it was clearly neither.) The personal record of my Clash-going friends is ambiguous, at best. In the years afterwards, Eugene would be a musician and non-profit administrator, politically liberal. Mark would be a cop and Trump voter, surrounded by brown-skinned Latino loved ones. Our kid brothers would reach higher professional and political heights as Democratic Party loyalists in multiracial urban power structures. I'm an academic who now listens to mostly black music, but that started years after The Clash.

But there was one night on the pier, the last time I ever saw The Clash, when the rain poured in from the river, and Joe saw us soaked and heaving below him – and breaking a long-standing agreement with Mick, he called 'White Riot' for an encore. For two astonishing minutes, I saw friends and family and strangers carried off our feet, sweeping from side to side and forward and back, a sea of happy, white, suburban humanity caught in a city storm. And when it was over, thousands of us walked back into Hell's Kitchen, under the West Side Highway, where, in the echoing acoustics, our voices rose as one and insisted again and again that we wanted a riot of our own.

Notes

1 Marcus Gray, *Route 19 Revisited: The Clash and London Calling* (London: Jonathan Cape, 2009); Sean Egan, *The Clash: The Only Band That Mattered* (New York: Rowman and Littlefield, 2015), p. 129.
2 http://www.photofeatures.com/clash/ppages/ppage15.html (accessed 18 November 2018).

3   The Clash on MV, *The Clash – Full Concert – 03/08/80 – Capitol Theatre (OFFICIAL)* (uploaded to YouTube November 2014), https://www.youtube.com/watch?v=CLKl6FIBH0U (accessed 12 July 2017).
4   Egan, *The Clash*, p. 175.
5   Ibid., p. 56.
6   Ibid., p. 106.
7   P. Merriam Clark, 'Clash Theory: Inside the Music of Strummer and Jones', *Spotidoc*, p. 15, http://spotidoc.com/doc/132599/clash-theory-1 (accessed 11 July 2017).
8   Johnny Green and Garry Barker, *A Riot of Our Own: Night and Day with The Clash – and After* (London: Orion, 2003), p. 136.
9   Quoted in Marcus Gray, *Last Gang in Town: The Story and Myth of The Clash* (New York: Henry Holt, 1996), p. 310.
10 Egan, *The Clash*, pp. 181, 183.
11 Quoted in Tom Pinnock, 'The End of The Clash – by Joe Strummer', *Uncut* (August 2012).
12 Egan, *The Clash*, p. 202.
13 Ibid., pp. 209, 215.
14 Antonino D'Ambrosio (ed.), *Let Fury Have the Hour: Joe Strummer, Punk, and the Movement That Shook the World* (New York: Nation Books, 2012); Barry J. Faulk and Brady Harrison (eds), *Punk Rock Warlord: The Life and Work of Joe Strummer* (Farnham: Ashgate, 2014). It should be noted that there is much of value in these books, though Justin Wadlow's essay in *Punk Rock Warlord* on 'Joe Strummer and the Promised Land' exemplifies both the hagiography and the sloppiness of some of this work: he describes the Bond's shows of May–June 1981, for example, as preceding the release of *Sandinista!*, which in fact occurred in December 1980.
15 Brian A. Cogan, 'From the 101'ers to the Mescaleros, and Whatever Band was in-between: Joe Strummer's Musical Journey (Or, Why Woody?)', in Faulk and Harrison (eds), *Punk Rock Warlord*, p. 32.
16 Barry J. Faulk and Brady Harrison, 'Introduction – John Woody Joe Mellor Strummer: The Many Lives, Travails and Sundry Shortcomings of a Punk Rock Warlord', in Faulk and Harrison (eds), *Punk Rock Warlord*, p. 2.
17 Kenneth J. Bindas, '"The Future is Unwritten": The Clash, Punk and America, 1977–1982', *American Studies* 34.1 (1993), p. 85.
18 Ibid., p. 84.
19 Ibid., p. 85.
20 Walidah Imarisha, 'Culture Clash: The Influence of Hip Hop Culture and Aesthetics on The Clash', in Faulk and Harrison (eds), *Punk Rock Warlord*, p. 157.
21 Alex Ogg, 'Saint Joe: An Apostate Writes', in Faulk and Harrison (eds), *Punk Rock Warlord*, p. 67.
22 Will Straw, 'Characterizing Rock Music Culture', in Simon During (ed.), *The Cultural Studies Reader*, 2nd edn (London: Routledge, 1999), p. 455.
23 Ibid., p. 457.
24 Egan, *The Clash*, p. 189.

25 Lester Bangs, *Psychotic Reactions and Carburetor Dung*, ed. Greil Marcus (New York: Anchor Books, 2003), p. 238.
26 Samuel Cohen, 'Washington Bullets: The Clash and Vietnam', in Samuel Cohen and James Peacock (eds), *The Clash Takes on the World: Transnational Perspectives on the Only Band that Matters* (London: Bloomsbury, 2017), p. 132.
27 Quoted in Imarisha, 'Culture Clash', pp. 155, 157.
28 Egan, *The Clash*, p. 189.
29 The Chuck D endorsement carries significant weight in the very American appreciations by D'Ambrosio and Imarisha cited above.
30 Quoted in Pinnock, 'The End of The Clash – by Joe Strummer'.
31 Justin Wadlow, 'The Last Gang in Town: The Clash Portrayed in New York and Paris', in Cohen and Peacock (eds), *The Clash Takes on the World*, p. 205.
32 Amiri Baraka, *Digging: The Afro-American Soul of American Classical Music* (Berkeley, CA: University of California Press, 2009).
33 Cohen, 'Washington Bullets: The Clash and Vietnam', p. 136.
34 Eric Lott, *Love and Theft: Blackface Minstrelsy and the American Working Class* (Oxford: Oxford University Press, 1993).
35 Greil Marcus, *In the Fascist Bathroom: Writings on Punk, 1977–1992* (London: Penguin, 1994), p. 307.

10
The one struggle: The Clash, Gary Foley, punk politics and Indigenous Australian activism

Alessandro Moliterno

On the evening of 23 February 1982, The Clash appeared on stage at Melbourne's Festival Hall. Towards the end of their set, the band launched into one of their well-known reggae covers, 'Armagideon Time'. At this point, they were joined on stage by the prominent Indigenous Australian activist Gary Foley. The music receded into an instrumental soundscape, as Foley took to the microphone and, with clarity and forthrightness, addressed the audience: 'At the time when all of this began, Aboriginal people discovered, explored and settled this country...'[1] The enthusiastic attention of the assembled fans was then directed towards a radical presentation of Indigenous politics. Foley proceeded to deliver a challenge to the historical orthodoxy of Australia, presenting instead a history of colonial persecution, the genocide of Australia's Indigenous peoples and the confiscation of their land – the very land on which the concert took place. Foley proclaimed that this oppression affected not only Indigenous Australian peoples, but also women, and the working classes who had been transported to the new colony. His speech then reached its climax, as Foley urged his audience to embrace solidarity and take action, tying three political causes of antiracism, feminism and workers' rights into 'one struggle'.[2]

Both by Foley's very presence on stage, and by his discourse, two seemingly disparate historical phenomena were now united – British punk rock and Indigenous Australian activism. The Clash had been perhaps the most successful band formed during the British punk movement in the latter half of the 1970s. From the outset, they had cultivated an image of political engagement that heavily influenced the conception of punk in the popular imagination. Gary Foley had already spent many active years advancing the struggle for Indigenous rights in Australia. This struggle had been ongoing since the arrival of European colonists in the late eighteenth century, and Foley was now at the forefront of the movement. When The Clash and

Foley joined forces in early 1982, Indigenous activists were deeply engaged in the process of organising a wave of protests intended to disrupt the Commonwealth Games, to be held in Brisbane later that year, and thereby draw international attention to their cause. Though barely registering in the Australian media, this collaboration constituted a very particular and perhaps critical episode in the history of music and politics.

This chapter explores the historical and political significance of this partnership. It examines the reception of The Clash's first and only tour of Australia, and addresses its political aspects, as the tour provided Foley with a platform for advocating the rights of Australia's Indigenous peoples. It will draw together two areas of historical inquiry. The first is the politics and authenticity of punk rock, and The Clash's position and influence within this. The second is the story of Indigenous Australian activism in the late 1970s and early 1980s which, at the time of The Clash's arrival, was in the process of redefining itself, adopting and evolving new strategies and tactics in pursuit of developing political goals. This chapter argues that The Clash's politics, largely established early on, were highly compatible with an evolving Indigenous Australian activism, and that despite its limited reach, the collaboration presented unique opportunities for Indigenous political expression while confirming political ideals that were central to the band's image.

Punk rock politics and authenticity

In his defining history of the movement, Jon Savage observed that punk rock in Britain 'thrust itself into politics, and politics came back to claim it'.[3] Through its controversial and offensive style, its relationship with the music industry, its crystallisation of the tumultuous late 1970s and its entanglement with various political movements, punk has at every stage been associated with politics. At the same time, the political aspects of punk rock have been seen, justifiably, as simultaneously unclear and problematic. The movement generated widespread controversy in British public life, which was already undergoing significant political and social change.[4] Meanwhile, punk raised questions regarding its political content and possibilities. As a primary example of British punk, The Clash reflected their time and have always been at the centre of these debates.[5]

More perhaps than any other band, The Clash have defined both the imagery and substance of punk politics. This is notable because although punk rock always appeared to be political, it has typically been difficult to ascertain exactly how.[6] The Clash's adoption of explicit stances in their music, performances and interviews allowed them to step into that vacuum, thereby determining the direction of much of the resultant discourse. At least on the surface, the band championed anti-racism, criticised the social and economic structures of society, attacked imperialism and maintained a rhetoric of strong engagement with their fans and the world at large. At the same time, they did not escape the scrutiny in terms of motives, behaviour and political authenticity that has been directed at the rest of the punk movement.

Interrogating the various characterisations of punk politics has generally fallen into two broad categories. The first is concerned with ascertaining exactly what punk politics were. From the beginning, articles appeared throughout the British music press under such titles as 'New Wave Neat Say Nazis',[7] raising questions, both for contemporaries and historians, concerning the political orientations of punk. What, for example, were the nihilistic or neo-fascist implications of a musical or cultural movement that appeared openly to embrace anarchy, or at least a type of anti-politics that violently rejected traditional values?[8] Was punk racist or anti-racist?[9] The second category relates to the degree to which punk could effectively challenge the established music industry. Consequently, some critics have focused less on political content and more on the degree to which punk ultimately constituted an 'unsuccessful musicians' revolt' against the music industry itself.[10]

The Clash were immediately embroiled in such questions. Their self-presentation and the way they were received by audiences and critics alike strove towards a more appealing version of 'punk rock politics'. Reviewers were often extremely critical.[11] Nevertheless, the group's popularity was soon established, and they featured on the cover of publications such as the *NME* and *Sounds*. In the process of attracting media attention, their politics took centre stage. From the beginning, the band expressed fears that Britain's youth, their audience, might constitute a valuable recruiting ground for the neo-fascist National Front. When asked during their first interview with the *NME*, in late 1976, 'What do you think people ought to know about you?', Joe Strummer responded: 'I think people ought to know that we're anti-fascist, we're anti-violence, we're anti-racist and we're pro-creative. We're against ignorance.'[12] The band professed a desire to utilise their platform and music as an alternative source of political ideas: 'We're hoping to educate any kid who comes to listen to us, right, just to keep 'em from joining the National Front.'[13] This aspiration, to use their careers to engage audiences in questions of an explicitly political nature and to embody a positive influence, became central to The Clash's image.

Certainly, their music contained ample political and social commentary. Beginning with their earliest concerts and interviews, this was crystallised in the recording of their eponymous first album in 1977. The album was brimming with songs demonstrating the group's rhetoric of political awareness and engagement, for example, 'I'm So Bored with the USA', 'London's Burning', 'Career Opportunities', their cover of Junior Murvin and Lee 'Scratch' Perry's 'Police and Thieves' (the first recorded demonstration of The Clash's close identification with the highly politicised reggae movement) and, perhaps most notably, 'White Riot'. The Clash took inspiration from political themes, including social alienation, inequality and unemployment, and advanced critiques of imperialism and capitalist social organisation. These ideas were developed further, particularly on the group's later albums *London Calling* (1979), *Sandinista!* (1980) and *Combat Rock* (1982).[14] Almost immediately, 'White Riot' gained a special, if controversial, place in The Clash's work as a signature attempt to address race politics in the UK. It was highly demonstrative of the group's attitudes towards political action, contrasting the political engagement demonstrated by members of Britain's African-Caribbean communities with the passivity of its white youth.[15] In the interview cited above, Strummer explained the song's argument, that 'white men' aren't prepared to deal with their problems, because 'everything's too cozy'.[16] Not only did anti-racism become a cornerstone of The Clash's political self-representation (epitomised in their appearance at the 1978 Rock Against Racism 'Carnival Against the Nazis'),[17] but also – and perhaps with more emphasis – a repudiation of political apathy. Strummer would later echo these sentiments when on tour in Australia.

The Clash's political image has not gone unquestioned, of course. Their politics have often been dismissed as merely a pose. Indeed, it could be argued that their adoption of such an overtly political image attracted greater scrutiny, as critics sought to ascertain how seriously The Clash's politics could be taken. In *The Last Gang in Town*, Marcus Gray attempts to unpack the dynamics between the realities and the mythologies that surround The Clash.[18] Gray takes both myth and reality seriously, arguing that, whatever the group's politics were, they must be contextualised within the tumultuous events and interactions of life in a band, which often forced external politics to the periphery.[19] In addition, the real-world implications of political music in general are notoriously difficult to delineate.[20] Considering the constraints of operating within the music industry, Simon Frith outlines this tension between the 'essentially petit bourgeois' nature of rock musicians and the desire for authentic expression, political or otherwise.[21] The music industry has repeatedly shown itself to be capable of absorbing radical political content – of 'turning rebellion into money'.[22] The Clash spent their entire career operating within these constraints and, furthermore, were clearly aware of them. At the same time, the group appear never to have abandoned their political ideals, and when the opportunity came to demonstrate them in Australia, the collaboration that unfolded seemed entirely natural.

Indigenous activism and land rights

While punk rock was taking shape in Britain, Indigenous Australians were busy entering a new phase in the long history of their resistance to colonisation. The Clash's tour of Australia coincided with one of many points of heightened activity within Indigenous activism, which was itself undergoing a significant period of change in its complex history. The collaboration between The Clash and Gary Foley should be viewed within these processes. From an outsider's perspective on Aboriginal history, there are two major developments that frame the political and social dimensions of this collaboration. The first is the shift in emphasis within Indigenous activism from pursuing legal equality and recognition in Australian society towards a starker assertion of Aboriginal identity and the inseparable demand for the acknowledgement of past injustices and the establishment of land rights. The second is the emergence of a younger cohort of Indigenous activists who, frustrated with political or conciliatory methods of advocacy, instead pushed for Aboriginal self-determination, setting more radical political agendas and making strategic use of symbolically charged protests.[23]

Indigenous Australians have resisted European invasion and colonisation since the arrival of the First Fleet in 1788.[24] The ensuing establishment of British colonies in Australia led to the confiscation of Aboriginal land and, despite constant and active opposition, British colonisation meant the extermination, subjugation and exploitation of Australia's Indigenous peoples.[25] The federation of the Australian states into a single nation in 1901 did not result in clear improvements on earlier colonial policies regarding Aboriginal Australians.[26] Even up until the 1960s, Indigenous Australians were subject to draconian legal restrictions, including on freedom of movement, the right to marry, to retain custody of their own children and the right to vote.[27] Bain Attwood notes that it was not until the 1960s that Indigenous Australians won some significant, though limited, advances in broadening their formal legal status.[28]

In 1967 a national referendum was held over proposed changes to the Australian constitution to include Indigenous Australians in the national census and allow the federal government to legislate for them directly. As Attwood and Markus have explained, the vote was widely misunderstood as a decision to extend citizenship to Indigenous Australians, who had already won this and other rights in most areas of the country.[29] Nevertheless, the referendum resulted in a huge majority in favour of the changes, and was widely viewed as a sign of progress in non-Indigenous attitudes towards race.[30] Unfortunately, however, discrimination and inequality continued to characterise the experience of Indigenous people in Australian society. From the mid-1960s, therefore, Indigenous activists shifted focus towards exposing the persistent racism in Australia and seeking Indigenous self-determination and land rights.[31]

There were two especially noteworthy episodes in this phase of development in Indigenous activism. The first was the Freedom Ride, in which activists, including Charles Perkins (later the first Indigenous chairperson of the Aboriginal Development Commission) travelled by bus through rural

Australia, documenting the segregation and discrimination still faced by Indigenous Australians.[32] The Freedom Ride demonstrated both the persistence of racist attitudes in the country and the limitations of the purported advances of the 1960s. The second episode was the establishment of the Aboriginal Tent Embassy in response to remarks made by the Prime Minister William McMahon during a public address in which he rejected Indigenous land rights claims. Shortly after the speech, a group of young Indigenous activists, including Foley, arrived at Parliament House with tents and placards, proclaiming the establishment of an Aboriginal embassy, demanding land rights and the recognition of past injustices.[33] This sparked rallies, legal action and clashes with police as the government attempted to remove the protestors.

The Tent Embassy was a widely publicised and highly symbolic protest that crystallised the developing methods and goals of Indigenous activism and shaped its future.[34] The more radical activism espoused by Foley and his colleagues represented growing dissatisfaction with methods of advocacy that politely sought a place for Indigenous peoples within broader Australian society.[35] Demonstrating this, the embassy protestors emphasised the injustice of European colonisation, genocide and dispossession, arguing that Indigenous Australians had a specific prior right to the land on which the Australian state had been built. As Foley stated during the embassy protests: 'We're going to get our bloody land even if we have to fucking well take it.'[36] Though land rights had been part of the agenda of Indigenous activism for some time, they now took centre stage.

The activism that Foley and his contemporaries were developing deepened the significance of international influences and tactics. Foley himself has written about the influence of the US Civil Rights and Black Power movements on young Indigenous activists in the late 1960s and 1970s.[37] Over the next decade, in addition to developing links with similar movements worldwide, Indigenous rights protestors continued to seek recognition on the international stage, making ingenious use of publicity and international embarrassment as a political tactic. In October 1982 Brisbane was scheduled to host the Commonwealth Games. Indigenous rights activists intended to disrupt the games with protests that would expand their international audience.[38] The fortunate timing of The Clash's tour, combined with their political interests and aspirations, made the band a natural ally of this political movement.

One struggle: synthesising punk rock politics and Indigenous activism

The Clash arrived in Australia in early February 1982. Their initial appearance before the Australian media occurred during a stopover en route to

New Zealand, before they returned to tour Australia. Shortly before the press conference, the band were approached by a group of Aboriginal activists, including Foley, who requested their support. The story was recounted by Paul Simonon in *The Clash*, a book of interviews compiled by the band:

> when we arrived I went straight to my room to catch up on some sleep ... but was woken up by a knock at the door. Three aborigines were standing there wanting a chat. They asked if they could come up on our stage to talk about their situation. So I got Joe and we had a meeting and of course said yes. We realized the power that we had 'cos we could let these guys talk to people who wouldn't normally pay any attention to them.[39]

When the group returned to Australia, Foley and some of his colleagues joined them. Together they played ten shows, visiting Sydney, Brisbane, Adelaide and Melbourne, and it became a semi-regular feature that, when The Clash played 'Armagideon Time', Foley would address the audience with 'a rousing political rap while The Clash backed him up with a tough reggae beat'.[40]

On the final night of their tour, The Clash appeared at Festival Hall in Melbourne. As the band reached the instrumental section of 'Armagideon Time', Foley approached the microphone and began to speak:

> At the time when all of this began, Aboriginal people discovered, explored and settled this country. Over thousands of years, five hundred Aboriginal nations developed a society here, which was in complete harmony with each other and this land. 50,000 years later, the British ruling class brought their own people here in chains, [crowd boos] and then they set about to exterminate the Aboriginal people here. This land was ours. This land belonged to the Aboriginal people. In 1778 there were three groups of people in this country who were oppressed. They were the English working class, they were the women that were brought down in the boats, and most of all they were the Aboriginal people. And today this country is pretty much the same.
>
> Whether all these blokes down here like to admit it or not they're just as oppressed as what we are, and they're not gonna get anywhere unless all of us work together on this thing. What happened to Aboriginal people continues to happen. But, if we're going to build an Australia of the future, where everyone is free, where no one is oppressed, then you people are going to have to understand that the struggle against racism, sexism and exploitation *is the one struggle*. [crowd cheers]
>
> Next time the unemployed people march, get out and march with 'em. And the next time women are marching for their rights, go down and march with 'em, and the next time Aboriginal people in this state march for their land rights, then be there with them too. There's only one

thing that Malcolm Fraser [the Australian Prime Minister] and what he represents is frightened of and that is unity...[41]

Apart from its eloquence, the speech was notable in its expression of three major points: the emphasis on Australian nationhood as the product of genocide and dispossession; the common cause to be found with those oppressed on the basis of their class and gender; and the ongoing persistence of those struggles. Foley's overarching rhetoric was collective action, based on political solidarity. His account of history foregrounded the injustice of colonialism while locating it within broader struggles whose existence would have been more obvious to his audience. The speech was a concerted attempt to push Indigenous politics from the periphery into the limelight, while simultaneously connecting it to commonly understood historical phenomena.

Foley's presentation of Australian history was extremely controversial in the context of the time, and it remains so to this day. It was not acknowledged, officially or in public discourse, that Australia, as a nation, was built on the legacy of genocide and dispossession that the historical record shows. The apparent enthusiasm of the audience is suggestive. Were Clash fans already more politically radical than the wider Australian population? Had the collaboration between Foley and the band, combined with the emotional quality of the performance, lent authority to this argument? Certainly, Foley was quoted as having received a 'phenomenal' response from the audience after one of the Sydney shows.[42]

The Festival Hall appearance showcased Foley's abilities as a performer and orator. His purpose on the tour was to engage a new audience with his main agenda: the struggle for Aboriginal rights. For many, this issue might already have been compelling, while its relevance to their own lives remained unclear. This was a major impediment faced by Indigenous activism, which would always find difficulties in gaining support where it was viewed as a fringe issue or, worse, as one that conflicted with the interests of non-Indigenous Australians. Indeed, the view that Indigenous rights, particularly land rights, could only be realised at the expense of the nation was a common argument made against them.[43] By locating this struggle within a broader history of colonialism and oppression, Foley displayed a nuanced understanding of the obstacles faced by this agenda, and the difficulty of pushing Indigenous rights from the periphery of politics into the centre. At one point, he directly addressed the audience as 'all these blokes down here', who were 'just as oppressed as what we are',[44] emphasising the relevance of this struggle to the lives of non-Indigenous Australians. By joining The Clash on tour, Foley could circumvent the media, with which Indigenous activism has had an uneasy relationship.[45] The disadvantage was the limited size of this audience, as the overall attendance at these concerts, in the thousands, was small compared with the reach of many media outlets. At the same time, this more intimate setting allowed Foley to communicate directly with this audience, who, at the time, responded with great enthusiasm.

Media coverage of the tour took place at two points: the original press conference during The Clash's stopover in Sydney, and reviews of the concerts that took place afterwards. The coverage from the Sydney press conference was largely dismissive or superficial. While it appears that the band did discuss politics, the media did not appear to take this aspect of the band seriously. In the *Sydney Morning Herald*, Strummer was reported as remarking 'What are we doing here when we've only sold 9,000 records? ... We know there's no use us being here. I've been told no one in Australia cares about politics. People just want to go down to Bondi Beach.' This was misunderstood as a comment about poor record sales: 'The band likes to think of itself as one of the last rock-and-roll outlaws. But yes, they are in it for the money.'[46] Melbourne's *Age* repeated Strummer's remarks, mentioning the discussion of 'racism, Aboriginals and riot', but did not go into further detail.[47] Reviews of the concerts were mixed but, despite the presence of Foley on stage, they tended not to mention The Clash's politics, or otherwise characterised them as inauthentic. The *Age* printed a short but scathing review of the 'low energy' concert at Festival Hall. This concluded with the statement: 'During the first of three encores the band was joined by activist Gary Foley in what could be called the "cheer and boo" session', omitting entirely anything that Foley actually said.[48]

While the Australian press were generally indifferent, the *NME* did address this aspect of the tour with some interest. In March 1982 the weekly printed a review of the tour and an interview with The Clash. Here, Foley's participation was not only acknowledged, but celebrated. Referring to one of the Sydney concerts, the article stated: 'Undoubtedly the highlight of the show, from the fourth night on, is "Armagideon Time" when The Clash bring on Gary Foley, the Aboriginal Land-rights Campaigner, who makes a short speech while the group play softly behind him...'[49] The article went on to quote Foley's speech at this concert:

> It's only 14 years since you people gave us the vote in this country, and we still have not got the land to give us economic independence. We need land, right. And we need it now. If you people can afford the time to come to a Clash concert, then you can afford the time, when aboriginal people march in this town, for their land-rights, then you should be there...[50]

It was here that Foley reported having received a 'phenomenal' response from the audience.[51] In the interview section of the article, Joe Strummer raised the issue of Indigenous politics briefly:

> Well, I'm only just hearing about Bjekle Peterson [sic] (the premier of Queensland), saying that if any aboriginals show up for the

Commonwealth Games in October, he's going to jail them. If that kind of guy is elected in charge of a State, then I don't know...[52]

Though the article was printed weeks later, and the sections that focused on Foley and Indigenous politics formed only a small component, the *NME* had dedicated more discussion to the events than any Australian newspaper. This is not surprising, given the obvious differences between the types of publication. The *NME*, and other British music papers, had a tradition of examining political discourse within popular music that the Australian daily newspapers lacked. The *NME* was distributed in Australia at the time, potentially extending the reach of Foley's message further than its indifferent reception by the Australian press. At the same time, the interview was mostly focused on other issues, suggesting that it was only one of the many things on the band's mind.

Overall, the media response might seem a disappointing outcome of the collaboration. The unwillingness of the press to examine the political aspects of The Clash's tour seriously, despite its ostentatious presentation, may have been simply a product of the editorial separation within those newspapers. It certainly raises questions, because the prominence of Indigenous rights activism at the time was considerable. The *Courier Mail*, for example, was regularly printing stories on Indigenous politics, most notably dedicating considerable space to the public spat that had been unfolding between members of the draconian Queensland government and the prominent Indigenous leader and public servant Charles Perkins.[53] Why the controversy generated by Perkins's support for the Games protests did not result in greater media attention for The Clash's involvement remains an open question.

After all, the collaboration between The Clash and Foley was perhaps a unique, if under-examined, episode in the struggle for Australian Indigenous rights *and* the story of The Clash. It is puzzling, for instance, that Marcus Gray mentions Foley in his history of The Clash without further examination.[54] Similarly, Foley has been quoted in a collection of essays on Joe Strummer, but only in the context of discussing Strummer's relationship to feminism.[55] Janie Conway-Herron, who was involved in the tour, describes its events in an article on the tensions of modern Australian identity, but does not discuss them in relation to The Clash's politics.[56] The episode also featured in a short 'Encounters' article in the Australian magazine, *The Monthly*.[57]

Gabriel Solis has produced a paper on the topic, in which he concludes that the tour did not produce historically significant effects, despite representing an opportunity to more clearly examine the politics of The Clash.[58] Solis draws attention to the involvement not only of Foley, but also of the Aboriginal reggae band No Fixed Address, who appeared as a support act on at least one evening of the tour. This demonstrates a revealing contrast between The Clash's active engagement in Indigenous politics and that of the Australian punk movement at large, which remained more a 'bohemian', rather than overtly political, phenomenon. This is a point that is perhaps underemphasised in Solis's analysis. The partnership between Foley's Aboriginal activism and The Clash demonstrated a certain ease of cooperation between seemingly, though not actually, disparate spheres that was notable for its rarity. And in this respect, the central question that emerges from this examination – perhaps one that cannot be answered sufficiently – is why it has remained so obscure for so long.

Conclusion

Solis observes that The Clash's Australia tour was not politically significant in terms of discernible outcomes. Indeed, it is difficult to find much evidence of greater interest or involvement in Aboriginal politics by non-Indigenous Australians as a direct result of the collaboration. At best, it could be argued that by uniting with the cause of Indigenous activism, The Clash marshalled the support of their audience, which may well have had flow-on effects. In the view of many, real progress in the struggle for Aboriginal rights has remained elusive. Yet in as much as there has been non-Indigenous support for the cause, The Clash's contribution, and the engagement of their fans, is part of that story.

Specific outcomes notwithstanding, Foley appeared impressed by his experiences with The Clash. When Joe Strummer died in 2001, Foley wrote an obituary entitled 'Good Bye, Joe', which included the following account:

> Aboriginal rights activist Gary Foley [referring to himself here in the third person] who was invited to join the 1980s Australian tour and promote Aboriginal land rights to audiences remembered the way Joe engaged his fans in political debate instead of just concentrating on sex, drugs and rock and roll.[59]

As the events of the tour faded into distant memory, Foley, who has campaigned for Indigenous rights right to the present day, continued to hold the band in high esteem. It has been suggested that despite the highly mythologised politics of The Clash, these were, ultimately, subsumed within the larger story of their musical career. The Australian tour was no different from any other in its everyday concerns and distractions. At the same time, The Clash's involvement with Indigenous activism demonstrated an impressive political curiosity and commitment. In the context of Australia in the 1980s, Indigenous activists often struggled to get their message across without distortion by the media or resistance from the wider Australian public. The Clash did not presume to speak for Aboriginal people, but instead invited Foley to present his case. This is significant, as Indigenous self-determination was a central pillar of Foley's politics, highlighting how crucial it was for Indigenous Australians to speak for themselves.

Foley's message, while advocating specifically for the rights of Indigenous Australians, intersected with key political themes expressed in The Clash's work discussed above. When Strummer asserted that Australians didn't care about politics, that there was 'no use for our message here', he was echoing his earliest statements in the NME concerning ignorance and political apathy. Foley was more than familiar with these realities as manifested in Australia. At the time of The Clash's tour, Indigenous activism presented a highly controversial historical and political perspective, and faced a daunting combination of racist or nationalist intransigence, opposition from financial and political interests, and antipathy and indifference from the media and public in general. Regardless of the uncertainties raised by the band's image, The Clash's involvement with Foley constituted not only an important, but an intelligent and, arguably, powerful act of solidarity, as well as an eloquent expression of Indigenous activism. It deserves its own place in history.

Notes

1 'The Clash – Live at Festival Hall', YouTube video of audio recording, 2:08:26, from The Clash's performance at Festival Hall, Melbourne, Australia, on 23 February 1982, posted by 'leonardo zidane', 3 November 2014, 1:28:19–1:28.35, https://www.youtube.com/watch?v=EzFxWPku4BY (accessed 25 February 2017).
2 Ibid., 1:28.19–1:32.37.
3 Jon Savage, *England's Dreaming: Sex Pistols and Punk Rock* (London: Faber and Faber, 1991), p. xix.
4 Dave Laing, *One Chord Wonders: Power and Meaning in Punk Rock* (Milton Keynes: Open University Press, 1985), p. iii; Mark Garnett, *From Anger to Apathy: The Story of Politics, Society and Popular Culture in Britain since 1975* (London: Random House, 2008). Garnett explores the 1970s within a broader examination of British decline.
5 Savage, *England's Dreaming*, p. xviii.
6 Laing, *One Chord Wonders*, pp. 125–8.
7 Julie Burchill, 'New Wave Neat Say Nazis', *New Musical Express*, 23 July 1977, p. 11.
8 Matthew Worley, 'Shot By Both Sides: Punk, Politics and the End of "Consensus"', *Contemporary British History* 26.3 (2012), p. 16.
9 Roger Sabin, '"I won't let that dago by": Rethinking Punk and Racism', in Roger Sabin (ed.), *Punk Rock: So What? The Cultural Legacy of Punk* (London: Routledge, 1999), pp. 206–10.
10 Simon Frith, *Sound Effects: Youth Leisure and the Politics of Rock 'n' Roll* (New York: Pantheon, 1981), p. 84.

11 Charles Shaar Murray, 'Sex Pistols Screen on the Green', *New Musical Express*, 11 September 1976, p. 41.
12 Miles, 'Eighteen Flight Rock and the Sound of the Westway', *New Musical Express*, 11 December 1976, p. 11.
13 Ibid.
14 See 'London Calling', 'Clampdown', 'Lost in the Supermarket', 'Guns of Brixton' on *London Calling* [album] (CBS, 1979); 'The Magnificent Seven', 'The Call Up', 'Washington Bullets' on *Sandinista!* [album] (CBS, 1980); 'Know Your Rights', on *Combat Rock* [album] (1982).
15 The Clash 'White Riot', *The Clash* [album] (CBS, 1977).
16 Miles, 'Eighteen Flight Rock and the Sound of the Westway', p. 11.
17 Ian Goodyer, *Crisis Music: The Cultural Politics of Rock Against Racism* (Manchester: Manchester University Press, 2009); John Street, *Music and Politics* (Cambridge: Polity, 2012), pp. 79–97. Goodyer's is the most in-depth work on Rock Against Racism; Street examines the movement in a broader context.
18 Marcus Gray, *Last Gang in Town: The Story and Myth of The Clash* (London: Fourth Estate, 1995).
19 Ibid., pp. 1–2.
20 For discussion of politics and music, see Street, *Music and Politics*, particularly pp. 1–8.
21 Frith, *Sound Effects*, p. 78.
22 The Clash, '(White Man) In Hammersmith Palais' (lyrics), *The Clash* [album].
23 Gary Foley, 'Black Power in Redfern: 1968–1972', 5 October 1971, the Koori History website, http://kooriweb.org/foley/essays/pdf_essays/black%20power%20in%20redfern%201968.pdf (accessed 25 February 2017).
24 See Henry Reynolds, *The Other Side of the Frontier: Aboriginal Resistance to the European Invasion of Australia* (Sydney: UNSW Press, 2006).
25 See Richard Broome, *Aboriginal Australians: Black Response to White Dominance 1788–1980* (Sydney: Allen and Unwin, 1982), p. 87; Ann Curthoys and John Docker (eds), *Aboriginal History Journal* 25 (2001). Broome notes that, by the twentieth century, Australia's Indigenous population had decreased by three-quarters. Curthoys et al. present a more recent examination of the question of genocide in Australia.
26 See Richard Broome, *Aboriginal Australians: A History since 1788* (Crows Nest, NSW: Allen and Unwin, 2010), pp. 309–16. Abuses and discrimination have been widespread and common. A prominent example is the Stolen Generations, Indigenous Australian children who were forcibly removed from their parents throughout most of the twentieth century.
27 Bain Attwood, Andrew Markus, Dale Edwards, Kath Schilling and Australian Institute of Aboriginal and Torres Strait Islander Studies, *The 1967 Referendum, or, When Aborigines Didn't Get the Vote* (Canberra: Aboriginal Studies Press, 1997), pp. 13–19.
28 Ibid.
29 Ibid., pp. ix–xi.
30 Ibid., pp. 55–63.
31 Bain Attwood and Andrew Markus, *The Struggle for Aboriginal Rights:*

A Documentary History (Crows Nest, NSW: Allen and Unwin, 1999), pp. 276–81; Gary Foley, 'A Short History of the Australian Indigenous Resistance: 1950–1990', in Allison Cadzow and John Maynard (eds), *Nelson Aboriginal Studies* (South Melbourne: Nelson Cengage Learning, 2011), pp. 114–27.
32 See Ann Curthoys, *Freedom Ride: A Freedom Rider Remembers* (Crows Nest, NSW: Allen and Unwin, 2002); Curthoys, 'The Freedom Ride and the Tent Embassy', in Gary Foley, Andrew Schaap and Edwina Howell (eds), *The Aboriginal Tent Embassy: Sovereignty, Black Power, Land Rights and the State* (Abingdon: Routledge, 2013), pp. 98–113.
33 Ibid.
34 Gordon Briscoe, 'The Origins of Aboriginal Political Consciousness and the Aboriginal Embassy, 1907–1972', in Schaap and Howell (eds), *The Aboriginal Tent Embassy*, pp. 42–53.
35 See Charles Perkins, *A Bastard Like Me* (Sydney: Ure Smith, 1975), pp. 189–90; Bain Attwood, *Rights For Aborigines* (Crows Nest, NSW: Allen and Unwin, 2003), pp. 307–49.
36 Foley, quoted in Attwood, *Rights for Aborigines*, p. 342.
37 Foley, 'Black Power in Redfern', pp. 3–12.
38 Wallace Brown, 'How We Will Stop the Brisbane Games', *Courier Mail*, 4 February 1982, p. 4.
39 The Clash, *The Clash* (London: Atlantic Books, 2008), p. 205.
40 Janie Conway-Herron, 'What Is Happening Is Real', *Coolabah* 35 (2011), p. 103.
41 'The Clash – Live at Festival Hall', 1:28.19–1:32.37.
42 Roz Reines, 'Tropic of Clash', *New Musical Express*, 27 March 1982, p. 16.
43 See Broome, *Aboriginal Australians: Black Responses to White Dominance*, pp. 206–8. The pastoral and mining industries lobbied fiercely against Aboriginal land rights claims using such arguments.
44 'The Clash – Live at Festival Hall', 1:28.19–1:32.37.
45 Scott Bennett, *Aborigines and Political Power* (Sydney: Allen and Unwin, 1989), pp. 133–49.
46 Susan Molloy, 'Four Rude Boys who Like to Clash', *Sydney Morning Herald*, 3 February, 1982, p. 9.
47 Dierdre Macken, 'The Not-so-loud Clash of Punk Symbols', *The Age*, 20 February 1982, pp. 11–12.
48 Rebecca Battles, 'Clash Low on Energy', *The Age*, 25 February 1982, p. 10.
49 Reines, 'Tropic of Clash', p. 16.
50 Ibid.
51 Ibid.
52 Ibid.
53 See Peter Morley, 'Joh Wants PM to Sack Perkins', *Courier Mail*, 2 February, 1982, p. 3.
54 Gray, *Last Gang in Town*, p. 407.
55 Amy Phillips, 'A Brother in Revolution', in Antonino D'Ambrosio (ed.), *Let Fury Have the Hour: Joe Strummer, Punk, and the Movement That Shook the World* (New York: Nation Books, 2012), p. 110.

56 Conway-Herron, 'What Is Happening Is Real', p. 103.
57 Shane Maloney and Chris Grosz, 'Gary Foley & Joe Strummer', *The Monthly*, December 2013, https://www.themonthly.com.au/issue/2013/december/1385816400/shane-maloney-and-chris-grosz/gary-foley-joe-strummer (accessed 25 February 2017).
58 Gabriel Solis, 'Punk Politics, Blackness, and Indigenous Protest: The Clash's Australian Tour, 1982', in Samuel Cohen and James Peacock (eds), *The Clash Takes on the World: Transnational Perspectives on the Only Band that Matters* (London: Bloomsbury, 2017), pp. 165–82.
59 Gary Foley, 'Good Bye, Joe', obituary for Joe Strummer, 13 January 2003, the Koori History website, http://www.kooriweb.org/foley/resources/story29.html (accessed 25 February 2017).

11
Brigade Rosse: The Clash, Bologna and Italian punx[1]

Giacomo Bottà and Ferruccio Quercetti

In 1978, Joe Strummer adapted the red T-shirt of campaign group Rock Against Racism with the stencilled logo of *Rote Armee Fraktion* enclosed in the words 'Brigade [sic] Rosse'. The customised garment, referring to both the German and Italian terrorist groups, is clearly visible in a few scenes of the film *Rude Boy* shot at the Rock Against Racism festival on 30 April 1978.[2] It is the same T-shirt that Strummer, it was rumoured, intended to wear on stage in Bologna in 1980.[3] At the time, Italy was at a crossroads: the shadow of *Anni di Piombo*[4] terrorism still lingered, but repression and national political pacification were beginning to take effect, slowly putting the so-called *Riflusso*[5] (withdrawal) into motion. That year, The Clash toured Italy for the first time, playing two shows, in Bologna on 1 June and in Turin two days later. Both shows had been organised by city councils on which the *Partito Comunista Italiano* (Italian Communist Party, hereafter PCI) held a majority. In Bologna, the gig belonged to a new wave of local cultural policies targeting young people. In the same period, the hardcore punk scene was taking shape, with bands often singing in Italian, embracing DIY culture and adopting tactics of political and civic resistance.[6] This new breed of Italian punks would come to the attention of quite a large audience on the occasion of The Clash show in Bologna.

This chapter deals with the Bologna concert, its organisation and its aftermath. We are interested in 'setting the scene', where the performance by The Clash does not work as the 'main act' but as an agency among others, within local and global sociopolitical frameworks adept at renewing cultural policies, at rebuilding a public space in the midst of terrorism and state repression, and at providing Italian youth with new means to subvert and operate. The data we collected are partly based on historical research and draw on archival materials, interviews and media texts. Our work is also connected to content analysis of relevant primary material, such as the flyer distributed at the gig by protesters, and the photos and video footage of the show currently available online.

Bologna 1977

Walking around Bologna's historic town centre in the spring of 1977, you might have encountered tanks patrolling the streets. On 11 March a confrontation between student groups led to a riot and the intervening police shot and killed Francesco Lorusso, a 25-year-old medical student and former member of the recently disbanded Marxist group *Lotta Continua*. A massive student revolt ensued: the local government proved unable to contain the upsurge and ultimately accepted the intervention of the military, sent in by the Minister of Internal Affairs. *Radio Alice*, the official radio of the *Movimento del 77*,[7] was raided by the police and permanently closed. All this engendered what looked like an irreparable fracture between the local government, led by the PCI, and a large section of the radical youth and student population, mainly organised in extra-parliamentary and predominantly leftist political groups.[8] In this context, starting from 1980, Mayor Zangheri and his administration launched a series of initiatives, which would later be gathered under the umbrella of the broader *Piano Giovani*[9] for Bologna. In 1980 the task of managing the first events and activities for the benefit of local youth was entrusted to Aureliana Alberici, Walter Vitali and Mauro Felicori.[10] Felicori expressed some of his views on the political motivations behind the administration's renewed interest in Bologna's radical youth in these terms: 'the political heart of the project lay in the desire – only partly admitted and never openly declared – to mend the rift between the old Left, local institutions and youth movements that had reached its peak in the conflicts of 1977'.[11]

In truth, by the late 1970s a large share of the Bolognese *Movimento* had already distanced itself from strict Marxist revolutionary doctrine. With their stress on creativity, irony and sarcasm, the Bolognese radicals expressed a desire to detach themselves from political violence. In fact, in spite of the March 1977 riots and the ambivalent position towards the Red Brigades expressed by a few during the *Convegno Nazionale sulla Repressione*,[12] the *Movimento* mainly opted for cultural practices to articulate dissent.[13] The local administration spotted in this local peculiarity an opportunity to rebuild the connective tissue between the town government and Bologna's youth and student population. Moreover, they saw a chance for the PCI to overcome the danger of intellectual obsolescence and to reinforce the party's position in the struggle over cultural hegemony, both at local and national level.

During his previous job at the National Secretariat of the PCI youth organisation in Rome, Walter Vitali witnessed the first incarnations of *Estate Romana*, the experimental and controversial summer festival launched in

1977 by the Rome municipality cultural division officer Renato Nicolini and supported by the recently elected, PCI-led city council. *Estate Romana* provided a blueprint for the promotion of events and the temporary use for multiple artistic purposes of public space.[14]

Ritmicittà

Among the many initiatives that the local government decided to put into action in Bologna was a music, dance and experimental theatre festival to be held in the city's main square, Piazza Maggiore. The festival would be called *Ritmicittà* (a pun combining 'rhythm' and 'city') and its organisational team included the local government and some music cooperatives. A number of theatre companies, dance groups, brass bands and jazz ensembles were invited to take part in the festival. According to the organisers, it was a conscious effort to establish dialogue between different creative communities and to introduce the citizens of Bologna to 'diverse fragments of reality' in their own city.[15] Moreover, a few local new wave, post-punk, experimental and punk bands were added to the line-up. By 1980 some of these bands were already known around Italy, partly because of their connections with the Bologna creative *Movimento* and partly because of their participation in previous events, such as the Bologna Rock Festival in April 1979[16] and Milan Rock 80 Festival in February the following year. Bologna bands Gaz Nevada, Skiantos, Luti Chroma, Confusional Quartet, Windopen and the Italy-based American blues artist Andy J. Forest took to the stage on the first three nights of the *Ritmicittà* festival. Out-of-town guests included the Milanese all-female punk rock band Clito and Café Caracas, a punk rock band from Florence. The most notable international guests were the avant-garde jazz group The Art Ensemble of Chicago. Nevertheless, in Felicori's recollection of the events that led to establishing the final line-up, Vitali was not yet satisfied with the festival programme, suggesting that it still needed 'an unambiguous gesture, a symbolic act, that will make clear that we really want to start a new season'.[17] This 'symbolic act' was suggested by *Lotta Continua* music journalist Massimo Buda:

> I called Massimo Buda on the phone at his Cervia home: 'Massimo we want to do something really big here in Bologna, please tell me what you think about it, please share your pipe dream.' Massimo replied with no hesitation whatsoever: 'That's easy Mauro: let's book The Clash.'[18]

Italian punk and The Clash

When punk was first introduced to an Italian mass audience, thanks to *Odeon*, a national television (*RAI*) pop culture show,[19] the *Movimento* didn't exactly know what to do with it. Punks were sometimes mistaken for fascists, partly because of their appearance (military gear, studded leather jackets, short haircuts, the use of Nazi symbols and regalia, and sunglasses) and partly because, at least initially, their provocation and nihilism were seen as dubious and hedonistic. The Clash were the first prominent and popular punk band that seemed to have embraced an identifiable political agenda. The band's lyrics, starting with their early social realist dramatisation of the British crisis, denounced imperialism at the global level and expressed solidarity with past and present struggles in various parts of the world. Nevertheless, the band's connection to British leftist politics was still very ambiguous. As Matthew Worley notes: 'Though enamoured by the image of the rock 'n' roll rebel and though attracted to the romanticism of a just cause, Strummer's commitment to "revolutionary rock" did not always sit easily with the expectations of those on the British left.'[20] However, the political sensibility that The Clash put across through their interviews, lyrics and visual imagery found political expression in the band's relationship with the music industry.

In 1978, however, another UK band, Crass, had already self-released the *Reality Asylum* EP and, in 1979, *The Feeding of the 5000* album, offering a new and uncompromising way of approaching punk from a radical standpoint. The band practised direct political action, played mainly in squats and engaged in seditious activities such as the *Thatchergate Tapes*.[21] The band led a collective lifestyle based on egalitarianism, no profit, animal welfare, pacifism, anarchy and a DIY ethic.[22] Programmatically, they also had a song in which they declared 'the name is Crass, not Clash' ('White Punks on Hope'). This politically driven take on punk was welcomed in Italy, and its enactment made it possible to build continuity between some individual veterans of the *Movimento* and the rising punk youth. It also offered 1980s youth a chance to create independent means to resist the status quo and develop political work.

The gig and its media aftermath

On 1 June 1980 The Clash played Piazza Maggiore, a fifteenth-century square in the centre of the city, enclosed by palaces and an old public library. Café Caracas from Florence and the English band Whirlwind opened the show, as the audience targeted them with bottles, beer cans and spittle. The Clash took the stage very late, because drummer Topper Headon, travelling on his own, got lost in traffic. They started their set with George Butler, Whirlwind's drummer, as a temporary replacement. Headon arrived in time to join in by the ninth song on the set-list, '(White Man) In Hammersmith Palais'. The band later delivered two encores and ended the 29-track set with 'White Riot'.[23] The Piazza Maggiore set-list was longer than usual to compensate for the confusing start of the show. Headon's roadie, Barry 'The Baker' Auguste, remembers the gig vividly in his own blog. In his recollection of the events, Headon's arrival onstage happened at another point of the set-list:

> Suddenly, Topper appeared at the side of the stage. He dashed onto the stage, grabbed a pair of drumsticks and the band crashed into 'London Calling.' The show immediately kicked into high gear with the band feeding off of Topper's energy and power. The crowd responded in kind – they went mental! Pent up frustrations were finally released for both audience and band alike and the hairs stood up on the back of my neck. It was one of the most intensely enthralling and ultimately rewarding shows the band ever played and they were truly thankful afterwards to the Bolognese fans for their patience and loyalty.[24]

The Italian national press wrote about the show in varied, sometimes contradictory terms. Some national newspapers approached the performance from a critical theory standpoint, emphasising how the 'metropolitan angst' exhibited by The Clash was allegedly part of the 'spectacle' of cultural production under capitalism: the band's decision to sign to the multinational record company CBS was cited as further proof in support of these opinions. As a confirmation of the sometimes unsympathetic attitude of the PCI towards the new cultural policies of the Bologna administration, the party's official newspaper, *L'Unità*, gave the gig a negative review. Journalist Michele Serra opined that:

> The Clash gig in its sclerotic and foregone rituality, in its alternative flyer violence, in its well-known hysteria, confirmed thoroughly the fearful limits and the stubborn closure of so-called 'rock culture', its disarticulated fury that turns into market product [...] its sexual provocation that looks like a pathetic pantomime of impotence, its gestural brutality that would like to express repressed animalism [...] or cursed lyrics that look like parodies of holy pictures.[25]

Serra also criticised the 'clash of cultures' between the band's metropolitan and spectacular imagery and the historical and urban setting of Bologna, a city that Serra described as a free and civilised community with an open and cultured public life. *Il Mucchio Selvaggio*, part of the emerging weekly and monthly music press,[26] covered the gig by reviewing the musical performance of the band and contextualising it within the punk movement.[27] On the fringe of the live review, there are references to the protest by local punks and attempts to describe the event in its subcultural dimension by analysing the punk look of some audience members. New wave rock magazine *Rockerilla* had a four-page feature article about the show by Massimo Buda, who was able to hang out with the band and to interview Strummer as well.[28]

Other approaches to the event came from two very different standpoints: national TV RAI and the newspaper *Lotta Continua*. RAI aired a twenty-minute special with edited live material from the gig and a post-gig interview (dubbed into Italian) with band members Topper Headon, Joe Strummer and Mick Jones. Reporter Gianni Minà asked them about their political agenda and their understanding of rock music. The band replied that they shouldn't be considered as left- or right-wing, but rather as a pro-working-class band and that their lyrics were based on 'social' and not 'social-ist' politics. When asked how they felt about playing a free show organised by the PCI, the band stated that they resented being 'politically manipulated', but they also stressed that such a gig would have been impossible in the right-wing UK, because Margaret Thatcher was 'full of shit'. Some emphatic voice-overs performed by actors, with translated lyrics from 'London Calling' and 'Guns of Brixton', accompanied parts of the live clips.[29]

Lotta Continua published a long interview with Joe Strummer on the day after the concert. Massimo Buda was finally able to enquire about the infamous Brigade Rosse T-shirt.[30] Strummer's answers emphasise a desire to be provocative and his personal antagonism towards the Rock Against Racism organisation, especially because of their involvement with the media corporation EMI. In addition, he also justified his previous sympathy for the *Rote Armee Fraktion*, the Irish Republican Army and *Brigate Rosse* as being motivated by an English standpoint and by his desire to identify with rebellion; he was, however, willing to condemn terrorist violence. Strummer also referred to his wanderings in Bologna city centre after the gig and to a long talk he had had with the Bologna *Crassian* anarcho-punks who had been staging a protest before and during the concert.

The protest

RAF Punk, one of the earliest Bolognese and Italian anarcho-punk bands, led the protest against The Clash show and the festival. As the group's drummer, Laura Carroli, remembers:

> We were just a small group of very young kids and we were not affiliated to any political youth organisation, therefore we could not enjoy access to certain public spaces. Our repeated demands for public rehearsal

rooms for us and other underground bands had been systematically ignored by the PCI-led administration and by the district authorities. Furthermore, the PCI administrators probably thought that public spaces should be assigned for political meetings rather than something they considered frivolous like our musical activity. We'd also been repeatedly screwed up by private landlords who had used us for cleaning up their garages and basements on the promise that we could later use them as rehearsal rooms [...] Obviously, that made us really angry too. We felt left out, exploited and alienated.[31]

Due to their youth, many new punks did not share the same political background and experiences of the already semi-established Bolognese punk and new wave acts playing at the *Ritmicittà* festival. According to Laura Carroli:

Many of our friends were just too young to have been active part of the *Movimento*: most of them were kids between thirteen and seventeen. I was slightly older than that and I had been actively involved in the *Movimento*. Jumpy [now Helena Velena, RAF Punk singer and lyricist] was younger than me but she was very precocious politically and she had been involved with *Radio Alice* as a speaker. Nevertheless, for both of us punk represented a welcome fracture with the *Movimento* of the time. We had seen the tail end of it all, the disappointment, the internal fights and the rioting, especially after the *Convegno Nazionale sulla Repressione*. Then heroin came and swept away many of us. We wanted to break free from all that and punk provided a vital regeneration, for us at least.

This mixed group of teenage kids and disillusioned members of the *Movimento* soon began to gravitate towards a new brand of punk ethos which was beginning to come to the fore around 1978–79. RAF Punk in particular found an important reference point in the animal rights, anarchist and DIY ideals of Crass. The band quickly embraced the Crass agenda, which included an outspoken dismissal of The Clash as a prime example of punk acts selling out to multinational corporations to attain rock star status. Due to their major label signing, political lyrics and rebel stance, The Clash were considered contradictory and ineffectual by the new anarcho-punks. As a result, when the *Ritmicittà* festival was launched and The Clash were announced as headliners, the Bolognese anarcho-punk scene reacted with anger:

Instead of listening to our demands the administration was giving us entertainment. We considered that a patronising and disingenuous move. They wanted to make peace with the *Movimento* and, at the same time, lure us as mere consumers of cutting edge music with a single big event.

> We had never asked for that. We'd rather have practice rooms where we could develop our own music all year long; we demanded spaces where we could put on shows for us and invite other bands, socialise, be active and make our scene grow day after day. We considered that as a much better way of spending public money than booking big stars and putting on festivals. On top of that there was our criticism of the commodification of political punk, which in our eyes was embodied by The Clash and their CBS deal.[32]

The outraged punks could count on the logistical support of the anarchists, the only political group that gave them shelter within the crowded Bolognese radical panorama. The small but solid anarchist infrastructure was crucial for the printing of flyers:

> I guess their political beliefs forced them to accept us for what we were. They let us gather and do our thing in their historical meeting place, the *Circolo Anarchico Berneri*, ironically located in one of Bologna's most conservative areas [...] They also had a small printing house and they let us use it to print our flyers at a very low price. Later on, the Anarchists gave us access to their own printing offset inside the *Circolo Berneri*. There we printed all our material, including our own journal – called *Punkzine* – and even the sleeves of our first record.[33]

On 1 June, the anarcho-punk protest group showed up in the Piazza Maggiore area and started distributing flyers to The Clash fans who had reached Bologna from all over Italy: 'We were so naive that we only printed 1000 flyers which was obviously not enough, given the number of punks who assembled in Bologna to see The Clash: as a result, before the square was only half full we'd already given out all our flyers.' Nevertheless, even after all the flyers had been distributed, the protesters kept engaging the arriving punks in discussions and arguments, individually or in groups, sharing the motivations behind their protest. The reaction of the gig-goers was mixed, as Laura Carroli remembers:

> The Clash fans and the assembled Italian punks were all so happy and excited to finally get the chance to see their favourite band that many of them were baffled by our protest. They could not understand how we could complain about The Clash playing for free in the main square of our city. Nevertheless, I think we seeded something in a few people's minds on that day.[34]

Carroli's impression is confirmed by the memory of Marco Philopat, a young attendee who would soon become a central figure of hardcore punk in Milan:

At The Clash gig in Bologna [...] I arrived proudly dressed up as Sid Vicious: white jacket, chains around my neck and arms with cuts and cigarette burns. To be in tune with the gig, I also got a Clash T-shirt. Before the start of 'London Calling', a group of local punks started mocking me and put a flyer in my hands, where Crass were repeatedly quoted [...] While I was running wild in front of the stage, in a remote area of my nervous system I was already feeling that those puppets made me feel good, but only to a certain degree. It was there that I started asking myself some questions.[35]

There is no footage of the 1 June protest. Nevertheless, in the video documentary *Mamma Dammi La Benza* (2005), Stefano 'Steno' Cimato, ex-RAF Punk and member of Nabat, and Giampaolo 'Jumpy' Giorgetti of RAF Punk (now Helena Velena) can be seen taking to the stage during the performances of unspecified local punk bands and talking into a microphone about their frontal opposition to 'the power' and to the municipality of Bologna.[36] In the same documentary, Steno expresses another point of view on the protest:

It's not that we did not like The Clash. They were an outstanding band and we did listen to their music. They have been really important for the punk scene. What we could not accept was the fact that the gig was held during the Communist Party recruiting campaign [...] we felt that our background, our values and our music had been taken away from us.[37]

The protesters even managed to get in touch with The Clash, albeit accidentally. On occasion, Helena Velena has reported a chance meeting with Joe Strummer while the latter was taking a walk in the city centre on the morning after the gig. She questioned the band's political stance and what she perceived as an evolution of their sound towards commercialism, to which, in Velena's recollection, Strummer replied 'Yes, but this record ['London Calling'] vibrates with the rhythm of the heart'.[38] Strummer's words represented some sort of epiphany for Velena: she suddenly realised that her attack on the band on the basis of their punk credentials and background was pointless since, from her standpoint, by 1980 The Clash had turned into something rather different, a rock band.

The protesters' flyer

The distribution of cyclostyled flyers had been common practice in Italian political activism since 1968, for instance during workers' strikes. In the late 1970s and early 1980s the *Brigate Rosse* communicated with the public via flyers exclusively. Leaflets were used to attract sympathisers, to lay claim to terrorist acts, to provide information about 'enemies of the people' and possible targets, and to offer narratives and justifications for their actions. The terrorists always signed their flyers with the star logo and the name of the group. Texts were typically typewritten. They were usually hidden before use and distributed anonymously in litter bins or telephone boxes.

The flyer by the young punks from Bologna adopts some of the graphic strategies of the *Brigate Rosse*: for instance, the use of black and white cyclostyle, the choice of A4 format and the typewritten text. However, there are also some striking differences, which are revealing of the huge paradigm change in Italian radical political action. First and foremost, in the punk flyer there is the ubiquitous presence of the circled A and cutout images are heavily employed. The flyer is printed on both sides, the first page dominated by a huge circled A. Some words run along the circle: *lifeless, punk rock* (with 'rock' crossed out) and *distruggi il potere non la gente* (destroy power not people). On the upper left side there are the logos of five local acts: RAF Punk, Uxidi, Anna FalkSS, The 69 A.C.I.D. Punk and Puke Punk. Nearly all the band names carry at least one circled A. Among the cutout images in the background we can recognise the Crass logo and some musicians, probably a live picture of the band and a picture of a man in what might be an electric chair. The typewritten text is divided into three typographical columns on this page, the first of them oblique to the page.

The second page is almost entirely covered by text, with a small portion of a picture at the bottom and a handwritten oblique text in capitals reading *PUNK E' ANARCHIA ATTIVA NON LURKERISMO PASSIVO* (punk is active anarchy not passive lurking). The text itself conveys the urgency behind its composition very effectively, both in the inclusion of mistakes and hand-made corrections and in the flow of thoughts. Compared to a flyer by the Italian revolutionary Left, this seems simpler and more impulsive; from a rhetorical point of view, there is little space for the political and critical theory that influenced the style of the revolutionary communists' written communications. The Clash are described as 'out-dated', a 'super-famous big group', 'instruments of power' and 'fucking inoffensive', their gig as 'organised to fuck us up' and as an instrument 'to gather votes' and 'ingratiate the youth masses'. The flyer also makes reference to the mainstream media attempt to normalise punk and its disruptive power by analysing and dissecting it. In opposition to all this, Bolognese punks propose to start a fanzine with interviews and reviews of punk bands (such as Crass, Eretics [*sic*], Epileptics and Crisis) and articles about Italian bands and DIY methods of clothing and hairstyling. The flyer ends with a plea to punks all over Italy to collaborate, write, start a band and keep the information going within the circle, avoiding interference from the system and from the mass media.

Conclusion

In a country that had yet to fully discover the first wave of the punk movement, the Piazza Maggiore show signalled the presence of a new generation of punks and gave them unexpected visibility.[39] Furthermore, by bringing so many Italian punks to Bologna, the gig also allowed the protesters to make first contact with many of those who would soon become active in the hardcore punk scene.[40] The new scene would later brand its members as 'punx' with the final letter chosen deliberately, in order to distinguish themselves from early first-wave 'punks'. With their uncompromising music and oppositional stance, hardcore punx kept the Italian tradition of political antagonism alive throughout the 1980s, safeguarding practices of dissent and political engagement through new forms of expression. In many cases, anarchism and anarcho-communist ideas replaced the political approach of the *Movimento*, while new issues such as animal rights were added to the list of causes worth fighting for.

The dismissal of The Clash concert by Michele Serra in the pages of *L'Unità* was based on a supposed contrast between the band's suburban combat aesthetics and Bologna's pristine architecture and benevolent and inclusive social setting: however, it can be argued that the band and the city shared some deep and subconscious similarities. The Clash had put themselves in the difficult position of standing for socialist ideals in a capitalist music industry, just as Bologna stood as an example of the administrative capabilities of the largest Communist Party in the Western world. Both the band and the city had to face heavy criticism from different sides of the political spectrum and both had to live up to very high expectations. The chaos and intensity of The Clash performance really matched the ferocity of the previous years in Bologna and offered some sort of catharsis for it: in the words of Steno, 'it was a ray of light'[41] and a long-lasting bond was established between the city and the band on that occasion.[42] In fact, the concert is still remembered by many members of the punk community and by music enthusiasts as a watershed moment. As Saverio Pasotti, guitar player in the band Windopen, has stated:

> The Clash show in Piazza Maggiore was a true starting point for so many musicians and young people in general: most of them were approaching that musical genre [punk] for the very first time. The square was packed and there were lots of teenagers. That concert left a mark on us [Windopen] too, and we were already somehow experienced, imagine how much impact it had on young people. It really changed the lives of many.[43]

However, unbeknown to all those who were in Piazza Maggiore on 1 June, much darker days lay ahead for the city. Just two months after the concert, the bombing of the central railway station would claim the lives of eighty-five people: a tragic reminder that the Years of Lead were still far from being over for Bologna and indeed for Italy more broadly.[44]

The concert did not, of course, stop political violence, nor it did single-handedly resolve the fracture between the PCI and radical youth. However, it offered a public arena, among others, where subcultural enactments, experiments in cultural policies, and real and imagined cities could be seen and heard interacting. Furthermore, it showed how music can transform lives at both the individual and collective level, when it beats to the *rhythm of the heart*.

Notes

1 The authors would like to thank the following for their essential contributions to this chapter: Laura Carroli, Stefano 'Steno' Cimato, Mauro Felicori, Luca Frazzi, Oderso Rubini and Angela Zocco. All translations from Italian by the authors.
2 Directed by Jack Hazan and David Mingay, 1980.
3 No witnesses can confirm whether Strummer actually wore the Brigade Rosse T-shirt on stage in Bologna or not. There are no photos or filmed footage of The Clash front man wearing the garment during that specific show. According to some accounts, he was dissuaded from wearing it by members of the organisation minutes before the beginning of the concert. See Alberto Piccinini, 'Un Punk e una Maglietta (delle BR)', *Rolling Stone Italia*, November 2012.
4 *Anni di Piombo* (years of lead) is a generic label commonly used to describe the complex political situation that characterised Italy between the end of the 1960s and the early 1980s. The term probably comes from *Die bleierne Zeit* (which translates from German as 'the leaden time', although the English title of the film is *Marianne and Juliane*), a 1981 film by German director Margarethe von Trotta, and was only used retrospectively to historicise that particular era.
5 In Italian political jargon, the term describes a mass retreat from civic engagement and political action towards personal concerns and private life. This happened in the wake of the political disappointments encountered by the radical left in the mid-to-late 1970s. See Paul Ginsborg, *A History of Contemporary Italy: Society and Politics 1935–1988* (London: Penguin, 1990).
6 In the case of Turin, see Giacomo Bottà, 'Lo Spirito Continua: Torino and the Collettivo Punx Anarchici', in The Subcultures Network (eds), *Fight Back: Punk Politics and Resistance* (Manchester: Manchester University Press, 2015), pp. 155–69.
7 The *Movimento del 77* is a complex, extreme left-wing political movement, which left aside most of the idealism of 1968 and started focusing on the 'needs' of its 'subjectivities', for instance by practising the *esproprio proletario* (collective actions of 'social shopping', in which goods were stolen for self-

financing purposes or to be distributed to the poor). Other common practices were the auto-reduction of ticket prices for popular music concerts and *non lavoro* (avoidance of work). See, for instance, Nanni Balestrini and Bruno Moroni, *L'Orda d'Oro 1968–1977: La Grande Ondata Rivoluzionaria e Creativa, Politica ed Esistenziale* (Milan: Feltrinelli, 2015).

8   See Oderso Rubini and Andrea Tinti, *Non Disperdetevi. 1977–1982 San Francisco, New York, Bologna: Le Città Libere del Mondo* (Rome: Arcana Editrice, 2003), pp. 215–25.
9   Youth Policy Plan.
10 See Rubini and Tinti, *Non Disperdetevi*, p. 222.
11 Oderso Rubini, *Largo all'Avanguardia: La Straordinaria Storia di 50 Anni di Musica Rock a Bologna* (Bologna: Sonic Press, 2011), p. 108.
12 The *Convegno nazionale sulla repressione* (National Conference on Repression) took place in Bologna in September 1977, as a response to the police and army violence of March 1977. More than 250,000 members of the *Movimento* gathered in Bologna, but no common plan for its future emerged from the proceedings.
13 See Rubini and Tinti, *Non Disperdetevi*, pp. 215–25.
14 Renato Nicolini, *Estate Romana: Un Effimero Lungo Nove Anni* (Reggio Calabria: Città del Sole Edizioni, 2011).
15 Massimo Buda, 'Come cambia il volto (non solo musicale) di una città. Ovvero del rock e della "politica"', *Lotta Continua*, 11–12 May 1980, p. 12.
16 The Bologna Rock Festival was organised by independent music cooperative Harpo's Bazaar on 2 April 1979, at Bologna's basketball stadium, with 6,000 attendees. See Oderso Rubini, *Largo all'Avanguardia. La Straordinaria Storia di 50 Anni di Musica Rock a Bologna* (Bologna: Sonic Press, 2011), pp. 90–5.
17 Ibid., p. 108.
18 Ibid.
19 Mara Persello, 'Peripheral Subcultures. The First Appropriations of Punk in Germany and Italy', in Paula Guerra and Tânja Moreira (eds), *Keep It Simple, Make It Fast! An Approach to Underground Music Scenes* (Porto: Universidade do Porto, 2016), pp. 93–8; and Marco Philopat, *Lumi di Punk: La Scena Italiana Raccontata dai Protagonisti* (Milan: Agenzia X, 2006).
20 Matthew Worley, 'Revolution Rock? The Clash, Joe Strummer and the British Left in the Early Days of Punk', in Barry J. Faulk and Brady Harrison (eds), *Punk Rock Warlord: The Life and Work of Joe Strummer* (Farnham: Ashgate, 2014), p. 82.
21 The *Thatchergate Tapes* was a hoax audio recording of a phone conversation between Margaret Thatcher and Ronald Reagan, regarding the Falklands War, created by members of Crass by mixing and cutting audio excerpts of the two politicians' speeches.
22 See George Berger, *The Story of Crass* (London: Omnibus, 2008).
23 The set-list included 'Clash City Rockers', 'Brand New Cadillac', 'Safe European Home', 'Jimmy Jazz', 'London Calling', 'Guns of Brixton', 'Train in Vain', 'Spanish Bombs', '(White Man) In Hammersmith Palais', 'Jail Guitar Doors', 'Somebody Got Murdered', 'Koka Kola', 'I Fought the Law', '48 Hours', 'Protex Blue', 'Police and Thieves', 'Bankrobber', 'Clampdown', 'Stay

Free', 'English Civil War', 'I'm So Bored with the USA', 'Complete Control', 'Armagideon Time', 'Tommy Gun', 'Garageland', 'Janie Jones', 'London's Burning', 'Capital Radio' and 'White Riot'.

24 https://thebaker77.wordpress.com/2013/12/19/bologne-calling-joe-strummer-memorial-tribute-show/ (accessed 21 March 2017).
25 Michele Serra, 'Prima di Bruciare Londra Meglio Conoscere Bologna', *L'Unità*, 3 June 1980.
26 To understand the late emergence of a popular music press in Italy, see Simone Varriale, *Globalisation, Music and Cultures of Distinction: The Rise of Pop Music Criticism in Italy* (London: Palgrave, 2016).
27 Stefano Lenti, 'THE CLASH Bologna 01/06/1980', *Mucchio Selvaggio* 31 (July–August 1980).
28 Massimo Buda, 'Clash', *Rockerilla* 6 (July 1980).
29 RAI TV has never re-run the TV special about The Clash. However, we were able to access the footage through the personal archives of music journalists Angela Zocco and Luca Frazzi.
30 Massimo Buda, 'Il Combattente del Rock che Confondeva James Dean con le BR', *Lotta Continua*, 8–9 June 1980.
31 Interview with Laura Carroli, Bologna, 12 September 2017.
32 Ibid.
33 Ibid. See also *Schiavi nella città più libera del mondo* (1982, Attack Punk), a compilation 7" featuring RAF Punk, Bacteria, Stalag 17 and Anna FalkSS. The Attack Punk label manager was RAF Punk's singer Jumpy Velena herself, and the title ('Slaves in the freest city in the world') was a rebuttal of Mayor Zangheri's famous public praise of Bologna's liberal virtues.
34 Interview with Laura Carroli, Bologna, 12 September 2017.
35 Marco Philophat, 'Non Esiste Autorità Al Di Fuori Di Te Stesso', in *DIY Crass Bomb L'Azione Diretta nel Punk* (Milan: Agenzia X, 2010), p. 10.
36 Authors' private correspondence with music journalist Luca Frazzi, March 2017.
37 *Mamma Dammi la Benza: Le Radici del Punk Italiano 1977–1982* (dir. Angelo Rastelli, 2005).
38 For instance in *Mamma Dammi la Benza: Le Radici del Punk Italiano 1977–1982* and in *Putiferio Clash*, https://youtu.be/L1FOozz1GlU (accessed 30 March 2017).
39 *Ciao 2001*, a weekly rock-pop magazine of the time, published the protesters' flyer in its report of the concert, thus giving the anarcho-punk scene unpredicted visibility.
40 Interview with Laura Carroli, Bologna, 12 September 2017.
41 Rubini and Tinti, *Non Disperdetevi*, p. 303.
42 Since 2002 Bologna has hosted the Joe Strummer Tribute, a festival dedicated to the band's musical and cultural heritage. Furthermore, one of the city's main urban parks and concert sites has been renamed after The Clash front man.
43 Pasotti in Rubini and Tinti, *Non Disperdetevi*, p. 147.
44 See Claudio Pescetelli, *Lo Stivale è Marcio, Storie Italiane, Punk e Non* (Rave Up Books, 2013).

Index

Abercorn restaurant bombing 52
abjection, sense of 13, 15, 77–8, 81, 91
Aboriginal rights 198–205
academic studies 4, 61–3
Adebayo, Dotun 96
Adorno, Theodor 17, 36, 171
'Albatross' (song) 138
Albertine, Viv 64, 114, 148
Albini, Steve 119
Alleyne, Mike 171
Angry Brigade 52
Anti-Nazi League 97, 100
artistry 49, 53–4, 61
Arulpragasam, Mathangi 81
Ashton, Frederick 55
Attali, Jacques 5–6, 139
Attwood, Bain 198
Auguste, Barry 213
austerity measures 27, 45
Australia 26, 194–205
authenticity
  politics of 180
  of punk 144–9, 155
authority, decline of 49
autobiographies 149, 154
autonomy of musicians 36, 42, 47

Back, Les 104
Baker, Danny 144–5
Bakhtin, M.M. 44
Bali 129–30
Ballard, J.G. 165
Bangs, Lester 187

'Bankrobber' (song) 71
Baraka, Amiri 189–90
'base and superstructure' model 36–8, 42, 45–9
'Battle of Bedford Street' 1–2
Baudelaire, Charles 80
Baulch, Emma 129–30
BBC World Service 173–4
the Beastie Boys 187
The Beatles (and Beatlemania) 39, 174, 180, 188
Benjamin, Walter 25–6, 79–81, 83, 108–11, 120–2
Berardi, Franco 111–12
Berry, Chuck 133
Bhaskar, Roy 37
Big Youth 115
black culture 91–2, 115, 117
Blackwell, Chris 171
Blur 165
Bologna 26, 112, 209–20
Boot, Adrian 2
boredom 163–4
  see also 'I'm So Bored with the USA'
Bragg, Billy 117, 119, 130, 141, 167
Brecht, Bertolt 141
Brexit 21, 23, 27
'bricolage' 90
Brixton riots (1981) 11
'Broadway' (song) 76–7
Brooker, Christopher 90
Brown, Wendy 79–80
Buda, Massimo 211, 214

Bulldog 100
Burchill, Julie 71
Burk, Greg 169
Butler, George 213

Cabut, Richard 19
'The Call Up' (song) 76–7, 182, 188
Callaghan, James 40, 43
Cameron, Mike 185, 187
capitalism 37–40, 49, 66
  resistance to 38, 40
'Car Jamming' (song) 13, 77
Carroli, Laura 214–16
Cashell, Kieran 74
censorship 55
Central School of Art 59
Centre for Contemporary Cultural Studies (CCCS) 148
Chimes, Terry 115
Chuck D 188
Cimato, Steno 217, 219
'Clampdown' 15–16
  see also 'Working for the Clampdown'
Clapton, Eric 93
Clark, P. Merriam 181
The Clash
  academic studies of 4
  ambivalence of 8
  Americanisation of 180
  characteristics of their music 5, 36–7, 41, 44–9, 75, 95, 104, 131–5, 161, 184
  commercial success of 13, 60, 134–5, 190, 194
  contradictions manifested by 4, 17, 47–8, 144
  criticisms of 3, 9–10, 12, 17, 35, 47, 60, 71, 80, 180–4, 215
  cultural significance of 4–5, 11–12, 17, 21
  distinctiveness of 41
  extensive touring by 182
  globalism of 173
  in historical context 24–7
  image of 151, 196
  influence of 3, 5, 26, 37, 49, 89, 130, 188
  involvement in films 3, 97, 144, 164, 169–70, 189
  literature on 149, 154, 178–83, 197, 200, 203

  playing at the Ulster Hall, Belfast 1
  political engagement of 2, 9, 12, 26–7, 35, 41, 44, 46, 61, 70–4, 89, 98–9, 131, 134, 188–9, 194–7, 203, 205, 212, 219
  recording career 6
  reputation and commemoration of 17–18, 23–4
  suspicions of selling-out 22, 60, 120, 144, 180, 190, 215–16
  tensions within the group 14, 47–8, 78
  see also fans of The Clash
The Clash (album) 7, 9, 70, 74, 131–4, 138
A Clockwork Orange (film) 165
club culture 161–2
Cochran, Eddie 130
Cogan, Brian 139
Cohen, Samuel 9, 76, 82
Cohen, Stanley 190
Combat Rock (album) 12–13, 15, 46, 48, 77–8, 179–80, 188–90, 197
consumer culture 147
Conway-Herron, Janie 203
Coon, Caroline 116
Cooper, Henry 21
corporate media 56–8, 61
Cost of Living EP 11, 181
countercultural movement 39–40, 46, 59–60, 114, 117 121
Crass 212, 215, 218
The Crickets 67
Critchley, Simon 24, 107
Cruikshank, George 90
cultural studies 4
Culture (reggae artists) 118
culture industries 20–1, 24–5, 74
Cut the Crap (album) 14, 48–9
Czezowski, Andrew 112, 114

Dammers, Jerry 102, 193
The Damned 54, 61, 151
Dean, Jodi 79–80
Debord, Guy 111
De Niro, Robert 189
Dennis, John 101
'Deny' (song) 133–4
Derrida, Jacques 27
Detroit 165
Devoto, Howard 155
Dickens, Charles 90

Diddley, Bo 182, 186
'Dig a Hole' (song) 93
'DIY' activities 147–8, 155
Dorsey, Lee 182, 186–7
Douglas, Mary 53
Dread, Mikey 96, 187–8
dub 169–70
Dunn, Kevin 129–30
Dylan, Bob 41, 116, 121, 178

'Earthquake Weather' (album) 77
Egan, Sean 180–2, 187–8
elite artists 55, 60
Engels, Friedrich 47
England and Englishness 167–8
'English Civil War' (song) 10, 43
The Exploited 130

Fabbri, Franco 42
Falklands War 15, 78
The Fall 164
fans of The Clash 26, 66, 98–100, 144–6, 149, 154–5, 216
    lapsed 3
Faulkner, William 61
Felicori, Mauro 210–11
feminism 63
La Fille Mal Gardée 55
'First Night Back in London' (song) 172–3
Fisher, Mark 19, 111
flyers 217–18
Foley, Ellen 64
Foley, Gary 194–5, 198–205
folk art 56, 58–9
Foote, Mickey 120
Ford, Tennessee Ernie 182
Ford Motors 43
Forde, Brinsley 99, 103
'48 Thrills' (song) 134
Fraser, Malcolm 200–1
Freedom Ride 198–9
Freud, Sigmund 79
Frith, Simon 5, 146, 197
From Here to Eternity (album) 144
Fudger, Marion 65
Furgerson, Paul 156

Gallagher, Mickey 75
Gallix, Andrew 19
Gange, Ray 99, 153
'Garageland' 9, 41–2, 73–5, 120, 134

Garvey, Marcus 93, 118
'Gates of the West' 11, 181, 189
Gaynor, Gloria 65
Gelbart, Matthew 174
gentrification 164, 183
'Ghetto Defendant' (song) 13
Gibbs, Joe 93, 116, 117
Gidley, Ben 103
'the gig that never happened' (Belfast, 1977) 1–3, 62
Gilbert, Pat 69, 93, 96, 120
Gillray, James 90
Gilroy, Paul 92, 97, 100
Ginsberg, Allen 13, 189
Giorgetti, Gianpaolo 217
    see also Velena, Helena
Give 'Em Enough Rope (album) 9–10, 42–3, 116, 180–1
globalism 173
'God Save the Queen' (song) 90, 112, 130, 174
Goering, Hermann 168
Goldman, Vivien 94
Good Vibrations (film) 2
Grainger, Percy 56
Gramsci, Antonio 133
Gray, Marcus 2–3, 24, 64, 92–3, 95, 117, 178, 197, 203
Green, Johnny 63, 96, 181–2
Grenfell Tower 76, 175
'Guardian Angels' on the New York subway 172
Guthrie, Woody 72

Haines, Luke 24
Hair (musical) 55
Harbour, Pearl 64
The Harder They Come 186
Harlesden Coliseun 150
Harper, Rob 112, 115
'Hate and the War' (song) 133
Hatherley, Owen 20
Headon, Nicky ('Topper') 14, 44, 47–8, 62, 77, 100, 153, 170–1, 212–14
Heath, Edward 6
Hebdige, Dick 90–2, 102, 147–8
Hegarty, Paul 139
heritage industry 90
Hesmondhalgh, David 60, 62
High Wycombe 150–1, 155–6
Hill, Joseph 118
Hinds, David 94

hip-hop 12, 47, 103–4, 188–9
Holmstrom, John 129
Horn, Gerd-Rainer 39
Howard, Robert 98
Huddle, Roger 101
Humphrey, Simon 120
Hynde, Chrissie 64, 148

'I Fought The Law' (song) 181
Ignorant, Steve 130, 141
image 151, 196
immersion 189
immigrant communities 8, 167
'I'm So Bored with the USA' (song) 12, 113, 133, 135, 163, 181
incomes policy 6
The Independent (newspaper) 154–5
indigenous peoples 194–205
Indonesia 129–30
internationalism 12
Israel 6
Italy 209, 219
    see also Bologna

Jackman, Vernon 185
Jacobsen, Eric 109–10
Jaguar cars 22
The Jam 61, 165
Jamaica 117–18
James, Wendy 64
Jameson, Fredric 19
'Janie Jones' (song) 131–2
Joe Strummer: The Future is Unwritten (film) 169
Johnson, Boris 20–1
Johnson, Linton Kwesi 99
Jones, Dylan 156
Jones, Mick 7, 9, 12–16, 20, 22, 40, 43–4, 47–8, 62–4, 69–78, 93, 95, 99, 101, 113–16, 119–20, 135–41, 150, 153–4, 164, 169–70, 175, 178–81, 188–91, 214
Jones, Stephen 156
Jones, Steve 90, 133, 166
Joyce, William ('Lord Haw Haw') 173–4
Jozajtis, Kris 156

Keegan, Kevin 21
Kelly, Danny 144–5
Kenny, Mary 173
Khamenei, Ayatollah 58
King, Stephen 117

The King of Comedy (film) 189
The Kinks 114, 130, 185
'Know Your Rights' (song) 12–13, 48, 77
Kristeva, Julia 172

Laing, David 61, 73
Lanchester Polytechnic 96
Leadville 165–6
Le Corbusier 165
'left melancholy' 25, 70, 73, 79–80, 83
'Leopardskin Limousines' 77
Lethal Bizzle 104
Letts, Don 18, 93, 95, 114, 116, 144, 153, 164, 169–70
Levene, Keith 131, 135–41
Levi's jeans 22
liberation theology 109, 118
Little Englishness 168
London 7–11, 22–3, 26, 39, 115, 122, 161–2, 167–8, 171–4
    flooding of 174–5
London Calling (album) 5, 11–12, 15, 17, 23, 35, 43–6, 74, 81, 91, 94, 119, 138, 173–4, 178–82, 197, 213, 217
London-ness of The Clash 186
'London's Burning' (song) 108, 134, 162, 164
Lorusso, Francesco 210
'Lost in the Supermarket' 74–5
Lott, Eric 190
Love, Courtney 53
Löwy, Michael 109
Lukács, Georg 141
Lydon, John 20, 90, 131, 139, 148, 166
Lynskey, Dorian 65

Macauley, Rocco 8, 121
McCartney, Linda 53
McDonagh, Martin 3–4
McLaren, Malcolm 89–90, 96, 111, 119, 166
McMahon, William 199
McNeil, Legs 129
'The Magnificent Seven' (song) 12, 47, 187–8
Malfa, Mark 179
Manley, Michael 93, 117
Marcus, Greil 191
market forces 10–11
Markus, Andrew 198

Marley, Bob 94, 171, 185
Marlow-on-Thames 150–1, 155
Marsh, Dave 129
Martin, Gavin 182
Martin, Nigel 156
Marx, Karl (and Marxist theory) 36, 38, 47, 49, 74, 109–10, 139
Mauresmo, Amelie 53
May, Theresa 161
media coverage 145
Melody Maker 56–7, 65
memoirs 148
M.I.A. 81–3, 104
Michon, Alex 113, 148
middle-class life 152
Milligan, Rowan Talliis 121
Minà, Gianni 214
miners' strike (1984) 35, 46
misogyny 64–5
Moon, Tony 148
Morrissey 165
Mosley, Oswald 173
Mulhern, Francis 35
multiculturalism 9, 11, 98
Murray, Andy 53
Murvin, Junior 11, 93–4, 117, 151
music hall tradition 90
music industry, the 25, 36, 146, 196
music's importance for understanding of the social world 5
Myers, Barry 93

National Front 7, 43, 196
national identity 89
Nazism 173
Needs, Kris 112–13, 119–20, 156
neoliberalism 15, 17–18, 27, 35–6, 43, 46–9, 78–9, 83
New Musical Express (NME) 187, 202–3
New Pop 46
'new social movements' 38, 40, 46, 108
New York 11–12, 26, 39, 48, 76, 172, 182, 184, 189
Newark, NJ 189–90
Nicolaeva-Legat, Nadine 55
Nicolini, Renato 210–11
'1977' (song) 8, 93, 113
No Fixed Address 203
Nolan, Seamus 121
nostalgia 19–20, 22
Notting Hill 162, 164, 169, 172

Notting Hill Carnival riots (1976) 8–9, 92–3, 95, 116–17, 169–70

official histories 149, 154
Ogg, Alex 184
oil crisis (1976) 6
Ono, Yoko 53
opening acts 187
Orwell, George 113
outernationalisation 26, 104
OZ trial (1971) 55

Panter, Horace 102
'Paper Planes' (song) 82–3, 104
Parsons, Tony 7, 71
Pasotti, Saverio 219
pastiche 19
Peach, Blair 101
Peacock, James 76, 82, 172
'Pearl Harbour' (tour) 181
Pearlman, Sandy 9, 42, 181
Peddie, Ian 79
Perkins, Charles 198–9, 203
Perry, Lee ('Scratch') 11, 94–5, 115–17, 170
Perry, Mark ('Mark P') 21–2, 59–66, 70, 118–19, 144
Petersen, Bjekle 202–3
Philopat, Marco 216–17
photo opportunities 2–3
Pink Floyd 59
place, sense of 161, 171
Platt, Edward 165–6
the Police 188
'Police and Thieves' 11, 27, 93–4, 115–17, 134, 151, 185, 196
policing 8–10, 52, 57
popular culture 19, 55–6, 104
post-war economic order 39, 46
predictability in music-making 42
Presley, Elvis 120, 178
protest songs 79
'Protex Blue' (song) 134–5
Public Image Limited (PiL) 131, 138–41
'punk hunting' 151–2
Punk (magazine) 129
punk rock 2, 10, 14–15, 18–21, 39–44, 49, 56, 59–63, 66, 73–4, 89–103, 107–10, 114, 121, 129, 185, 191, 194, 212
  investigations into 146
  political aspects of 195–6

Punk Rock Movie 114
Punk '77 110–14, 119–22
'Punky Reggae Party' 94
Pussy Riot 58
Putin, Vladimir 58

Queenan, Joe 91

Rachel, Daniel 137
racism 8–9, 16, 93–100, 151, 187
  see also Rock Against Racism
radical politics 9
rap music 188
Rastafarianism 91, 93, 95, 116–18
Rat Patrol from Fort Bragg 182
Reagan, Ronald 15, 48, 78
Reddington, Helen 149
Redgrave, Steve 152
reductionism 36
reflexivity 148
reggae music 26, 89–103, 114–17, 169–71, 185–7, 196
Reid, Jamie 21, 89–90, 111, 174
Reilly, Mark 156
'Remote Control' (song) 132–3
Reynolds, Simon 47, 140–1
Rhodes, Bernie 7–8, 14, 43, 111–18
rhythm and blues (R'n'B) 39, 113
Riley, Mykaell 93–4
Ritmicittà festival 211–15
Rizzle Kicks 104
Rock Against Racism (RAR) movement 89, 93, 97–103, 151, 209, 214
'Rock of the Casbah' 14, 48, 190–1
rock music 42, 94, 103, 174, 185
  ideology of 146
  professionalised criticism of 146–7
Roger, Ranking 103
Rolling Stone (magazine) 146
The Rolling Stones 119, 185, 187
Rome 112
Ronan Point collapse (1968) 165
Rotten, Johnny 54, 61, 90, 93, 114–15
Route 19 178–9
Roxy club, Covent Garden 112, 114
Rude Boy (film) 97, 99–100, 153, 209

'Safe European Home' (song) 9, 43, 95, 116, 189
Sandinista! (album) 11–12, 46–7, 75–6, 168, 172, 179–80, 188, 197
Sassoon, Donald 40

Saunders, David ('Red') 97, 101
Savage, Jon 14, 90, 95–6, 107, 164, 195
Scelsa, Vin 186
Scorsese, Martin 189
Scritti Politti 47
sectarian divisions 2
self-actualization 148
Serra, Michele 213, 219
Sex Pistols 54–5, 61, 89–93, 113, 115, 119, 130, 133–4, 139, 151–2, 155–6, 166, 180
sexism 53, 63–5
Shahan, Cyrus 108
Shakespeare, William 90
Sharp, Cecil 56
Shelley, Pete 155
Shelton, Syd 98, 101
'Should I Stay or Should I Go?' 81, 190
Simmel, Georg 172
Simon, Kate 121
Simonon, Paul 8, 11, 14, 44, 47–9, 54, 93, 95, 100, 113–19, 131, 136, 150, 153–7, 169–73, 178, 190, 200
Sinker, Mark 90–1
Sioux, Siouxsie 61, 63, 113
Situationist International (SI) 110
The Slits 65, 114
Slumdog Millionaire (film) 82
Smith, Mark E. 119
Smith, Patti 115
Smith, Pennie 173
Sobczak, Eugene 179
social commentary 168–9
Social Contract 43
Solis, Gabriel 203–4
'Something about England' (song) 76, 168
Sony (company) 22
Sound System 22
'Spanish Bombs' (song) 12, 27
The Specials 102–3
Spencer, Neil 96
Springer, Jacqueline 53
Springsteen, Bruce 163
squatting 162, 169
State of Emergency 93, 116
Stevens, Guy 44
Sting 188
'Straight to Hell' (song) 13, 15, 70, 77–9, 82–3, 104, 190

Straw, Will 184
Strongman, Phil 114
Strummer, Joe 2, 4, 7–10, 12–14, 16–17, 22, 35, 40, 43–9, 52–3, 62, 64, 66, 69–78, 82, 93–8, 101–2, 108, 112–20, 131, 134–6, 144, 150–6, 161–2, 168–75, 179–91, 196–7, 202–5, 209, 214, 217
  criticisms of 183
  different personae of 72
subcultures 147–9, 184
suburban punks 155
superstructure *see* 'base and superstructure' model
Sutch, Screaming Lord 155

Technics hi-fi 22
Temple, Julien 90, 113, 165
terrorism 12
Thames Barrier 174–5
Thatcher, Margaret (and Thatcherism) 10–11, 15–16, 23, 35, 43–8, 77–8, 214
'This is England' (song) 14
Thompson, Ben 82
Thornton, Sarah 145
'Tommy Gun' (song) 10, 43
Tosh, Peter 193
Townshend, Pete 101
trade unions 6, 35, 37, 43, 46, 48
Traverso, Enzo 81
Trinity College, Dublin 18
Truman, James 182
Two Tone 102–3

Ulster Hall 1–2
underpasses 165
unemployment 11, 48
United States 39, 47, 77–8
'Up in Heaven (Not Only Here)' (song) 76, 175
U2 183

Vaughan Williams, Ralph 56
Velena, Helena 215, 217

Victoria Park Carnival (1978) 97, 151, 197
Vietnam War 12–13, 77
violence, political 52
Vitali, Walter 210–11

Wadlow, Justin 189
Walter, Chris 179, 186
war, glorification of 91
Ward, Ned 161–2
'Washington Bullets' (song) 12
Watt-Roy, Norman 47
Watts, Billy 156
Watts, Ron 155–6
Webb, Kate 98
'weekend punks' 152–3, 155
Western Avenue (A40) 165–6
Westminster Council 175
Westway 7, 76, 162–9, 173, 175
Westway to the World 144, 164
Westwood, Vivienne 89–90, 166
'What's My Name' 131–7
Whirlwind 212–13
'(White Man) in Hammersmith Palais' (song) 95, 100, 169–70, 189, 213
'White Riot' (song) 8–9, 41, 73, 92–6, 112–17, 121, 133, 150, 170, 191, 196–7, 213
The Who 14, 22, 130, 185
Wicke, Peter 41–2
Wilkinson, David 140
Williams, Pharrell 58
Williams, Raymond 37, 45
Williams, Richard 65
Wilson, Harold 40
'winter of discontent' (1978–79) 6, 43
Woolf, Virginia 53
'Working for the Clampdown' 15–18, 45
working-class attributes 152
Worley, Matthew 212
Wozniak, Steve 22
Wright, Patrick 91

Žižek, Slavoj 107–8

EU authorised representative for GPSR:
Easy Access System Europe, Mustamäe tee 50,
10621 Tallinn, Estonia
gpsr.requests@easproject.com